Implementing SAP® BusinessObjects Global Trade Services

Happy Reading
Rajen

SAP® Essentials

Expert SAP knowledge for your day-to-day work

Whether you wish to expand your SAP knowledge, deepen it, or master a use case, SAP Essentials provide you with targeted expert knowledge that helps support you in your day-to-day work. To the point, detailed, and ready to use.

SAP PRESS is a joint initiative of SAP and Galileo Press. The know-how offered by SAP specialists combined with the expertise of the Galileo Press publishing house offers the reader expert books in the field. SAP PRESS features first-hand information and expert advice, and provides useful skills for professional decision-making.

SAP PRESS offers a variety of books on technical and business related topics for the SAP user. For further information, please visit our website: *www.sap-press.com*.

Sönke Jarré, Reinhold Lövenich, Andreas Martin, Klaus G. Müller
SAP Treasury and Risk Management
2008, 722 pp.
978-1-59229-149-6

Sabine Schöler, Olaf Zink
SAP Governance, Risk, and Compliance
2008, 312 pp.
978-1-59229-191-5

Aylin Korkmaz
Financial Reporting with SAP
2008, 672 pp.
978-1-59229-179-3

John Jordan
Product Cost Controlling with SAP
2008, 572 pp.
978-1-59229-167-0

D. Rajen Iyer

Implementing SAP® BusinessObjects Global Trade Services

Galileo Press

Bonn • Boston

Galileo Press is named after the Italian physicist, mathematician and philosopher Galileo Galilei (1564–1642). He is known as one of the founders of modern science and an advocate of our contemporary, heliocentric worldview. His words *Eppur se muove* (And yet it moves) have become legendary. The Galileo Press logo depicts Jupiter orbited by the four Galilean moons, which were discovered by Galileo in 1610.

Editor Stephen Solomon
Developmental Editor Kelly Grace Harris
Copyeditor Julie McNamee
Cover Design Jill Winitzer
Photo Credit Image Copyright Benjaminet, 2008. Used under license from Shutterstock.com
Layout Design Vera Brauner
Production Editor Kelly O'Callaghan
Assistant Production Editor Graham Geary
Typesetting Publishers' Design and Production Services, Inc.
Printed and bound in Canada

ISBN 978-1-59229-246-2
© 2010 by Galileo Press Inc., Boston (MA)
1st edition

Library of Congress Cataloging-in-Publication Data
Iyer, Rajen.
    Implementing SAP BusinessObjects Global Trade Services / Rajen Iyer. -- 1st ed.
        p. cm. -- (SAP essentials)
    ISBN-13: 978-1-59229-246-2 (alk. paper)
    ISBN-10: 1-59229-246-1 (alk. paper)
    1. Exports--Management--Computer programs. 2.
Imports--Management--Computer programs. 3. Business logistics--Computer programs. 4. SAP ERP. I. Title.
    HF1414.4.I94 2010
    658.70285'53--dc22
                    2009028937

Contents

Acknowledgments 11

1 Global Trade and SAP BusinessObjects Global Trade Services   13

1.1	Import, Export, and ERP Systems	14
1.2	Trade Checks and Services	16
	1.2.1 Trade Compliance	18
	1.2.2 Customs Declaration and Transit Procedures	19
	1.2.3 Classification and Duty	20
	1.2.4 Letter of Credit	21
	1.2.5 Electronics Compliance Reporting	22
1.3	Trade, Supply Chain, and Supply Chain Extensions	23
	1.3.1 Export Process	24
	1.3.2 Import Process	25
	1.3.3 Preference Management	27
1.4	System Architecture and Landscape	28
1.5	Summary	31

2 Feeder Systems   33

2.1	Feeder System Foundation	34
	2.1.1 SAP ECC SAP BusinessObjects Global Trade Services Plug-in	36
	2.1.2 SAP ECC Configurations	41
	2.1.3 System Communication	44
	2.1.4 Master Data	45
2.2	SAP BusinessObjects Global Trade Services System Foundational Configurations	49
	2.2.1 SAP BusinessObjects Global Trade Services Netweaver	51
	2.2.2 Cross-Application Components	55
	2.2.3 System Communication	56
2.3	Summary	57

3	**SAP BusinessObjects Global Trade Services Baseline Settings**		**59**

3.1	SAP BusinessObjects Global Trade Services General Configurations		59
	3.1.1	SAP BusinessObjects Global Trade Services System Setup	61
	3.1.2	Change History and Transfer Logs	62
	3.1.3	Number Ranges	63
	3.1.4	Organizational Structure	65
	3.1.5	Partner Structure	66
	3.1.6	Legal Regulations	68
	3.1.7	Numbering Scheme	71
3.2	Compliance Management Fundamentals		72
	3.2.1	SAP BusinessObjects Global Trade Services Documents and Business Processes	73
3.3	Embargo Service Checks		78
	3.3.1	Embargo Service Setup and Configurations	79
	3.3.2	Activations Specific to Embargo Service Checks	81
	3.3.3	Control Settings for Embargo Service Checks	82
3.4	Summary		82

4	**Enabling Embargo and Sanctioned Part List Screening**		**83**

4.1	Embargo Applications		84
	4.1.1	Embargo Country – Global	84
	4.1.2	Legal Regulation and Country of Destination or Departure	85
	4.1.3	Legal Regulation and Specific to Country of Departure and Destination	86
4.2	Configuration of the Sanctioned Party List		88
	4.2.1	Activating the Business Partner at the Business Partner Function Level	89
	4.2.2	Determination Procedure	90
	4.2.3	Activate Legal Regulation	90
	4.2.4	Address Comparison	91
	4.2.5	Control Settings	94
4.3	SPL Content Loading and Associated Processes		99
	4.3.1	Loading	100
	4.3.2	Monitoring	100
	4.3.3	Indexing	101

4.3.4 Screenings 103

4.3.5 Operational Effectiveness 105

4.4 Tactical Reporting 106

4.4.1 Reports on Embargo Business Partners and Documents ... 106

4.4.2 Reports on SPL Screening of Business Partners 107

4.4.3 Reports on SPL Screening of Documents 110

4.5 Summary 112

5 Classification **113**

5.1 Numbering Schemes: Design and Application 114

5.1.1 Export and Import Lists 114

5.1.2 Harmonized Tariff Numbers and Commodity Codes 116

5.1.3 Other Numbering Schemes 119

5.2 Product Content and Classification 120

5.2.1 Content 121

5.2.2 Product Classification 122

5.3 Summary 126

6 Legal Control: Export and Import **129**

6.1 Export Legal Control Setup: Baseline Configuration 129

6.1.1 Country Group 130

6.1.2 Item Category Activation and Depreciation Group 131

6.1.3 Numbering Schemes 131

6.1.4 License Types 133

6.1.5 Control Settings 136

6.1.6 Allowed Status 139

6.1.7 Time Zones 139

6.1.8 Partner Groupings 139

6.1.9 Determination Procedures: Legal Control and License Types 140

6.1.10 Address Comparison for License Types 141

6.2 Legal Import Control 142

6.2.1 Import Licenses 143

6.3 Operational Effectiveness 145

6.3.1 Legal Control and Operational Effectiveness 146

6.3.2 Export/Import Data Setup 148

6.3.3 Trade Reporting and Monitoring 151

6.4	ITAR and Agreements	153
	6.4.1 Business Scenarios, Associated Configurations, and Data Setup	153
	6.4.2 Configurations Steps	154
	6.4.3 Data Setup	156
6.5	Summary	158

7 Customs Management: Application and Use 159

7.1	Foundations of Customs Management	160
	7.1.1 Legal Regulations	160
	7.1.2 Numbering Schemes	160
	7.1.3 Document Structures	161
	7.1.4 Import Customs Declarations	165
	7.1.5 Customs Codes	166
	7.1.6 Authorization	168
7.2	Configuring Customs Management	169
	7.2.1 Activation	170
	7.2.2 Control Settings	170
	7.2.3 Preference Settings	170
	7.2.4 Customs Duty Setup	171
7.3	Communication Setup: Post-Processing Framework	173
	7.3.1 Automated Export Submission Scenario	173
	7.3.2 Post-Processing Framework	174
	7.3.3 Defining Condition and Output Parameters	177
	7.3.4 Messages: Definition for Communication Process	178
	7.3.5 Process Template	178
	7.3.6 Message Parameters	180
	7.3.7 Middleware Communication Setup	181
7.4	Cockpit Setup	184
	7.4.1 Messages	187
	7.4.2 Classifications	187
	7.4.3 Master Data	188
	7.4.4 Identification Numbers	190
7.5	Summary	190

8 General Add-On Functionality and Features 191

8.1	Text Determination	192

8.1.1   License Text 193
8.1.2   Product Text 195
8.2   Customs Product 195
8.3   Case Management and Email Notification 197
8.3.1   Record Management 197
8.3.2   Email Notification 202
8.4   Default Data and Incompletion Checks 203
8.4.1   Default Data 203
8.4.2   Incompletion Checks 206
8.5   Application Integrations: HR, FI, and EH&S 207
8.5.1   SAP ERP HCM Integration 208
8.5.2   SAP FI Integration 218
8.5.3   SAP EH&S Integration 219
8.6   Summary 223

9   Preference Processing or Preferential Treatment **225**

9.1   Preferential Treatment and Determination Configuration 226
9.1.1   Feeder System or SAP ERP Setup 227
9.1.2   SAP BusinessObjects Global Trade Services Configuration . 231
9.2   Preference Processing Business Processes 242
9.2.1   SAP Feeder System Process 242
9.2.2   SAP BusinessObjects Global Trade Services Cockpit
         Process 245
9.3   Summary 255

**10 Intrastat Reporting with SAP Electronics Compliance
     Reporting (SAP ECR)** **257**

10.1   Data Setup for Intrastat Reporting 258
10.1.1   SAP BusinessObjects Global Trade Services Data Setup ... 259
10.1.2   SAP ECR Data Preparation and Processes for Feeder
          Systems 264
10.1.3   SAP ECR Processing Within SAP BusinessObjects
          Global Trade Services 268
10.2   Business Process Procedure for Intrastat Reporting 271
10.2.1   SAP BusinessObjects Global Trade Services Configuration ... 271
10.2.2   Feeder System Configuration 278
10.3   Summary 285

11 Functionality Release, Upgrade, Archiving, and Technical Overview of SAP BusinessObjects Global Trade Services 287

11.1 Functionality Releases and Delta Features 288
  11.1.1 SAP BusinessObjects Global Trade Services 1.0 Versus SAP BusinessObjects Global Trade Services 2.0 288
  11.1.2 SAP BusinessObjects Global Trade Services 2.0 Versus SAP BusinessObjects Global Trade Services 3.0 289
  11.1.3 SAP BusinessObjects Global Trade Services 7.x 289
  11.1.4 SAP BusinessObjects Global Trade Services 8.0 290
11.2 Data Retention and Archiving 291
  11.2.1 Archiving Objects 292
  11.2.2 Archiving General Steps and Procedures 292
11.3 SAP BusinessObjects Global Trade Services Table Structure 299
  11.3.1 Linking Product and Classification Information 299
  11.3.2 Transaction Information 301
11.4 BAdIs, User Exits, and Copy Control 302
  11.4.1 BAdIs 302
  11.4.2 User Exits 303
  11.4.3 Copy Control 304
11.5 Summary 306

12 Data Transfer Between Standard, and Non-SAP Interfaces, and Best Known Methods 307

12.1 Master and Transactional Data Interface 308
  12.1.1 Change Pointers 308
  12.1.2 Non-SAP Interface 311
  12.1.3 Content Load and Screening Interface 314
12.2 Best Known Methods for Managing Your Trade System Project Implementation 316
  12.2.1 Supply Chain Processes: Preparation Work 317
  12.2.2 Requirement Analysis 322
  12.2.3 Scoping 323
  12.2.4 Managing the SAP BusinessObjects Global Trade Services Project 325
  12.2.5 Build and Testing Approach 327
12.3 Summary 328

The Author 329
Index 331

Acknowledgments

I would like to dedicate this book to all of the International Trade Business and System professionals whose dedication and passion to the profession constantly inspires and motivates me. I would also like to thank our customers, who constantly challenge us to deliver innovative products, services and solutions.

I would like to thank SAP PRESS for giving me an opportunity to present my experience and knowledge on SAP BusinessObjects Global Trade Services and the associated Trade System solutions with this book.

I hope this book allows business and SAP professionals to make the best use of their investment with SAP BusinessObjects Global Trade Services and provides them with the references, documentation, and best practices they need for rapid and robust implementations.

Global trade is integrated very tightly with the supply chain and processes involving the import and export of goods and services. As such, understanding the key interfaces and the architecture of SAP BusinessObjects Global Trade Services is important in making implementation decisions.

1   Global Trade and SAP BusinessObjects Global Trade Services

Global trade is the exchange of capital, goods, and services across international borders or territories. With the rise of a global economy, international trade is increasing and becoming crucial as a major source of economic revenue to a large number of countries around the world. Globalization is also driving the outsourcing of manufacturing, services, and intellectual property management. Most world-class, multinational organizations across a wide variety of industries are building significant infrastructures and processes to support increased globalization. As part of that development, organizations are looking closely at the lowest common denominator of global trade: import and export.

Supply chain typically originates with customer demand and is either manufactured internally or outsourced to vendors. This process involves moving goods and services between different partners and locations. The outbound transactions that cross borders need to adhere to the export laws of the country from which the goods and services are shipped. The inbound transaction involves following the import law of the country to which the goods are imported. The transactions could be generated out of any logistics or ERP system. The import and export checks for these transactions are carried out within the SAP BusinessObjects Global Trade Services system. Trade checks and services are performed on business partner, product classification, and transaction for license exemption or license requirement. Trade service might involve determining the declaration requirements for the exporting or importing country and any preferential law that might apply.

Today's supply chain processes are no longer confined to the typical logistics or ERP system; they extend beyond your sales, procurement, inventory, and goods movement processes. This allows you to enhance your relationship with your customer using the SAP Customer Relationship Management (SAP CRM) application, with suppliers using SAP Supplier Relationship Management (SAP SRM) and with transport with SAP Transportation Management System (SAP TM). These supply chain extension trade service checks can be either routed through the SAP ERP system or directly to the SAP BusinessObjects Global Trade Services system. The system architecture involving SAP BusinessObjects Global Trade Services can function as a central trade system with multiple systems feeding into it for trade checks.

1.1   Import, Export, and ERP Systems

To begin, let's discuss the basics of exporting and importing. In a typical simple supply chain process, most companies have customers, vendors, financial institutions, and other partners. In most instances, when an organization sells a product to an international customer, it needs to cross borders to fulfill the order. The export laws of the country from which the goods are shipped are applied to this outbound movement. Similarly, when an organization sources goods and services from a vendor located in another country, the import laws of the receiving country are applied.

There are generally four critical elements that make up an import/export transaction:

▶ Business partner, which could be a customer, individual, partner, or vendor

▶ Country, where the product is either shipped from or received into

▶ The goods, services, or products that need to be classified for export and import control for license exemption or requirement or no control

▶ Trade declaration for import and export reporting to customs

Figure 1.1 depicts the trade services that are performed against the ERP system as the feeder system.

The logistics or ERP system is also called the feeder system in the SAP Business Objects Global Trade Services terminology. The business partner, product, and business processes originate the feeder system. The source system can be any ERP system, where the key trade interfaces are

▶ When materials are created or changed; in SAP BusinessObjects Global Trade Services, these are identified as Product Create, Change.

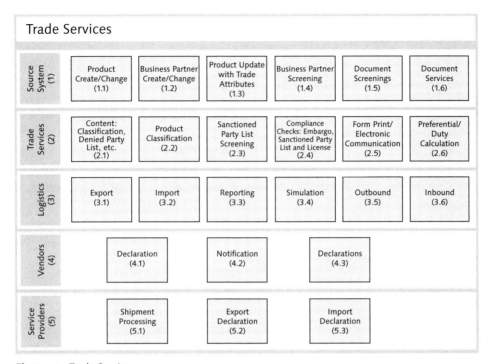

Figure 1.1 Trade Services

▸ When customers are created or changed; in SAP BusinessObjects Global Trade Services, these are identified as *Business Partner* Create, Change.

▸ When a *product* is updated with a trade attribute, for example, the export classifications and *import tariff number.*

▸ When business partners are screened against *denied party list screening.*

▸ When document compliance check or screening for *sanctioned party lists, embargos,* or *license determination is performed.*

▸ When document services provides the documents generation for customs declarations.

The key functional elements in SAP BusinessObjects Global Trade Services are

▸ Content for classification, denied party list, duty, preferential rules

▸ Product classification, which provides the classification assignment from export and import processing

▸ Sanctioned party list screening of business partners against denied party list content

15

▶ Compliance checks consisting of sanctioned party list screening, embargos, and license determination for transactions

▶ Form printing and electronic communication for customs declaration

▶ Preferential processing, valuation, duty calculation/drawback

Any logistics process involves one of the trade services. Outbound transactions, for example, include sales order, and order delivery note; inbound transactions, for example, include purchase order and inbound delivery. Reporting is part of the trade process for a logistics transaction, for example, the *Intrastat* and *Extrastat*. Simulations are functions that allow you to do a mock-up run and check on business transactions.

1.2 Trade Checks and Services

When companies use an ERP system to perform their supply chain transactions, they will have to perform export or import checks based on the goods being sent out or received into the country. These trade checks can be performed using the SAP GRC Global Trade Services application. Any transaction within the ERP system has the product and business partner information; from a global trade point of view, these products are identified for export or import classification and checked for license for permission to export or import. Additionally, business partners are screened for appearance on the denied party list.

When a customer requests a part or service, for example, the contract is acknowledged with an order, which is presented as a sales order in the ERP system. If this part has to be shipped to a different country and crosses borders in the process, export regulation of the departing country apply. This supply chain process checks for trade compliance within an SAP BusinessObjects Global Trade Services system. Similarly, if the company plans to purchase goods from a vendor located in a different country, it must comply with import regulations.

SAP BusinessObjects Global Trade Services has four major components:

▶ Compliance Management

▶ Customs Management

▶ Risk Management

▶ Electronic Compliance Reporting (ECR)

The trade business processes can be put into high-level functional bands as follows (see Figure 1.2):

▶ Product Classification

▶ Business Partner

▶ Export Management

▶ Import Management

▶ Trade Preference

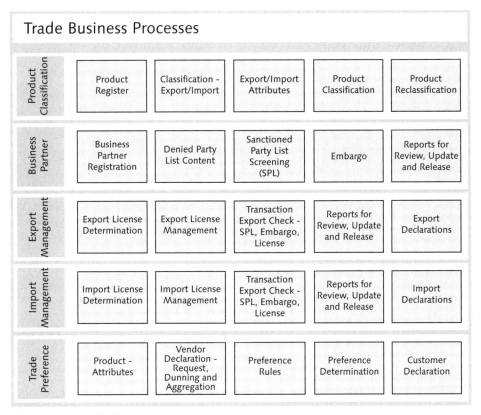

Figure 1.2 Trade Business Process

Product classification is performed at the SAP BusinessObjects Global Trade Services system after the products are transferred from the feeder system, which can be a SAP system or non-SAP system. The content for classification can be uploaded in SAP BusinessObjects Global Trade Services for import and export by number, and following the load, these numbers are assigned to the product. The product classifications are used for determining the export or import control and trade declarations. Business partners are screened for trade compliance with the denied party list and reviewed for any matches. Export management involves performing the compliance service check and trade declarations. Similarly, for import management, you need to perform the import compliance check and import declaration. Trade preference allows you to manage the trade agreements and laws that might benefit in determining better duty rates for trade goods between countries with trade agreements. In the next section, we will consider the trade compliance that is performed against your outbound or inbound transactions.

1.2.1 Trade Compliance

SAP BusinessObjects Global Trade Services Compliance Management addresses the screening of business partners when they are created and when they are used within a transaction, sales order, delivery note, or purchase order. This functionality is called *sanctioned party list screening* and uses the denied party list content to screen the business partner addresses. *Import legal control* addresses the import check requirements for products and services that are imported into a particular country, based on the importing country regulations. *Export legal control* addresses the export licensing requirements for products and services. The *embargo check* functionality is applied across both *export* and *import legal controls*. Embargo checks are based on the country of departure for import transactions, and the country of destination for export transactions.

The product number identifies enterprises' materials or services; these parts are classified for export or import purposes. Products are classified according to their respective government guidelines and regulations; for example, in the United States, the export regulation (*Export Administration Regulation*) uses the *Commerce Control List* (CCL). Export control classification numbers are defined with CCL. An ECCN (export control classification number) is an alphanumeric code; in combination with the country chart, it provides the reason for control by destination country.

Legal control license determinations for products are based on the product classification for imports or exports. License determination is based on the legal regulation of the departure country for exports, and it is based on the destination country for imports, as well as the partner country, classification number, and license type. The license types represent the control these products have based on different attributes, which will be explained in more detail in Chapter 6, Legal Control: Import and Export.

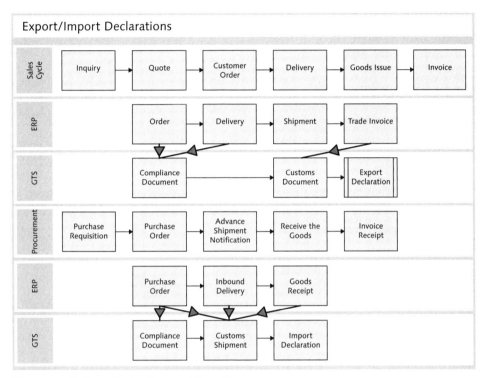

Figure 1.3 Customs Declarations and Reporting

1.2.2 Customs Declaration and Transit Procedures

SAP BusinessObjects Global Trade Services Customs Management is a module that you can use to standardize electronic communication processes, including customs declarations. Communication in Customs Management takes place by printing messages or creating *Electronic Data Interchange* (EDI) messages. You can connect SAP BusinessObjects Global Trade Services to customs authorities all over the world to manage foreign trade activities. SAP BusinessObjects Global Trade Services can communicate and set up electronic customs processes with European, US, and Australian customs authorities, and address the different filing formats, data transmission requirements, and other features.

In SAP BusinessObjects Global Trade Services Customs Management, you have two options: a printed form or an electronic communication. With a printed form, you have the option to print, mail, or fax. With electronic communication, the system converts the data into an *intermediate document* (IDoc) and sends the IDoc output file (text) to middleware. The middleware acts as a translator to convert the IDoc file into the format in which the receiving system expects it. Customs declarations can be created for export or import.

SAP BusinessObjects Global Trade Services also has functionality to support transit procedures. Transit is a facility available to operators that allows the movement of goods across international borders under customs control while ensuring that any changes due on those goods in their country of destination are secured. There are different types of transit; for example, community transit is a system that provides for the movement, under customs control, of goods that are not in free circulation through the community and also for the movement of free circulation goods in certain circumstances. Transit procedure is comprised of two separate procedures, the *external community transit procedure* (T1) and the *internal community transit procedure* (T2).

1.2.3 Classification and Duty

Trade compliance classification controls legal license requirements or exemptions; products are classified with respect to export and import declarations. Export classifications for export declarations are also called *commodity codes*, and import classifications are called *harmonized tariff numbers,* which are part of the *Harmonized Tariff System* (HTS). US commodity codes are called Schedule B. Schedule B are only qualified or updated with 6 digits from a 10-digit code; in other words, when looking at a 10-digit code, you will see the 6 digits update and the rest filled with zeros. HTS is an internationally agreed-upon code for traded products used for identifying imported products. Every country has different lengths for HTS; the first 6 digits are usually uniform; normally the initial 6 digits are the same, and the subsequent digits are more country-specific.

Classifications are maintained based on the numbering scheme in SAP Business Objects Global Trade Services and can be assigned for export or import purposes. Some product imports involve import duties based on the country of origin. SAP BusinessObjects Global Trade Services provides the functionality to capture the content and provide a calculation in the document and simulation.

1.2.4 Letter of Credit

SAP BusinessObjects Global Trade Services Risk Management has *letter of credit* functionality (see Figure 1.4). In a sales transaction, in compliance with the terms of payment that the exporter has requested, the importer opens a letter of credit at the bank of its choice. After approving the request for the letter of credit, the opening bank can contact the confirming bank's branch in the exporter's country to open the letter of credit on behalf of the importer and for the benefit of the exporter.

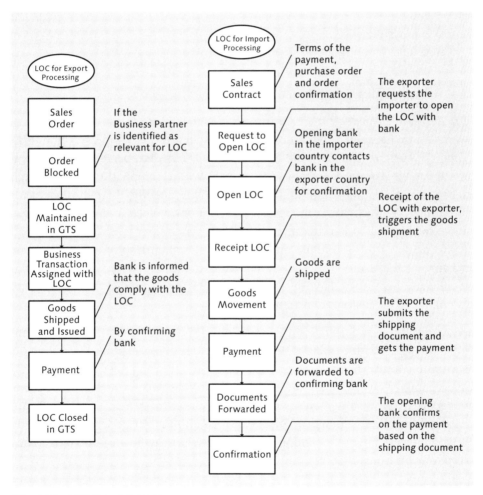

Figure 1.4 LOC Export Process

The letter of credit receipt gives the exporter the assurance of the importer's ability to pay, and the goods shipment is released. The exporter submits the shipping document and the letter of credit to the confirming bank, which checks the shipping documents for any discrepancies and pays the exporter the stipulated amount. The documents are forwarded to the opening bank in return for payment, and the opening bank then negotiates with the importer payment according to the stipulated terms in exchange for the shipping documents.

There are three different types of documentary letters of credit:

- Revocable
- Irrevocable confirmed
- Irrevocable unconfirmed

1.2.5   Electronics Compliance Reporting

Intra European Community Trade Statistics (Intrastat) is a system for collecting statistics on the exchange of goods among member states of the European Union (EU). When the customs check on the EU internal borders disappeared, the opportunity to use the data from customs declarations for the compilation of the foreign exchange of goods statistics also disappeared. Consequently, the requirement for collecting data directly from the economic operator involved in the intra-community exchange of goods came into force. This system provides direct collection of information from economic operators and communities engaged in internal exchange of goods and registered in the Value Added Tax (VAT) system. Statistics on the exchange of goods with non-EU countries are compiled by the Extrastat system, based on customs declarations.

Arrivals for Intrastat declaration include goods dispatched from another EU member state. *Dispatches* for Intrastat declaration include goods exported from one EU country to another. Operations that are subject to reporting need not necessarily have a commercial character. Return of goods and dispatch of replacement goods are reported in the direction in which the returned or replacement goods are actually dispatched. In practice, this means that an Intrastat declaration has to be prepared for the flow of incoming goods (arrivals) or the flow of outgoing goods (dispatches) for the following transactions:

- Selling from stock

- Procure to stock

- Inter-company selling

- Returns

- Inter-company stock transfer

The main components of Electronic Compliance Reporting (ECR) are Intrastat and Extrastat, commodity codes or classification, and master data. The Intrastat component allows you to edit documents, and display, import, or delete a worklist. Commodity codes or classifications let you maintain commodity codes and assign them to the products. Master data provides the functionality to edit the provider information, default values, and business partners.

1.3   Trade, Supply Chain, and Supply Chain Extensions

If you look at today's trade systems and solutions, you would find that each business unit has its own ERP and foreign trade implementation. Data are spread across companies on many platforms and in different systems, so it is difficult to introduce change or to standardize these locally managed trade processes. SAP BusinessObjects Global Trade Services is a centralized trade solution with the data shared across the entire enterprise. The process is managed centrally and operated locally, making it relatively easy to change.

SAP BusinessObjects Global Trade Services allows you to standardize your compliance processes and deploy them across your enterprise. Global trade processes cross enterprise boundaries, and SAP BusinessObjects Global Trade Services can be an intermediary system connecting the internal and external systems. For example, your brokers helping clear customs, carriers moving goods, and customs authorities providing clearance might want to have access to the information across the trade data and processes. The end-to-end processes that we will discuss in the following section involve export, import, and preferential determination. Export management helps you manage the compliance mandate with outbound transactions, and import allows you to bring in the goods within the country. Trade preference allows you to benefit from the trade agreements between the exporting and importing countries.

1.3.1 Export Process

Export control is a critical aspect of international trade. Countries impose controls for various reasons, ranging from national security to foreign policy requirements to international treaty obligations, as well as for terrorism concerns and issues related to human rights.

Typically, an *export* is defined as a product that is transferred — physically or electronically — to a foreign nation. It includes hardware, software, and technical data, as well as items resulting from technology, training, and servicing. Exporting and re-exporting products is prohibited when the exporter knows or suspects the goods are going to an embargoed destination or to denied parties (customer, vendor, or partner) or persons.

Export control consists primarily of performing the compliance checks for your outbound transaction from the business partner you are dealing with, countries you are shipping to, and the product that might have export restrictions. Business partners are screened against the denied party list content within the sanctioned party list screening, as master data and within the transactions, when applied. Business partners are also checked for embargoes countries and blocked for review and appropriate action. Transactions can be reviewed for authorized release.

Another important element of export control is legal control license determination. Products that are to be used in the export transaction need to be classified for export purposes. Products are classified according to government guidelines and regulations, and assigned with an export control classification number (ECCN) or also called export classification number (ECN). In the United States, the classifications for export control are referenced from the Commerce Control List (CCL) as a part of the Export Administration Regulations (EAR).

The Bureau of Industry Security (BIS) maintains the CCL within EAR, which includes products (commodities, software, and technology) subject to export licensing. BIS also maintains the Commerce Country Chart (Table 1.1), which details license requirements based on the destination and reason for control. So, in combination with CCL and the Commerce Country Chart, it allows you to determine whether a license is required for items on CCL to any country in the world.

Countries Reason for Control	Guyana	Hungary	Iceland	Indonesia
Chemical and Biological Weapon	CB1/2	CB1	CB1	CB1/2
Nuclear Nonproliferation	NP1		NP1	NP1
National Security	NS1/2	NS1	NS1	NS1/2
Mission Technology	MT1	MT1	MT1	MT1
Crime Control	CC1/3			CC1/2
Regional Stability	RS1/2	RS1	RS1	RS1/2

Table 1.1 Commerce Country Chart

Export checks are performed during end-to-end supply chain transactions; for example, an inquiry from the customer is followed by a quote, and after the customer confirms the requirement, you sign the contract with the sales order and then ship the goods with a delivery note. Within your warehouse the goods are picked, packed, and shipped, and a post goods is issued for account entry. When the goods are issued, they are technically out of the inventory, and the next step in the process is to prepare for customs declaration. Customs declaration is triggered with the creation of a billing document, for example, the proforma. Key documents created in ECC are transferred or replicated in the SAP BusinessObjects Global Trade Services for trade service checks. For example, sales orders and delivery notes are transferred to SAP BusinessObjects Global Trade Services for compliance checks under Compliance Management, and billing documents are transferred to SAP BusinessObjects Global Trade Services for customs declaration under Customs Management.

Pricing conditions in the transactions are used for license value decrement. The same pricing condition values in the billing document are used for export document declarations of values and valuation. The preferential treatment within Risk Management uses the pricing condition from the SAP ECC document to capture the duty calculation.

1.3.2 Import Process

The importer has the responsibility to ensure imported goods meet admissibility requirements, including proper marking, safety standards, and so on. They must obtain all necessary permits in advance of goods' arrival, observe all duty rates when goods arrive, and make sure all requisite documentation is filed with the proper authorities throughout the import process. To ensure that your company receives goods on time, customs clearance procedures must be strictly adhered to. When entering a country, goods face a host of import processes to clear customs, including inspection, appraisement, classification, and liquidation.

Some countries require an importer to have a license, permit, documents, and associated certificates, depending on the importing country laws, the country it is being shipped from, and the country of origin of the product. Like Export Management, the Import Management implementation in SAP BusinessObjects Global Trade Services involves functionality across different modules: *Compliance Management* for import license and product classification, *sanctioned party list screening and embargo checks* for inbound transactions, *Customs Management* for import HTS numbers and commodity codes, and *import declarations and documentations*. Customs Management also addresses duty calculations.

If your company has trades between countries that have trade agreements, you want to make use of any preferential treatment and take advantage of the trade agreements. This is achieved by implanting preferential processing with Risk Management. These preferential processing determinations are used as an advantage within import declarations for duty preferences.

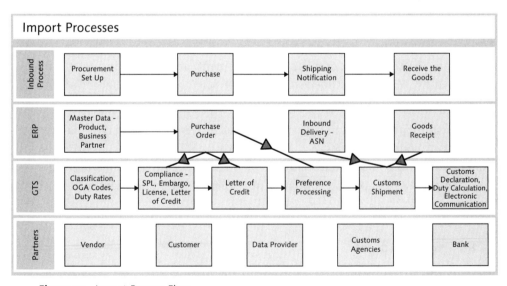

Figure 1.5 Import Process Flow

1.3.3   Preference Management

Preferential processing in SAP BusinessObjects Global Trade Services Risk Management helps exporters fulfill all of the legal requirements for customs tariff preferences and show that their goods are eligible for preferential treatment, thus enabling their customers to import these goods either duty-free or at a reduced rate of import duty. By providing evidence of eligibility for preferential treatment, exporters therefore gain a significant competitive advantage.

Preferential processing involves maintaining the following:

- Vendor declaration
- Material or Billing of Material for usage indicator, if it is manufactured internally or sourced externally
- The result of the threshold value for preferential treatment, stored in the product master
- The threshold value of product with its ex-works price (depending on the result, the product is either eligible for preferential treatment or not)

If you have a bill of material (BOM), the preferential status is set for the main component in the product master. Results are determined and saved for each main component. On the sales document, the determined threshold value is compared with the ex-works price and recognizes the preference situation for the current delivery (the ex-works price must be greater than or equal to the threshold value). If the system determines a positive preference status, it allows you to print a preferential statement.

Vendor Declarations Management provides functionality for requesting vendor declarations and sending reminders. Vendor declarations can be requested through email, or uploaded using XML format, through web-based interface with supplier access and self-update. These vendor declaration needs to be updated in the system, which allows you to aggregate them. The system allows you to issue or revoke vendor declarations, depending on the customer's purposes. For declaration to customs, the goods need to be classified according to a numbering schema. The numbering schema for the European Union is called *combined nomenclature* (CN). Imported and exported goods are identified by their classification number, starting with the subheading of the nomenclatures under which they fall. This determines which rate of customs duty applies and how the goods are treated for statistical purposes.

Countries sign trade agreements to eliminate barriers to trade in goods and services between countries and to liberalize significant conditions for investment within that free-trade area. Trade preferences benefit from imports, in terms of lower or no duties and, from an exporting point of view, better competitiveness because the customer pays less.

Preferential processing in SAP BusinessObjects Global Trade Services Risk Management helps the exporter fulfill the legal requirements for customs tariff preferences and show that their goods are eligible for preferential treatment, thus enabling the customer to import these goods either duty-free or at a reduced rate of import duty. There are several ways for your product to qualify as originating in your country or economy zone. For North America Free Trade Agreement (NAFTA), the methods might be based on one of the following:

▶ Rules of origin or tariff shift, which means you apply enough labor to the product or its components to change its commodity code

▶ De-minus rule (maximum of 7% non-originating goods), which allows a product to qualify for preferential treatment if no more than 7% of the product is composed of non-originating goods

▶ Certificate of Origin (based on your vendor declaration), which your vendor provides to certifying that the product or its components originates in your country or economic zone

Preferential processing starts with identifying the product procurement indicator. If sourced externally, a request of vendor declaration is made. The vendor declaration is used for getting the preferential treatment on the imported product. Subsequently, it is processed within the supply chain, and, while shipping the product out, the declaration documents are generated and shipped along with other export documents. The documentation and declaration are generated within the Customs Management customs shipment document for export declarations.

1.4   System Architecture and Landscape

SAP BusinessObjects Global Trade Services is a standalone system; the presentation layer can be a SAP Enterprise Portal (SAP EP) or the SAP GUI. SAP EP may use BSP Web UI, SAPGUI, or Web Dynpro as a user interface to the SAP BusinessObjects Global Trade Services system. The SAP BusinessObjects Global Trade Services-specific applications are *SAP SLL-LEG* (legal and logistics) and *SAP application component*

AP. You need to ensure the relevant release based on the version implemented, as documented in the master guide. The SAP BusinessObjects Global Trade Services application sits on SAP NetWeaver, which is comprised of the ABAP Stack for SAP NetWeaver BW, SAP ABA, SAP PI Basis, SAP Basis, and Java stack for Adobe Document Services. Below SAP NetWeaver, you have the database. SAP BusinessObjects Global Trade Services interfaces with SAP R/3 or SAP ERP, and they communicate with each other at the application and SAP NetWeaver level.

SAP BusinessObjects Global Trade Services is built on the ABAP and SAP NetWeaver components, similar to SAP ERP, so you have the option of installing and running in the same SAP NetWeaver system. When you do that, you need to make sure that SAP BusinessObjects Global Trade Services is defined as a separate client from SAP ECC because for SAP ECC to be identified as a logical system to communicate with SAP BusinessObjects Global Trade Services and vice versa, the two should be identified as separate logical systems. In other words, if SAP ECC has to communicate with the SAP BusinessObjects Global Trade Services system, they have to identify each other as a logical system. Alternatively, it's possible to have SAP BusinessObjects Global Trade Services and SAP ERP, SAP SRM, SAP SCM, or SAP HCM be in separate SAP NetWeaver systems. This is the recommended system architecture for performance reasons, where you install the SAP BusinessObjects Global Trade Services and SAP ECC on separate boxes.

With SAP Service Part Management, you can interface SAP CRM with SAP BusinessObjects Global Trade Services. For transactions created in the feeder system — for example, sales orders, purchase order, delivery and billing orders — a remote function call (RFC) communication is made to SAP BusinessObjects Global Trade Services for a trade service check.

SAP BusinessObjects Global Trade Services can be your central system, and SAP ERP, a non-SAP system, or SAP CRM might be connected and talk to it for trade services checks. Alternatively, SAP SRM and SAP CRM can connect with SAP ERP, which can talk to SAP BusinessObjects Global Trade Services. For example, a purchase requisition created in SAP SRM can flow through SAP ERP to SAP BusinessObjects Global Trade Services for a trade service check. And when the purchase requisition is converted into a purchase order in SAP ERP, it makes a call to SAP BusinessObjects Global Trade Services for a trade service check.

SAP ERP uses *Application Linking and Enabling* (ALE) to send master data over to SAP BusinessObjects Global Trade Services and *RFCs* for transferring transactional data. ALE uses the stages data and transfers over to the identified data element to the SAP BusinessObjects Global Trade Services system. RFC is a real-time function, and transfer and trade service checks are performed instantly.

There are other systems that access SAP BusinessObjects Global Trade Services for data upload and content. For example, denied party list and classification content data are uploaded into the SAP BusinessObjects Global Trade Services using an XML interface program. You can also use the middleware or SAP NetWeaver Exchange Infrastructure (SAP NetWeaver XI) interface to do the data transfer.

For external applications or partners to have access to SAP BusinessObjects Global Trade Services, you can use the pre-delivered function module for different functions and applications called Business Application Programming Interface (BAPI) and expose them to the Web services. SAP BusinessObjects Global Trade Services provides customs communication services, which enables electronic communation between exporters and importers with customs authorities by sending EDI/EDIFACT/XML.

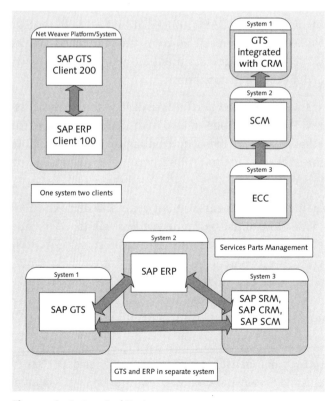

Figure 1.6 System Architecture

Trade processes are embedded within the supply chain application, or an ERP application is interfaced with a standalone trade application. SAP Foreign Trade is an example of the first scenario, and SAP BusinessObjects Global Trade Services is an example of the second scenario. In both cases, trade processes go hand-in-hand with the supply chain process, and the supply chain process needs to comply with trade rules and regulations. The trade system and services are built to meet the trade requirement based on the system settings and business rules, which reflect the country-specific trade laws and the content to support the rules and regulations.

1.5 Summary

This chapter introduced trade systems and services, including how the trade processes are embedded into the supply chain processes and the different systems that feed into the trade system for the service check. The end-to-end process involves export, import, and preferential processing with the compliance and customs declarations. We went over functions and processes that support the end-to-end trade system. The supply chain extension can be interfaced with SAP ERP or directly to the SAP BusinessObjects Global Trade Services system. Finally, the chapter concluded by discussing the system architecture and the recommendation for setting up the system pipeline. In the next chapter, we will discuss the configuration and system settings of Compliance Management, starting with the foundation and backbone of the compliance module. This will help you understand Compliance Management configurations and business process setup.

SAP BusinessObjects Global Trade Services is a standalone application that interfaces with a feeder system for master data and transactional screening. You should plan on configuring and setting up a feeder system, such as SAP ECC, when you set up your SAP BusinessObjects Global Trade Services configurations.

2   Feeder Systems

SAP BusinessObjects Global Trade Services is a standalone system that interfaces with a feeder system for supply chain or logistics transactions. The feeder system represents your enterprise resource system, logistics system, and SAP or non-SAP system, all of which act as a basis for master data and transactional data. The key master data are your business partners and products, where business partners can be you customers, vendors, employees, bank, and so on. Transactional data represents your outward goods movement, triggered by a sales order, delivery, or shipment, or your inward goods movement, triggered by a purchase order, inbound delivery, or goods receipt. These supply chain transactions are initiated in the feeder system, which can be SAP ERP, SAP Customer Relationship Management (SAP CRM), SAP Supplier Relationship Management (SAP SRM), or any non-SAP ERP system. These systems act as the originating system for transactions and master data.

With SAP BusinessObjects Global Trade Services implementation, you need to review your end-to-end supply chain and consider how trade processes will affect it. If you plan on implementing SAP BusinessObjects Global Trade Services with an existing live ERP system, you need to look at incorporating these trade processes within the regulation ERP transactions. With SAP ECC, you have configurations and technical objects built into the SAP BusinessObjects Global Trade Services plug-in. Apart from the SAP BusinessObjects Global Trade Services plug-in, specific settings, technical changes (BAdI activation, etc.), and configuration, you need to set up configurations or prepare the system that helps the trade processing of documents (e.g., defaulting foreign trade data in the delivery document).

Figure 2.1 displays the key interfaces between the feeder system and the SAP BusinessObjects Global Trade Services system. The feeder system could be a SAP ERP, SAP CRM, SAP SRM, or a non-SAP logistics system.

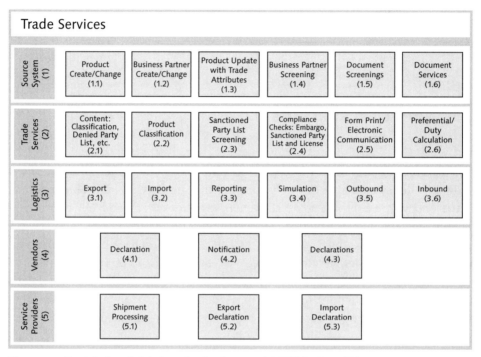

Figure 2.1 Key Interface Points from Feeder System with SAP BusinessObjects Global Trade Services

With the understanding of the feeder systems and their interfaces to SAP BusinessObjects Global Trade Services, let's consider the detail behind this feeder system and the key elements that constitute the feeder system set up. Understanding this will help you build a strong foundation.

2.1   Feeder System Foundation

Within SAP ECC feeder systems, SAP BusinessObjects Global Trade Services-specific plug-ins deploy sets of programs to facilitate communication with SAP ECC and the SAP BusinessObjects Global Trade Services system (see Figure 2.2). The system is configured to initiate communication and data transfers to SAP Business-Objects Global Trade Services and associated programs, facilitating ongoing communications. Transaction /SAPSLL/MENU_LEGALR3 provides the configuration needed to set up the system communication between SAP ECC and SAP Business-Objects Global Trade Services, as well as the configurations needed for programs and transactions to transfer master and transactional data.

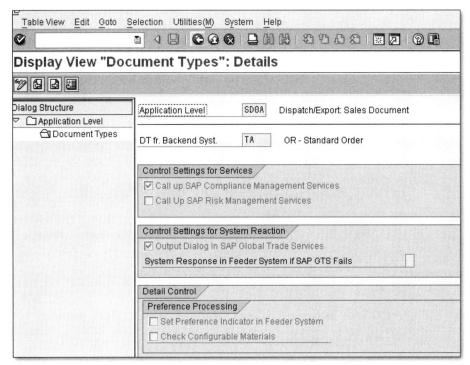

Figure 2.2 The Feeder System Interfaces with SAP BusinessObjects Global Trade Services Functions and Components

There are setups specific to the document that is identified for SAP BusinessObjects Global Trade Services screening within the SAP ECC configuration, which can be accessed via DISPLAY IMG • SALES AND DISTRIBUTION • FOREIGN TRADE/CUSTOMS • SAP GLOBAL TRADE SERVICES – PLUG-IN. Here you can also find BAdI and user exits, which you can make use of based on your business requirement for data transfer to SAP BusinessObjects Global Trade Services. Because SAP ECC is the system of record for all logistics transactions, there might be data that standard document transfers do not bring to SAP BusinessObjects Global Trade Services; this is when you have to use BAdIs. We will go over some of those examples and cases in

Chapter 11, Functionality Release, Upgrade, Archiving, and Technical Overview of SAP BusinessObjects Global Trade Services.

The foreign trade configuration in the SAP ECC system can be used with the SAP BusinessObjects Global Trade Services plug-in to prepare a document before it is sent to SAP BusinessObjects Global Trade Services. For example, the default data proposal for sales and delivery document within SAP ERP or R/3 can help you check for incomplete data. The configuration can be found under SALES AND DISTRIBUTION • FOREIGN TRADE/CUSTOMS • CONTROL FOREIGN TRADE DATA IN MM AND SD DOCUMENTS • TRANSPORTATION DATA. This helps get the trade-relevant data into the SAP ECC document. So when the document is saved with the default data in the SAP ECC system, the information is transferred to SAP BusinessObjects Global Trade Services.

For outbound transactions, your Sales and Distribution and Logistics Execution configurations influence SAP BusinessObjects Global Trade Services processes. For example, the pricing maintained in the SAP ECC billing document acts as a base for duty calculation and representing values in the trade documents. Similarly, business processes such as consolidation have an influence on the SAP BusinessObjects Global Trade Services customs document generation and trade documentation and declarations. As a result, the SAP ECC processes and configurations are very important, and lay the foundation for many of the trade processes. In the following sections, we discuss these processes and configurations in more detail.

2.1.1   SAP ECC SAP BusinessObjects Global Trade Services Plug-in

The SAP ECC SAP BusinessObjects Global Trade Services plug-in provides the programs, transactions, and configurations needed to set up the interface between the SAP ECC and the SAP BusinessObjects Global Trade Services systems. There are two key areas within SAP ECC that you need to set up for SAP BusinessObjects Global Trade Services:

▶ SAP Global Trade Services: Plug-in and other associated configurations
▶ SAP Global Trade Services: Legal Menu

The communication between SAP ECC and SAP BusinessObjects Global Trade Services is identified by application level and document type. In the configuration, check the control settings for one of the SAP BusinessObjects Global Trade Services service checks; Compliance, Customs, or Risk. Compliance checks are performed for transactions that enable goods movements (sales orders, purchase orders, and delivery notes), and customs checks are invoked for customs declarations.

If you are migrating from the SAP Sales and Distribution Foreign Trade (SAP SD FT) module to SAP BusinessObjects Global Trade Services, you should turn off the legal control check of documents and switch to transferring these documents to SAP BusinessObjects Global Trade Services. The configuration to switch on or off SAP SD FT checking falls under REFERENCE IMG • SALES AND DISTRIBUTION • FOREIGN TRADE/CUSTOMS • LEGAL CONTROL • DOCUMENT CONTROL. You can pick the order or delivery for activation. The activation is based on the combination of order type and item category in SAP ECC.

Plug-in-specific configurations can be found under REFERENCE IMG • SALES AND DISTRIBUTION • FOREIGN TRADE/CUSTOMS • SAP GLOBAL TRADE SERVICES – PLUG-IN. Broadly, you have two sets of configurations:

▸ Control for transfer of data from SAP ECC to SAP BusinessObjects Global Trade Services

▸ BAdI and user exits

The SAP ECC plug-in delivers the pre-activated BAdI for different application areas, for example, purchasing documents, material documents, and sales documents. The key configuration is found in SAP GLOBAL TRADE SERVICES – PLUG-IN • CONTROL DATA FOR TRANSFER TO SAP GLOBAL TRADE SERVICES • CONFIGURE CONTROL SETTINGS FOR DOCUMENT TRANSFER. Document types in SAP ECC fall under different application levels based on their functional area; for example, purchasing documents (NB and UB) fall under MM0A, and sales documents (TA) fall under SD0A. Based on the different application areas, you will find different control settings for service checks, system reactions, and other details.

Let's look at an example of some document activations from different functional areas. Figure 2.3 displays the configuration settings for a sales order document transfer to SAP BusinessObjects Global Trade Services. By checking the CALL UP SAP COMPLIANCE MANAGEMENT SERVICES CHECKBOX, you are turning on the compliance check for this sales document. Similarly, you can check the RISK MANAGEMENT SERVICES checkbox to invoke risk management checks in SAP BusinessObjects Global Trade Services. By checking the output dialogue in the SAP Global Trade Services checkbox, you can have the system display a window with the SAP BusinessObjects Global Trade Services block status. This occurs if any order headers or line items are found blocked within SAP BusinessObjects Global Trade Services. The System Response in Feeder System if SAP BusinessObjects Global Trade Services Fails checkbox allows you to select between two options: either to allow the processing of a document (e.g., to allow the processing of a sales order through delivery and invoice), or to stop the processing of a document through the supply chain. If you want to allow the processing of a document, you need to choose Option A from the dropdown list. Within the Detail control, you have check to send the preference indicator back to the SAP ECC document (this is used with SAP BusinessObjects Global Trade Services Risk Management). If you check the Configurable Materials check box, the system sends the communication back from SAP BusinessObjects Global Trade Services to SAP ECC for configurable parts, based on preference determinations in SAP BusinessObjects Global Trade Services.

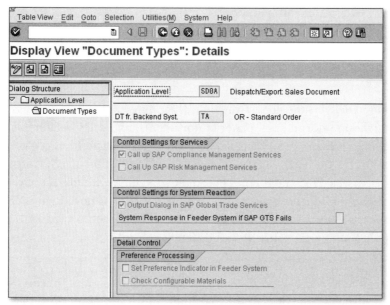

Figure 2.3 Sales Document: SAP BusinessObjects Global Trade Services Service Checks Within the SAP ECC Plug-In

In Figure 2.4, we see a purchasing document with one additional service check for SAP Customs Management. Because purchasing documents can be used as importing pre-clearance documents, SAP BusinessObjects Global Trade Services allows you to submit these documents not only to Compliance Management but also to Customs Management. The detail control specific to preference processing is to generate a worklist for vendor declaration. If you check this box, the worklist preparation for vendor communication for requesting declarations is triggered when a purchase order is created.

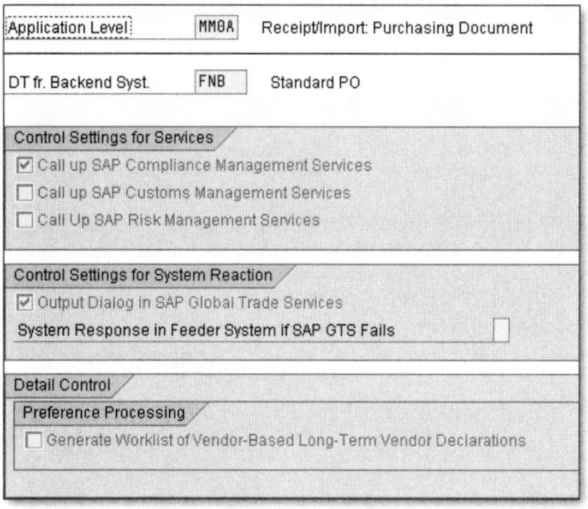

Figure 2.4 Purchasing Document: SAP BusinessObjects Global Trade Services Service Check Within SAP ECC Plug-In

With material documents, you can set up the interface for invoking Customs Management for customs declaration of the goods moving in or out of your warehouse, and Risk Management for preferential processing. Within the detail control for Customs Management, configure MANUAL PROC. CUSTOMS WAREHOUSE for the purpose of tracking bonded goods movements. Track inward movement with TRANSFER TO INWARD PROCESSING (see Figure 2.5). Here you can select the appropriate category of goods movement, which could be Scrapping, Returns, and so on.

Other application levels have subsets or variations of these services; for example, if you follow the menu path MM0B (RECEIPT/IMPORT: INBOUND DELIVERY DOCUMENT) • INBOUND DELIVERY, you can check to perform Customs Management. This will ensure the inbound delivery is transferred for customs declaration. If you follow the menu path SD0B (DISPATCH/EXPORT: OUTBOUND DELIVERY DOCUMENT) • OUTBOUND DELIVERY, you can perform Compliance Management, Risk Management, and set the system to display a pop-up window if the document is blocked. Figure 2.6 displays a SAP BusinessObjects Global Trade Services block pop-up window for a sales order.

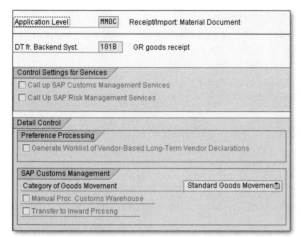

Figure 2.5 Material Document: SAP BusinessObjects Global Trade Services Service Check within SAP ECC Plug-In

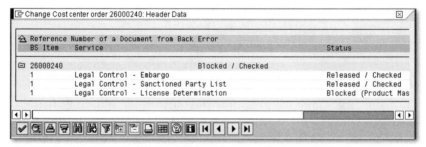

Figure 2.6 SAP BusinessObjects Global Trade Services Service Check: Block Dialog with Transactional Processing

For export purposes, billing documents are used for generating export declaration documents. With the application area SD0C, you will find configuration settings for transferring billing documents (to invoke Customs Management and Risk Management), sending preferential indicators back to the feeder system, sending configurable materials communication from SAP BusinessObjects Global Trade Services to SAP ECC, and generating long-term vendor declaration for customer purposes.

Just as a purchase order is the trigger to generate an import goods vendor declaration, a billing document is the trigger to generate an export transaction vendor declaration. Figure 2.7 displays the setting for proforma billing documents for transfer to SAP BusinessObjects Global Trade Services.

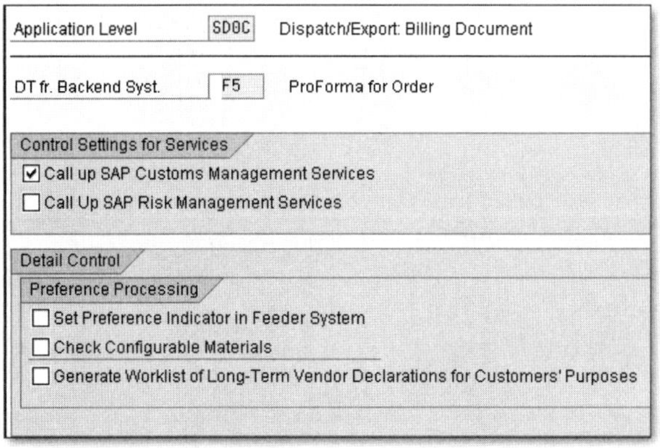

Figure 2.7 Billing Document: SAP BusinessObjects Global Trade Services Service Check with ECC Plug-In

2.1.2 SAP ECC Configurations

Apart from the SAP ECC plug-in configurations, there is another related configuration within SAP ECC that is needed for setting up processes on the SAP ECC side. In the following sections, we discuss two cases where this configuration would be applicable.

Case 1

While processing a sales order, there may be a situation where you want to save the document but not process the sales order; in other words, you want to stop the system from creating a delivery note. This is controlled by SAP ECC, and SAP BusinessObjects Global Trade Services can influence it. To stop the delivery note creation, SAP offers copy control codes, which allow you to check the status of a document before creating the delivery document. During the delivery note creation, SAP ECC makes a remote function call (RFC) to SAP BusinessObjects Global Trade Services; if the call returns a block, further processing of the document is stopped.

The SAP BusinessObjects Global Trade Services codes are applied to the order requirement of the item category, from the source document (the sales order) to the delivery document. We recommend making a copy of the existing copy control, appending the SAP BusinessObjects Global Trade Services code, and then saving it into a new custom copy routine. This copy routine is applied to the item order requirement.

Figure 2.8 displays the copy control requirement from the source document type DL (Order Type Scheduling Agreement) to the target EL (inbound). The menu path is REFERENCE IMG • LOGISTICS EXECUTION • SHIPPING • COPY CONTROL • SPECIFY COPY CONTROL FOR DELIVERIES.

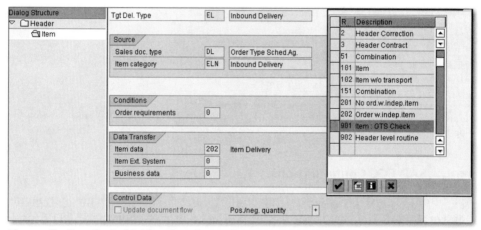

Figure 2.8 Copy Control Settings from Source Document to Target Document

Pick, pack, and post goods issue use requirements in conjunction with the incompletion control for deliveries. The requirements can be configured through REFERENCE IMG • LOGISTICS EXECUTION • SHIPPING • COPY CONTROL • DEFINE COPY REQUIREMENTS. The incompletion control for deliveries is set up under REFERENCE IMG • LOGISTICS EXECUTION • SHIPPING • BASIC SHIPPING FUNCTIONS • INCOMPLETION CONTROL FOR DELIVERIES. The following steps define the incompletion control for SAP BusinessObjects Global Trade Services requirement checks:

1. Define Status Group with the checks you want to perform in different areas (e.g., during pick, post goods issue, etc.).

2. Define an incompletion procedure with the fields you want to check within the procedure, and assign the status group.

3. Assign the incompletion procedure to the item category.

Case 2

Data within SAP ECC can be pre-populated on the SAP ECC side and sent to SAP BusinessObjects Global Trade Services customs documents, for example, INCO term, country of origin, and so on. These are critical data needed by SAP Business-

Objects Global Trade Services to process the customs declarations, and SAP BusinessObjects Global Trade Services depends on SAP ECC to provide this information. This can be controlled by defining incompletion schemes for foreign trade data. You can find this configuration via the following menu path: Reference IMG • Sales and Distribution • Foreign Trade/Customs • Control Foreign Trade Data in MM and SD Documents • Incompletion Schemas for Foreign Trade Data.

You can also use the default data determination within the ECC document, proforma or delivery, for example, the customs office for export declaration, mode of transport, and so on. This is configured under Reference IMG • Sales and Distribution • Foreign Trade/Customs • Transportation Data.

Overall, SAP ECC Materials Management, Sales and Distribution, and Logistics Execution closely integrate with SAP BusinessObjects Global Trade Services. They also interface as master data with SAP Human Capital Management (SAP HCM) and SAP Human Resource Management (SAP HRM) for personal screening, and SAP Financials for financial institution screening. Master and transaction data flow from SAP ECC to SAP BusinessObjects Global Trade Services for trade checks. (We will go over SAP BusinessObjects Global Trade Services-specific data and processing in later chapters; in Section 2.1.4, Master Data; and in more detail in terms of functions and business process behind it in Chapter 12, Section 12.1, Master and Transactional Data Interface.)

The data from SAP ECC are essential in performing the SAP BusinessObjects Global Trade Services checks. The key data elements from the SAP ECC point of view are as follows:

- Compliance
  - Parties involved within the transactions; for example, customers, vendors, and so on
  - Countries from where the data are shipped and received
  - Product details, that is, transacted
- Customs
  - Parties involved, countries, product details
  - Value of the goods and other transactional costs
  - Country of origin

- ▸ Transportation details, routes
- ▸ Commercial terms
- ▸ Risk/preference
  - ▸ Product details
  - ▸ Sourcing details

We recommend that you plan on making SAP ECC configuration changes because there are always changes in SAP ECC required for a complete SAP BusinessObjects Global Trade Services system implementation.

2.1.3 System Communication

System communication between SAP ECC and SAP BusinessObjects Global Trade Services is set up for master data and transactional data transfers. Master data transfers use Application Linking and Enabling (ALE), and transactional data transfers use remote function calls (RFC). The following setup can be accessed via /SAPSLL/ MENU_LEGALR3 • Basic Settings • Under System Connection to SAP Business-Objects Global Trade Services.

1. Define the logical system to represent the feeder system (SAP ECC) and the receiving system (SAP BusinessObjects Global Trade Services) in the SAP ECC system.

2. Assign the client to the SAP ECC logical system created in the preceding step. This allows you to recognize the client by the logical systems.

3. Maintain RFC destination for RFC calls. Here you define the source logical system and the destination logical system.

4. Maintain RFC destination for method calls. Here you need to define the source logical system communication to target the logical system through a pre-delivered BAPI. Select the source system, and click on Standard BAPI Destination. In the pop-up window, enter the destination logical system (see Figure 2.9).

5. Maintain ALE distribution. Here you need to create an ALE model for the master data transfer between SAP ECC and SAP BusinessObjects Global Trade Services. Define a model view with the source and target system, and assign a pre-delivered BAPI. Adding a BAPI involves maintaining the sender and receipt system, and assigning CustomsDocumentIF as an interface object and SynchronizeIfR3 as a method.

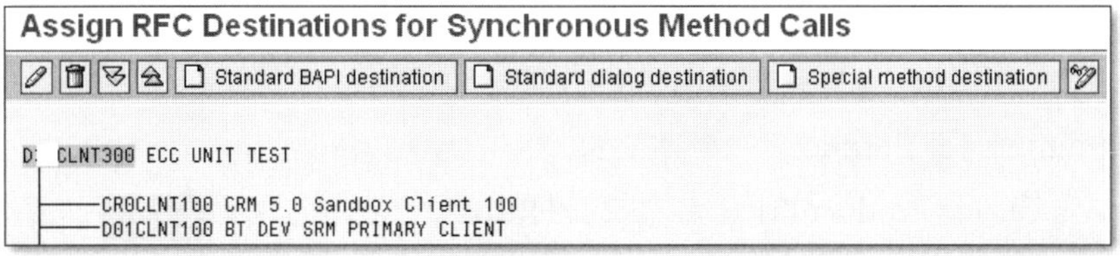

Figure 2.9 RFC Destination Connection for Method Calls

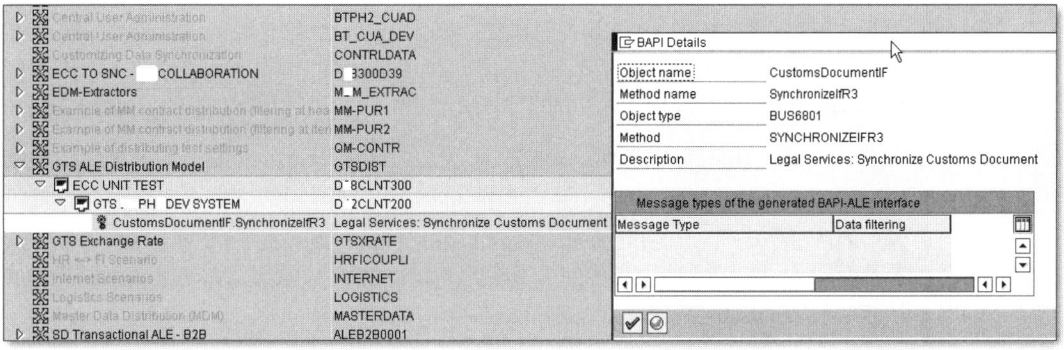

Figure 2.10 ALE Model Setup for Sender and Receipt System

2.1.4 Master Data

Master data transfers from SAP ECC to SAP BusinessObjects Global Trade Services use the ALE model and the system communication setup. The initial transfer of master data uses the RFC connection with the system connections, as explained in the previous section. Use TRANSACTION /SAPSLL/MENU_LEGALR3, and go to the Master Data tab, which has a section called Initial Transfer of Master Data for SAP BusinessObjects Global Trade Services. As the name signifies, this is only used for initial transfer and conversion. For ongoing transfers, the process used is called change pointers. The new records created or changed are captured with change pointers.

A *change pointer* is based on the concept of message types identified for master data, and it captures the fields that are identified in the message types. The message types for standard master data are pre-delivered as follows:

▶ Material Master Message Type: /SAPSLL/MATMAS_SLL

▶ Customer Master Message Type: /SAPSLL/DEBMAS_SLL

- ▶ Vendor Master Message Type: /SAPSLL/CREMAS_SLL
- ▶ Address Master Type: /SAPSLL/ADRMAS_SLL
- ▶ Change pointers for Product BOM: /SAPSLL/BOMMAT_SLL
- ▶ Change Pointer for Product Price: /SAPSLL/PRCMAT_SLL
- ▶ Change Pointers for Procurement and Sales: /SAPSLL/PSDMAT_SLL

Fields of interest are identified within the message types. Changes are captured in Table BDCP, statuses in Table BDCPS, and the aggregation of change pointers (BDCP, BDCPS) in Table BDCP2. Let's go through some of the key steps for defining change pointers within the SAP ECC system:

1. Activate the change pointer globally. Use Transaction BD61, and check the Change Pointers Activated – Globally checkbox.

2. Activate change pointers for message types. Use Transaction BD50, and add the message types you want to activate (e.g., /SAPSLL/MATMAS_SLL for material master). Then click on Activate.

3. Validate the default message type fields that come with pre-delivered message types. Use Transaction BD53, and enter the message type. Click on Change to review the pre-delivered fields. The fields in Figure 2.11 are selected with the message type (either manually or automatically); the light gray fields are not selected. If you want to select a field, check the field, and click on Select. If you select any additional fields, you must use the user exit and write an ABAP code to pull in this added field for transfer to SAP BusinessObjects Global Trade Services.

4. Identify and map the message type's fields. Use Transaction BD52, and enter the message type in the pop-up window. Ensure that the fields in the message types shown in the previous steps are listed here.

5. Assign the Function module to message type. Use Transaction BD60, select the message type (e.g., /SAPSLL/MATMAS_SLL), and ensure that the reference message type, function module, classifiable object, and ALE object type are correct. Figure 2.12 displays configuration settings for Message Type /SAPSLL/CREMAS_SLL. Table 2.1 displays the settings for standard message types.

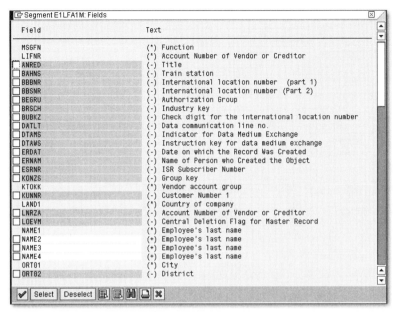

Figure 2.11 Message Type Default Fields

Message Type	Reference Message Type	Function Module	Clas-sifiable Object	ALE Object Type
/SAPSLL/ MATMAS_SLL	MATMAS	/SAPSLL/CREMAS_ DISTRIBUTE_R3	MARA	MATNR
/SAPSLL/ DEBMAS_SLL	DEBMAS	/SAPSLL/DEBMAS_ DISTRIBUTE_R3	KNA1	KUNNR
/SAPSLL/ CREMAS_SLL	CREMAS	/SAPSLL/CREMAS_ DISTRIBUTE_R3	LFA1	LIFNR
/SAPSLL/ BOMMAT_SLL	/SAPSLL/ BOMMAT_ SLL	/SAPSLL/BOMMAT_ DISTRIBUTE_R3	MARA	MATNR
/SAPSLL/ PRCMAT_SLL	/SAPSLL/ PRCMAT_SLL	/SAPSLL/PRCMAT_ DISTRIBUTE_R3	MARA	MATNR
/SAPSLL/ PSDMAT_SLL	/SAPSLL/ PSDMAT_SLL	/SAPSLL/PSDMAT_ DISTRIBUTE_R3	MARA	MATNR

Table 2.1 Message Types Mapping for Functional Modules

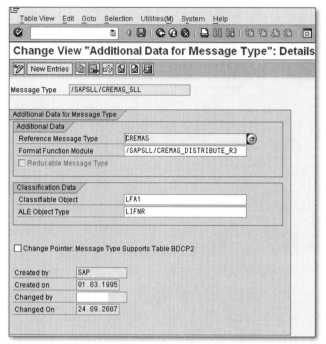

Figure 2.12 Message Type Configuration Setting for Function Module with Change Pointer

Change Pointer Processing

Change pointer processing involves setting up jobs for capturing any ongoing changes and transferring them to SAP BusinessObjects Global Trade Services (see Figure 2.13). As shown earlier in Figure 2.12, the change pointer triggers an entry into Tables BDCPS and BDCP. The status on the change pointer entry into the table is blank; once processed, the status is updated with an X.

Change pointer processing involves running Program RBDMIDOC, which can be run online or in the background by using Transaction SA38 or SE38, respectively. When you enter and execute the program, it will ask for a message type. After you enter the message type, you can either click on Execute (for online processing), or go to menu item PROGRAM • EXECUTE IN BACKGROUND (to schedule the program in the background). We recommend scheduling in the background if there are more than 500 records.

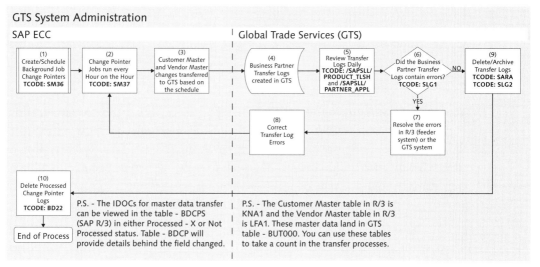

Figure 2.13 Change Pointer Processing Flow

Program execution pulls the change pointer entry for the specific message type and pushes the data into SAP BusinessObjects Global Trade Services. Following successful completion, the system updates the table with a processed status in Table BDCP, indicated by an X. You can review the transfer results within SAP BusinessObjects Global Trade Services by logging on and executing the SAP BusinessObjects Global Trade Services area menu (TRANSACTION /SAPSLL/MENU_LEGAL • SYSTEM MONITORING under TRANSFER LOGS • GENERAL click on CUSTOMS PRODUCTS). Here you can verify the successful transfer of the product master data and business partners. Similarly, you can verify for customer and vendors with business partners.

2.2 SAP BusinessObjects Global Trade Services System Foundational Configurations

SAP BusinessObjects Global Trade Services implementations involve system installation and basic setup. In this section, we discuss configurations that we can categorize as *foundational*, meaning that they apply across modules and are mandatory for all implementations.

Because SAP BusinessObjects Global Trade Services systems are built on a SAP NetWeaver platform, just like SAP ECC, SAP NetWeaver and cross-application components are similar. It is important that the common SAP NetWeaver and cross applications of SAP ECC and SAP BusinessObjects Global Trade Services are in sync (see Figure 2.14).

The system communication setup allows you to establish the communication between your feeder system and other downstream systems. General setting configurations are configurations that apply to all modules of SAP BusinessObjects Global Trade Services, so, once configured, they can be applied to all modules as they get activated or enabled.

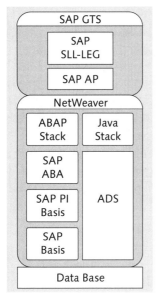

Figure 2.14 SAP BusinessObjects Global Trade Services System Installation Components

For establishing a sound communication and interface with your SAP ERP system, you need to consider the following critical configuration components.

2.2.1 SAP BusinessObjects Global Trade Services Netweaver

There are settings within SAP BusinessObjects Global Trade Services NetWeaver that need to be in synchronization with SAP ECC NetWeaver. These fall under REFERENCE IMG (SPRO) • SAP NETWEAVER, and are as follows:

- ▶ Countries

- ▶ Geographical codes

- ▶ Currencies

- ▶ Units of measure and ISO codes

In the following sections, we discuss these settings in more detail.

Countries

Country definitions in SAP BusinessObjects Global Trade Services should map to the definition in SAP ECC. Normally the two-digit codes are pre-delivered by SAP and should be the same in SAP BusinessObjects Global Trade Services and SAP ECC. What you need to double-check is the country-specific checks. Figure 2.15 displays the different fields that are configurable for country checks. If you have a mismatch between SAP ECC and SAP BusinessObjects Global Trade Services, it might cause a problem when transferring the master data. For example, if postal codes are mandatory in SAP BusinessObjects Global Trade Services and not in SAP ECC, the record might come over from SAP ECC without the postal code, and it might fail to update in SAP BusinessObjects Global Trade Services. Another common error in transfer is a mismatch in the postal code length and checking rule.

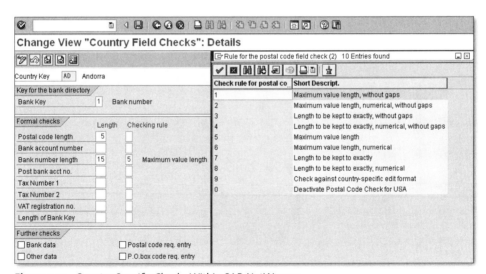

Figure 2.15 Country-Specific Checks Within SAP NetWeaver

As you can see in Figure 2.15, the checking rule applies to the postal code format. If in SAP ECC NetWeaver, the postal code configuration is defined mandatory with length 5 and checking rule 1, than the same setting must be defined for SAP BusinessObjects Global Trade Services NetWeaver for that specific country. It is essential for these country settings within the SAP ECC and SAP BusinessObjects Global Trade Services be in sync. This configuration step can be accessed via SAP REFERENCE IMG • SAP NETWEAVER • GENERAL SETTINGS • SET COUNTRY-SPECIFIC CHECKS.

Geographical Codes

Another important parameter that should be in sync is the geographical code or the region code. There is a utility provided by SAP that allows you to compare configuration table entries in the source and target systems. While you are in the configuration, go to UTILITIES • ADJUSTMENT. When the window pops up, enter the RFC connection, and pick the source logical system from the dropdown list. The pre-requisite is that the RFC connection is set up from SAP BusinessObjects Global Trade Services to SAP ECC, as you are calling the SAP ECC table entry for comparison with the SAP BusinessObjects Global Trade Services table entry. This utility allows you to compare the difference between the two systems and sync them accordingly (see Figure 2.16). The configuration for regional setup can be found under SAP REFERENCE IMG • SAP NETWEAVER • GENERAL SETTINGS • INSERT REGION.

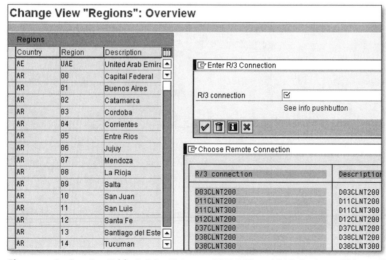

Figure 2.16 Syncing Table Entries Between SAP ECC and SAP BusinessObjects Global Trade Services

Units of Measure and ISO Codes

The unit of measure (UOM) assigned to materials is transferred to SAP Business-Objects Global Trade Services along with the material number and description. The UOM is a key parameter in determining the quantity and weight of a product. (The UOM used in the SAP ECC material master should also be mapped for successful transfer of materials.) As shown in Figure 2.17, the UOM has a three-digit code, with a commercial code, technical name, description (long and short), and, most importantly, the International Organization for Standardization (ISO) code. The ISO code for a particular UOM maintained in SAP ECC should match the UOM maintained in SAP BusinessObjects Global Trade Services.

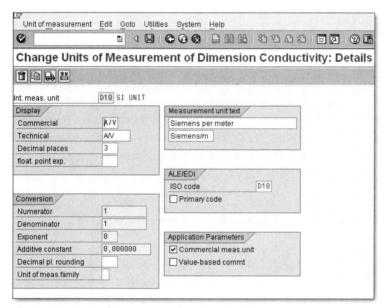

Figure 2.17 Units of Measure Configuration Definitions

This configuration can be found under SAP Reference IMG • SAP NetWeaver • General Settings • Check Units of Measure. This proposes configuration settings for dimensions, ISO codes, and UOMs. Click on ISO Codes to maintain ISO codes, and you can map the ISO codes into the UOM.

Currencies

Currencies are used as part of your transaction to represent the price or cost of the product sold to your customer or procured from the vendor. When the documents are transferred from the SAP system to the SAP BusinessObjects Global Trade Services system, these currencies codes are transferred along with the document. The currency configuration mapping in the SAP BusinessObjects Global Trade Services allows the system to understand the code and do the translation for reporting purpose. Currencies from the transactions are translated appropriately for duty calculation and customs reporting. The configuration step can be found under SAP REFERENCE IMG • SAP NETWEAVER • GENERAL SETTINGS • CURRENCIES • CHECK CURRENCY CODES AND ENTER EXCHANGE RATES. Ensure the currency codes and the exchange rates are in sync in both the SAP ECC and SAP BusinessObjects Global Trade Services systems.

2.2.2 Cross-Application Components

Following the configuration sync up with SAP NetWeaver, as a next step, we need to perform configuration steps with the cross-applications. Cross application is another component that is available with the installation of SAP ECC and SAP BusinessObjects Global Trade Services. Here you need to validate the business partner roles. Business partner roles are mapped with your customer or vendors and need to be identified in SAP BusinessObjects Global Trade Services for screening and processing within the documents. The configurations are pre-delivered, but it is important to verify that the key business partner roles exist in the system.

Table 2.2 displays the important business partner roles, IDs, and descriptions that are pre-delivered and mapped in the SAP BusinessObjects Global Trade Services system.

BP Role	BP Role ID	Purpose
Business Partner (General)	00000	General Business Partner for customers and vendors
Employee	BUP003	Employee role
Organization	BUP004	Organization units
Financial Service	FS0000	Financial service business partner
Customs Office	SKKCOF	Customs office for export or import
Customs	SLLCPC / SLLCPS	Customs business partner
Data Provider	SLLCAP	Content data provider

Table 2.2 Business Partner Roles, IDs, and Descriptions

BP Role	BP Role ID	Purpose
Foreign Trade Org	SLLFTO	Foreign trade org to map SAP ECC company codes
Administrative Unit	SLLMGR	Administrative unit for vendor declarations
Legal Unit	SLLSIT	Legal units to map plants

Table 2.2 Business Partner Roles, IDs, and Descriptions (Cont.)

This configuration can be accessed via SAP REFERENCE IMG • CROSS-APPLICATION COMPONENTS • SAP BUSINESS PARTNER • BUSINESS PARTNER • BASIC SETTINGS • BUSINESS PARTNER ROLES • DEFINE BP ROLES.

2.2.3   System Communication

For SAP BusinessObjects Global Trade Services to receive communication from a feeder or sender system, you need to define system communication within SAP BusinessObjects Global Trade Services. The configurations involve following two steps:

1. Define the logical system for the feeder system by creating a logical system definition for the feeder system and the SAP BusinessObjects Global Trade Services system. Here you might also want to define the other logical system, from where you expect data to flow into SAP BusinessObjects Global Trade Services.

2. Assign the system client. Figure 2.18 displays the typical client assignment and details behind the configurations.

There are two additional settings provided in SAP BusinessObjects Global Trade Services that follow the logical system definition and assignment. First you need to set the definition of the logical system group, and then you need to assign the group to the logical system group. This involves defining logical system groups and assigning the systems to one or more groups. While assigning organizational parameters within SAP BusinessObjects Global Trade Services, you will have to choose between assigning them to a logical system or to a logical system group. We recommend using a logical system group because, in the future, if you have added another feeder system and would like to include it in the SAP BusinessObjects Global Trade Services service check, you can do it by simply defining the logical system and assigning it to the group. The prerequisite for this is that your organizational data are common across your enterprise.

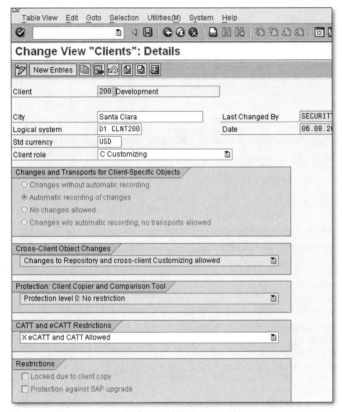

Figure 2.18 Assignment of Logical System to Client

The two steps in the configuration involve (a) defining a logical system group for SAP BusinessObjects Global Trade Services, and (b) defining one or more feeder systems. Logical system groups not only allow you to group the feeder system but also the SAP BusinessObjects Global Trade Services systems. So to group the feeder system and SAP BusinessObjects Global Trade Services system, you need to define two logical system groups, one to group the feeder system and another to group the SAP BusinessObjects Global Trade Services system. The configuration for the system connections can be found under REFERENCE IMG • SAP GLOBAL TRADE SERVICES • SYSTEM CONNECTION TO FEEDER SYSTEM.

2.3   Summary

In this chapter, we reviewed the key configurations required to set up system communication, master data, and document transfers to SAP BusinessObjects Global Trade Services for service checks. Feeder system configuration involves setting up the configuration within the SAP BusinessObjects Global Trade Services plug-in and associated configurations, which define your supply chain process for trade service checks. We also discussed the importance of keeping relevant SAP NetWeaver configurations in sync, so that the system communications are maintained in SAP ECC and SAP BusinessObjects Global Trade Services.

In the next chapter, we discuss the foundational configurations for SAP Business-Objects Global Trade Services, similar to SAP ECC, which we reviewed in this chapter. Following that, we review the general configurations for Compliance Management and embargo checks. With this knowledge, we can move on to more complex service enablement, such as sanctioned party list screening, license determination, and letters of credit.

Companies typically choose to implement compliance to start with, giving them an opportunity to build a robust base. The baseline settings for compliance provide a foundation for other SAP BusinessObjects Global Trade Services functionality and modules. The foundation of compliance is shared across all of the compliance components, and embargo setup allows you to understand the compliance in very simple form.

3 SAP BusinessObjects Global Trade Services Baseline Settings

In the previous chapter, we discussed configurations for common settings in SAP BusinessObjects Global Trade Services and SAP ECC. In this chapter, we move on to SAP BusinessObjects Global Trade Services-specific configurations. We start with the baseline settings, which are required for all modules or functions, and then move on to module-specific configurations. The baseline provides the configuration settings that are shared across all of the SAP BusinessObjects Global Trade Services components. These baseline settings are more general, which allows you to define settings that can be share or used in different functionality within SAP BusinessObjects Global Trade Services. Following the understanding of the baseline, we will go over the foundation configuration for Compliance Management. These foundational configurations are shared across all of the compliance modules, for example, embargo, sanctioned party list, and legal control. The best way to understand the concept of compliance module setup is through the embargo services. Embargo set up is the simplest functionality within the compliance, and we will go over the setup in this chapter.

3.1 SAP BusinessObjects Global Trade Services General Configurations

The SAP BusinessObjects Global Trade Services General settings allow you to build the baseline and set up the system with configurations that will be shared or used by multiple modules and functions (see Figure 3.1). In this section, we discuss the general settings of SAP BusinessObjects Global Trade Services, which can be broadly categorized into the following:

▶ SAP BusinessObjects Global Trade Services system setup

▶ Change History and Transfer log

▶ Number ranges

▶ Organizational structure

▶ Partner structure

▶ Legal regulations

▶ Numbering scheme

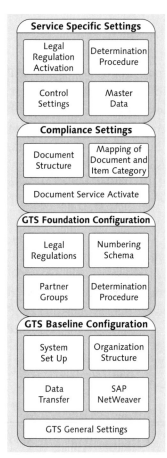

Figure 3.1 Configuration Approach in SAP BusinessObjects Global Trade Services Implementation

3.1.1   SAP BusinessObjects Global Trade Services System Setup

Like any other SAP system, after SAP BusinessObjects Global Trade Services is installed, you must set the time zone. Time zones play a key role in capturing activities or updates within the SAP BusinessObjects Global Trade Services system; for example, when you have a business partner screened for a sanctioned party list screening, the system captures the time the business partner was screened for audit purpose. Similarly, if you have content loaded within SAP BusinessObjects Global Trade Services, you can have the system capture the time the load was carried out. This is maintained under SAP Reference IMG • SAP Global Trade Services • General Settings • Maintain System Time Zone.

You also must activate the content services for system document storage. This involves setting content services with HTTP and Internet Communication Framework (ICF) to call the SAP system work process. These are required for attaching documents in electronic communications or for uploading data into SAP BusinessObjects Global Trade Services documents (e.g., attaching a scanned document to a license). The configuration can be found under SAP Reference IMG • SAP Global Trade Services • General Settings • Activate HTTP Services for Document Storage (Using SAP Content Server). When you click on this configuration setting, it prompts you with Maintain Services. In Hierarchy Type, key in "SERVICE"; in Virtual Host, key in "DEFAULT_HOST"; then click Execute. This lists all of the Virtual Hosts and Services, and expands the folder *sap\bc.* Keep your cursor on *contentserver,* and go to the following menu: Service/Host • Activate. Figure 3.2 displays the service activation for content services.

Typically, SAP ECC is the system of record for the material master. It is important that we define the format and length for the product within SAP BusinessObjects Global Trade Services in sync with SAP ECC. Review the default settings within the following configuration: SAP Reference IMG • SAP Global Trade Services • General Settings • Define Output Format for External Product Number. The output format should be 40 in length, and the boxes titled Save Lexicographically and Show Leading Zeros should be unchecked. We recommend that you make your SAP BusinessObjects Global Trade Services product format the same as the SAP ECC product or material format; thus, if you have an SAP ECC product with 30 length and Show Leading Zeros checked, the same setting should be mapped in SAP BusinessObjects Global Trade Services; in other words, you need to change the default settings from 40 to 40 in the SAP BusinessObjects Global Trade Services system.

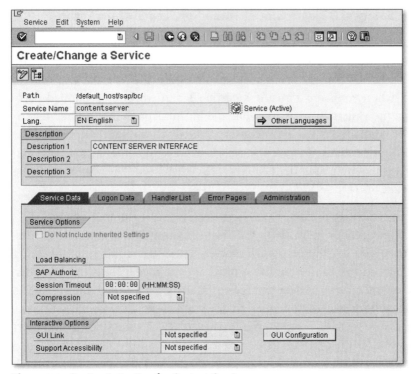

Figure 3.2 Service Activation for Content Services

3.1.2 Change History and Transfer Logs

Data within SAP BusinessObjects Global Trade Services can be categorized into two areas: data that are dependent on the feeder system (e.g., the master, vendor, and transactional data), and data that are maintained in SAP BusinessObjects Global Trade Services manually or through interfaces, which are specific to trade. During the system setup, you must decide on what data you want to track the change history. The default pre-delivered tables that are tracked within SAP BusinessObjects Global Trade Services can be found under: SAP GLOBAL TRADE SERVICES • GENERAL SETTINGS • CONTROL SETTINGS FOR THE GENERATION OF CHANGE DOCUMENTS. We recommend that you do not make any changes to the pre-delivered settings, but if you want to track changes on any additional tables, you can add them here.

There are also pre-delivered transfer log profiles within SAP BusinessObjects Global Trade Services for data transfers from feeder systems and for data upload or maintenance within SAP BusinessObjects Global Trade Services. These logs capture the data transfer details — success or failure — which can be used for confirmation of transfer and error analysis. The log profile setup is a two-step configuration. In the first step, you define the log profile; and in the second step, you assign the log profile to objects.

Similar to the change history function, transfer logs also create entries in tables and need housekeeping. The key difference here is that with change history, you might want to retain the log for future audit purpose, whereas with transfer logs, the use of the log has a specific time limit. For example, after you confirm the correct transfer of a material master, the log can be deleted from the system. For effective system log storage space use, you might want to look at changing some of the pre-delivered settings for the log profile.

Let's look at an example of a log profile for a business partner master data distribution. In this case, you might want to define the parameters as follows:

▶ Log Persistence: A - Save Log Only if Error Occurs.

▶ Log Backup: A - Save Current Log and Delete Olds Logs

▶ Log Scope: B - Reduced Log

The configuration entries for this log profile can be found under SAP Reference IMG • SAP Global Trade Services • General Settings • Define Control Profile for Logging. The assignment of a control profile configuration step is next to this configuration in the Display IMG. The second entry is pre-delivered, and you can keep it as is without any changes.

3.1.3   Number Ranges

Similar to any SAP ERP implementation, number ranges are key foundational settings following the installation of SAP BusinessObjects Global Trade Services. Number range configurations can be found under SAP Reference IMG • SAP Customizing Implementation Guide • SAP Global Trade Services • General Settings • Number Ranges.

For business partner objects, you need to maintain a minimum of two setup number ranges, one for business partner transfers from the feeder system, and one for organizational data. Number ranges for organizational data are flagged as external and set up as alphanumeric; this allows you to maintain the organizational data with some intelligence for easy search. These number ranges are used for assigning

SAP BusinessObjects Global Trade Services internal numbers for objects created or transferred from other feeder systems. Business partners, customs products, and documents must be configured irrespective of which module or functionality you plan on implementing. Figure 3.3 displays the typical number range settings for business partners.

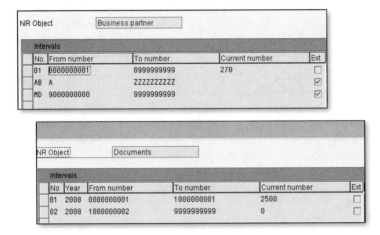

Figure 3.3 Number Range Defaults for Business Partners

Document number ranges are used for registering SAP BusinessObjects Global Trade Services-equivalent documents for feeder reference documents; for example, when a sales order is created in SAP ECC with the appropriate SAP BusinessObjects Global Trade Services service turned on, an equivalent SAP BusinessObjects Global Trade Services document is created with an SAP BusinessObjects Global Trade Services internal document number. Document number ranges have years as a key association, so you might want to plan on number ranges for future years. Similar to document number ranges, number ranges for vendor declarations also need to be maintained by year.

Depending on which functionality you are implementing, you might need to maintain number ranges for the following:

▶ General (applies to all modules)

    ▶ Business partners

    ▶ Products

    ▶ Documents

- ▶ Compliance/Customs/Risk
  - ▶ Licenses
- ▶ Customs Management
  - ▶ Outbound processing authorizations
  - ▶ Periodic declarations
  - ▶ Internal package numbers
  - ▶ EDI messages
- ▶ Risk Management
  - ▶ Vendor declarations
  - ▶ Preference models
  - ▶ Bills of product

3.1.4 Organizational Structure

There are two key organizational structures that need to be mapped as part of your foundational configurations: the foreign trade organization (FTO), and the legal unit (LU). The FTO maps to the SAP ECC company code, and the LU maps to the SAP ECC plant. The configuration for organizational structure can be found under SAP REFERENCE IMG • SAP CUSTOMIZING IMPLEMENTATION GUIDE • SAP GLOBAL TRADE SERVICES • GENERAL SETTINGS • ORGANIZATIONAL STRUCTURE.

Define Foreign Trade Organizations allows you to maintain FTOs. While creating an FTO, make sure you pick the appropriate business partner role (SLLFTO – Foreign Trade Organization). The business partner role for an LU is SLLSIT – Legal Unit. One of the best practices is to build intelligence in the naming for FTOs and LUs; this will help you identify these organizational data while processing information within SAP BusinessObjects Global Trade Services, or when searching for relevant FTOs. For example, for creating an equivalent FTO for Company Code 1000, you might want to create an FTO called FTO_1000. This will help you identify the FTO that maps to the company code and enable you to search all FTOs by using the FTO* wild character.

> **Note**
>
> For SAP NetWeaver BW reporting, you must maintain entries for all FTOs within the configuration setting Control Settings at FTO Level for SAP NW Business Warehouse (SAP NetWeaver BW).

Following the definition of the FTO and LU, ensure that these are mapped to the feeder system organizational data; the FTO should be mapped to the company code, and the LU should be mapped to the plant. You have two choices for mapping the organizational data; you can choose to map it at the logical system level or the logical system group level. Based on your design choice, you need to pick the right mapping, either to map these organization data to logical system or logical system group. As mentioned earlier, logical system group mapping has its advantages; consider its pros and cons, and decide appropriately.

> **Note**
>
> These organizational data, unlike SAP ECC or SAP ERP, are considered master data. However, their mappings to SAP ECC organizational data (company code and plant) are captured as configurations and can be moved across systems (development to quality to production) as configurations. The prerequisite is that you must maintain the RFC between the source system (e.g., SAP BusinessObjects Global Trade Services development) and the target system (e.g., the quality system). You also must define and map the source logical system in the target logical system, so that when the data are transferred, the target system can recognize them.

Following the mapping of the SAP BusinessObjects Global Trade Services organizational data (FTO and LU) to the SAP ECC organizational data, you need to assign FTO to LU. This enables you to recognize the transaction flowing from the feeder system, which has the company code that financially owns the transactions and the plant that ships or receives goods. If the country of LU is different from the country of FTO, the system gives a warning.

3.1.5   Partner Structure

Partner functions and types are another important configuration that needs to be defined and mapped to the SAP ECC partner functions and types. The purpose of the partner type definition within SAP BusinessObjects Global Trade Services is to recognize these SAP ECC partners when they are transferred within a document. While defining a partner function within SAP BusinessObjects Global Trade Services, you decide on its name, short description, and long description. We recommend that you keep the partner function name similar to SAP ECC for consistency. Select to what indicator you want to assign the partner function: (a) Import, (b) Export, or (c) Import and Export. There are partner functions that might be assigned exclusively to export (e.g., Sold To and Ship To in a sales document) or import (e.g., Vendor in a purchase order). However, some partner functions might be used in both sales (outbound/export) and purchasing (inbound/import). For these, you should select the Import/Receive and Export/Dispatch Indicator. Finally, the partner function should be mapped to the partner type. This is used for external communication; for example, when you send declarations to customs authorities or EDI communications to your partners (brokers, vendor). The configuration for this can be found under SAP REFERENCE IMG • SAP CUSTOMIZING IMPLEMENTATION GUIDE • SAP GLOBAL TRADE SERVICES • GENERAL SETTINGS • PARTNER STRUCTURE • DEFINE PARTNER FUNCTIONS. Make sure that all of the SAP ECC partner functions are listed for mapping in SAP BusinessObjects Global Trade Services.

The next step within the partner structure configuration is the Define Groups of Partner Functions. We will cover the configuration settings and purpose of this configuration for embargo checks and other services in Section 3.3.3, Control Settings for Embargo Service Checks, because they will make more sense in that context.

Following the configuration of the partner function, you need to assign the partner function to the feeder system partner functions. If you decided to map to the logical system group level for other organizational parameters, then you need to map the partner types to the logical system group as well. If you decided to map to a logical system, than you need to keep the partner type mapping consistent.

> **Note**
>
> With the mapping of organizational data (FTO, LU), partner functions, and document types (discussed in Section 3.1.4, Organizational Structure), SAP BusinessObjects Global Trade Services provides features to automatically pull these data from SAP ECC. The only caveat is that the data you pull are assigned to the default organizational data keyed for SAP BusinessObjects Global Trade Services mapping. This feature allows you to avoid entering the SAP ECC data manually in SAP BusinessObjects Global Trade Services and thus avoid any manual errors. While executing the automatic transfer of SAP ECC configurations for SAP BusinessObjects Global Trade Services mapping, you can choose to run in simulation and review the results before the actual run. For the actual run, you can choose to overwrite existing records or only write new records. Automatic transfer will bring all of the configuration entries for relevant data from SAP ECC to SAP BusinessObjects Global Trade Services. You can then go in manually to change the default mapping and also delete the ones you don't want to maintain in the mapping in SAP BusinessObjects Global Trade Services.

Figure 3.4 displays the pop-up window that appears for partner function transfers from SAP ECC. You have the choice to run this transfer for contact person, customer, or vendor, and it can be run separately with a default partner function for each role. Following the update, you can go to the manually assigned partner function to change the default assignment.

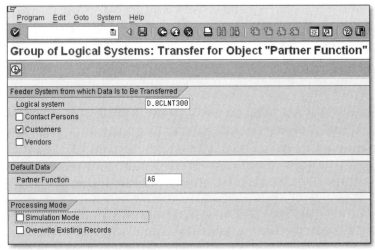

Figure 3.4 Transfer Organizational Data Between SAP BusinessObjects Global Trade Services Systems

3.1.6 Legal Regulations

SAP BusinessObjects Global Trade Services are configured, and trade processes are defined, according to the definition of legal regulation. *Legal regulation* refers to the legal entity against which the rules are defined for trade checks and processing. In other words, if you want to enable an export license determination check for shipping products across borders, you need to check the export regulations of the exporting country. As such, the regulations for license checks in SAP must reflect the exporting countries' rules and regulations.

The legal regulation definition is the starting point of the specific SAP BusinessObjects Global Trade Services service enablement. Table 3.1 explains the key parameters in defining legal regulation.

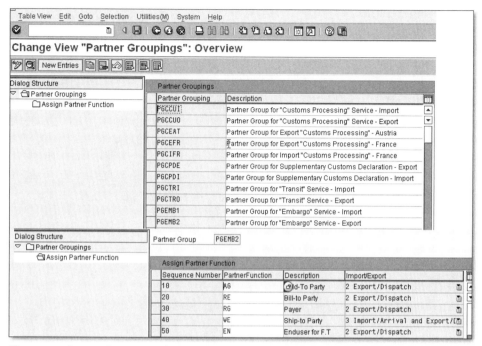

Figure 3.5 Partner Grouping and Partner Types Within a Particular Group

Legal Regulation	Type of Legal Code	Purpose	Import/ Export	Pre-Delivered Configurations
Sanctioned Party List Screening	03 – Prohibition and Restrictions	Sanctioned Party List Screening	Export	SPLUS
EMB	03 – Prohibition and Restrictions	Embargo Screening	Export	EMBUN
Customs	01 – Customs Processing	Customs Declarations	Export/Import	ACE for US ATLAS for DE
License	00 – German Foreign Trade Regulations	Legal Control for License Determination	Export/Import	EAR for US AWV for DE

Table 3.1 Pre-Delivered Configurations for Different Legal Regulations

Legal Regulation	Type of Legal Code	Purpose	Import/ Export	Pre-Delivered Configurations
Preference	06 – Preference Law	Preference Processing – NAFTA and EU	Export/Import	NAFTA PANEG for EU
Transit	07 – Transit Process Import/Export	Transit Processing and Declarations	Export/Import	TRS*
Letter of Credit	09 – Letter of Credit	Letter of Credit Processing	Export/Import	LOC
Electronics Compliance Reporting	10 – External Application	Intrastat and Extrastat Reporting	Export/Import	ENSEU

Table 3.1 Pre-Delivered Configurations for Different Legal Regulations (Cont.)

Every legal regulation must be updated with the origin country against which the rules are applied. For example, if we were applying US Export Administrative Regulation, the origin country would be the United States, as the laws pertaining to US export would be applied to this regulation. Legal regulation configuration can be found under SAP REFERENCE IMG • SAP CUSTOMIZING IMPLEMENTATION GUIDE • SAP GLOBAL TRADE SERVICES • GENERAL SETTINGS • LEGAL REGULATIONS • DEFINE LEGAL REGULATION.

Note

While creating the SAP BusinessObjects Global Trade Services client, we recommend that you create the client as a copy of Client 000, which copies the pre-delivered configurations. This expedites the implementation. With legal regulation, you again might want to make use of the pre-delivered configuration or create a new entry as a copy from the standard pre-delivered configuration. This ensures that the key dates associated with the deadline type assignments are copied over.

Following the definition of the legal regulation, you need to ensure that the legal regulation is activated. Depending on the export or import country, you must list all of the countries for which the regulation might be active. For example, a US-based company that operates in other countries should check export laws and regulations for these countries, in addition to the United States.

SAP BusinessObjects Global Trade Services 3.0 introduced the idea of country groups, which allows you to group countries for export or import processing. (We will explore the pros and cons of using the country group when we specifically discuss the different services within the SAP BusinessObjects Global Trade Services.) This setting is part of the legal regulation settings, and, if you decide to use it, you need to define and assign it to an associated legal regulation.

There are pre-delivered determination procedures for all of the key legal regulation services. We will explain the applications and where to adopt custom procedures, if needed, based on your specific needs. Embargo settings will be reviewed in Section 3.3.2, Activations Specific to Embargo Service Checks.

3.1.7   Numbering Scheme

A numbering scheme represents the structure for import and export classification numbers. When defining numbering schemes, you must decide on this structure. The structure definition consists of level (sequence number), length (length of the number or character), and maintenance (exact length or range). A typical structure is shown in Figure 3.6.

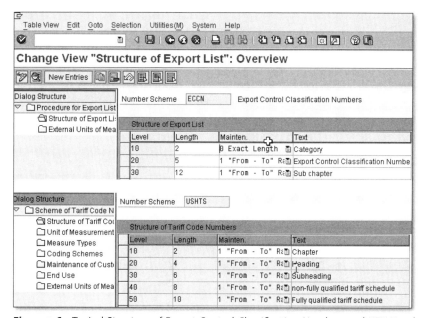

Figure 3.6   Typical Structure of Export Control Classification Numbers and HTS Numbering

An *export control classification number* (ECCN) is used for classifying products from an export control point of view. ECCNs are alphanumeric and are used in the Commerce Control List (CCL) to represent products for export control reasons. We will discuss the different characters that constitute the ECCN in Chapter 6, Legal Control: Export and Import. ECCNs are used for determining whether a product needs a license to ship it across borders.

As ECCNs are used for export control, the *Harmonized Tariff System* (HTS) is used for import classification of products. The format of the numbers in HTS is based on the international Harmonized Commodity Coding and Classification System, established by the World Customs Organization to facilitate international trade. The number of digits varies from country to country, but the first six digits are usually identical. The HTS number starts with two-digits, which represent the chapter to which it belongs; chapters are then divided into headings, and headings are further divided into subheadings. Regulation provides documentation on the product classification with chapters on the specifications. The rest of the number represents the complete HTS number, also known as the *fully qualified* HTS number. We will discuss how the number is used with product classification and determination for preferential processing and duty calculation in Chapter 9, Preference Processing or Preferential Treatment, where we cover customs management and preferential processing.

With regards to the definition of the numbering scheme, the HTS definition has some additional settings. External UOMs for data loads are required for UOMs that are applicable to the HTS number; if these are not maintained, the system gives you an error message during content upload. We recommend that you copy pre-delivered numbering schemes and then make the necessary changes; for example, for the United States, use the USHTS numbering scheme.

3.2 Compliance Management Fundamentals

The general setting configurations of Compliance Management are shared across all of the compliance modules and functions. It is important to understand the fundamentals of these configurations because they will help you leverage other functionalities within other SAP BusinessObjects Global Trade Services modules.

The shared settings primarily involve the definition of transaction processing for trade services checks within SAP BusinessObjects Global Trade Services. Similar to documents in SAP ECC, these settings represent the different supply chain processes (sales order, rush order, purchase order, delivery). In SAP BusinessObjects Global Trade Services, the document types represent the transactional processes within SAP BusinessObjects Global Trade Services, which are in turn used to activate or control the trade service checks.

3.2.1 SAP BusinessObjects Global Trade Services Documents and Business Processes

In SAP ECC or SAP ERP systems, you have documents that represent the transactions, for example, sales document, delivery to represent the outbound sales transaction and logistics process, and purchase order to represent the procurement from your vendor. Similarly, you have documents within the SAP BusinessObjects Global Trade Services system to represent the transactions within the system, for example, EXORD represents the export order, EXDLV represents Export Delivery, and so on. These allow you to map the feeder system document to the appropriate SAP BusinessObjects Global Trade Services documents for right trade service checks.

Some of the pre-delivered SAP BusinessObjects Global Trade Services documents are as follows:

▶ **EXPDLV**
Export Customs Document: Outbound Delivery Document Level

▶ **EXPINV**
Export Customs Document: Billing Document Level

▶ **EXPORD**
Export Customs Document: Sales Document Level

▶ **IMPORD**
Import Customs Document: Purchase Order Document Level

Some of the key parameters that are important in defining the SAP BusinessObjects Global Trade Services documents are listed here and shown in Figure 3.7:

▶ **Import/Export indicator**
Indicate whether the document will perform export or import trade service checks.

▶ **Number Range Numbers**
Assign the number range you defined in the general settings. These numbers are SAP BusinessObjects Global Trade Services numbers assigned to the document transferred from the feeder system. Document number ranges are year-specific, so it is important you have the number ranges created for future years, or at the turn of the New Year your documents from feeder systems would not be transferred and saved to SAP BusinessObjects Global Trade Services because the number ranges for the new year do not exist in the system. As these are internal number ranges within SAP BusinessObjects Global Trade Services, and the system allows you to retrieve documents by the feeder system reference number, it is recommended that you keep one document number range for all SAP BusinessObjects Global Trade Services documents. This helps you more easily manage the document number ranges.

▶ **Log Control**
This allows you to control the log maintenance of document transfers from feeder systems and data retention in SAP BusinessObjects Global Trade Services. You can reference the pre-delivery settings and keep the values as they are.

▶ **Check functions**
Check the SAP NetWeaver Business Intelligence checkbox if you want to transfer documents from SAP BusinessObjects Global Trade Services to SAP NetWeaver BW. By checking this, the documents become available for SAP NetWeaver BW extraction. Check the Start Follow-On Function in FS checkbox if you want to allow further processing of documents when they are released in the feeder system. Check the Mail Dispatch in Case of Technical Incompleteness checkbox if you want to generate email when a document is technically incomplete.

▶ **Control Data**
Pick from the possible selection (Document Type or Combination of Document Type and Legal Regulation) based on the level of control you want the service determination to use. Pick the Calculation Profile (Export or Import) for Customs Management documents. Note that for Compliance Management documents, these are left blank.

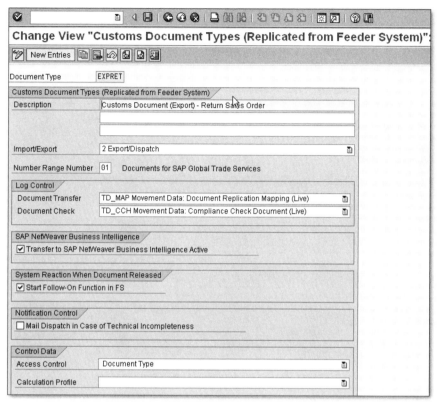

Figure 3.7 Typical Structure of a Numbering Scheme for Export Control Number and Harmonized Tariff System

The configuration menu path for these settings is SPRO • SAP REFERENCE IMG • SAP GLOBAL TRADE SERVICES • SAP COMPLIANCE MANAGEMENT • GENERAL SETTINGS • DOCUMENT STRUCTURE • DEFINE DOCUMENT TYPES.

If you have certain supply chain transactions or processes for which you want to perform specific service checks, define a custom SAP BusinessObjects Global Trade Services document type (see Figure 3.8). For example, if you have a service order, you might want to perform a sanctioned party list screening and embargo but exclude it from license determination checks. Then you might want to create an SAP BusinessObjects Global Trade Services document type to map to this document type from SAP ECC. In the next section, we will see how these document types are used to control the service activation.

Service activation allows you to select the document you want to activate for different services; for example, you might want to activate a regular sales order for sanctioned party list, embargo, and legal control, and use the service order for only sanctioned party list and embargo.

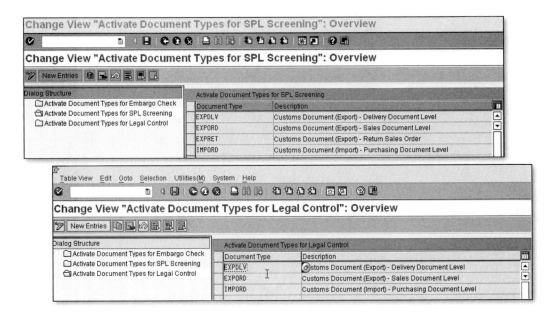

Figure 3.8 SAP BusinessObjects Global Trade Services Customs Document Definition

Service Activation

Following the definition of the SAP BusinessObjects Global Trade Services documents, you need to decide the services you want to activate. The standard predelivered has the export order, export delivery, and import order activated for embargo checks, sanctioned party list, and legal control checks.

If you have a document you want to exclude from a service check, you should make sure that this does not appear in the service. Within the service activation, you only want to list the document types that are relevant for that service. In other words, within the Legal Control folder, you want to only list the SAP Business-Objects Global Trade Services document types that you want the legal control service to be performed with. For example, if you have a return order for which you want to perform the embargo check and sanctioned party list so it appears in the both the services and in the legal control, you don't have the document mentioned.

The configuration menu path for this setting is SPRO • SAP REFERENCE IMG • SAP GLOBAL TRADE SERVICES • SAP COMPLIANCE MANAGEMENT • GENERAL SETTINGS • DOCUMENT STRUCTURE • ACTIVATE DOCUMENT TYPES.

Assignment of Feeder Document Types

Now you must assign the feeder system document types to the SAP BusinessObjects Global Trade Services documents you defined. For example, you might want to map the sales order document to the SAP BusinessObjects Global Trade Services document type EXORD. Similar to the organizational data mapping we saw earlier, here you have the option to map it to a logical system or a logical system group. If you decided to map the organizational data to the system group, you should continue this practice.

> **Note**
>
> If you have the document types in the SAP ECC plug-in activated and want to only map those documents in SAP BusinessObjects Global Trade Services, you can check the Activate Document Types Only checkbox. With automatically-transferred document types, you can pull the document types activated in the SAP ECC plug-in and mapped to the SAP BusinessObjects Global Trade Services document type, based on the application level selected (MM0A – Receipt/Import Purchasing Document, SD0A – Dispatch/Export Sales Document, or SD0B – Dispatch/Export – Outbound Delivery). You can run this in simulation mode and uncheck it when updating the configuration tables.

The configuration menu path for this setting is SPRO • SAP REFERENCE IMG • SAP GLOBAL TRADE SERVICES • SAP COMPLIANCE MANAGEMENT • GENERAL SETTINGS • DOCUMENT STRUCTURE • ASSIGNMENT OF DOCUMENT TYPES FROM FEEDER SYSTEMS • ASSIGN DOCUMENT TYPES AT FEEDER SYSTEM GROUP LEVEL.

Item Category Definition, Activation, and Mapping

Similar to document types, you need to define item categories in SAP Business-Objects Global Trade Services. The combination of document types and item categories allows you to control the document type service check activation. For example, if you have a regular sales order in which if you have a service item, and these service items don't involve any physical shipment of parts, then you can exclude them from a license check. Similarly, you can define an item category that you want to exclude from the relevant service. After you map it to the feeder system item category, it is transferred to SAP BusinessObjects Global Trade Services and excluded from that particular service check.

The configuration menu path for this setting is SPRO • SAP Reference IMG • SAP Global Trade Services • SAP Compliance Management • General Settings • Document Structure • Define Item Categories.

When activating item categories for legal control, make sure that Value Depreciation, Quantity Depreciation, and Depreciation Group are updated. This allows you to check and depreciate value and quantity from transactions to an assigned license. If you want the document to refer to the preceding document (e.g., deliveries refer to sales orders), check the Adopt Legal Control Data from Preceding Item checkbox. The configuration menu path for this is SPRO • SAP Reference IMG • SAP Global Trade Services • SAP Compliance Management • General Settings • Document Structure • Activate Item Categories.

While mapping item categories, you need to map the item category to the SAP BusinessObjects Global Trade Services item category, as is the case with application level and order types. The configuration menu path for this setting is SPRO • SAP Reference IMG • SAP Global Trade Services • SAP Compliance Management • General Settings • Document Structure • Assignment of Item Categories from Feeder System • Assign Item Category at Feeder System Group Level.

3.3   Embargo Service Checks

Countries that export or import goods perform embargo service checks for the countries with which they do business, based on the list they maintain within the SAP BusinessObjects Global Trade Services cockpit. From a configuration point of view, embargo activation is the most basic, and should help you understand how Compliance Management works. In the following sections, we will go over the Embargo setup for the Embargo Service activation and associated configurations. Having understood the baseline and the compliance foundation, these next sections will give you an overview and concept behind the compliance function enablement.

3.3.1   Embargo Service Setup and Configurations

The determination procedures for active legal regulation are pre-delivered for all of the services in SAP BusinessObjects Global Trade Services (Compliance, Customs, Risk Management, etc.), and you can view the pre-delivered assignment as the first configuration step on different service checks. The definition details behind these configurations can be found under the following menu path: SPRO • SAP REFERENCE IMG • SAP GLOBAL TRADE SERVICES • GENERAL SETTINGS • LEGAL REGULATIONS • DEFINE DETERMINATION PROCEDURE FOR ACTIVE LEGAL REGULATIONS.

Select the determination procedure of interest, and click on the folder titled Assignment of Determination Strategy (see Figure 3.9); you should see the sequence number and the determination strategy assigned. The default strategy is ALR001 – Determine Legal Regulation at Country Level. The other available strategies are described in Table 3.2.

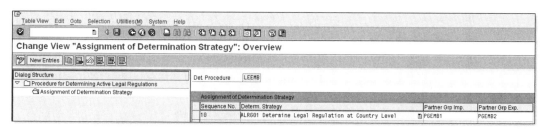

Figure 3.9   Document Type Activation for Different Services

Determination Procedure	Service Check
ALR002 – Determine Legal Regulation: Country/Country Level	Checks based on the combination of departure and destination country
ALR003 – Determine Legal Regulation: Country/Country Group Level	Checks based on the combination of departure and destination country group
ALRG11 – Determine Legal Regulation: Country Group Level	Checks based on the departure or destination country group
ALRG13 – Determine Legal Regulation: Country Group/Country Level	Checks based on the combination of departure country group and destination country
ALRG13 – Determine Legal Regulation: Country Group/Country Group Level	Checks based on the combination of departure and destination country group
ALR001 – Determine Legal Regulation at Country Level	Checks based on the departure or destination country

Table 3.2 Determination Procedure Defaults Available in the System

The country group option allows you to group countries, which allows you to use the group for activation; in other words, if you want to add a country, you can simply add to the group, and the activation is enabled. Figure 3.9 displays the determination strategy assigned by default, which is Legal Regulation Activation by Country. If you choose to pick Country Group/Country, then you need to appropriately activate it within the Country Group folder (Country Group/Country subfolder). Legal regulation activation is done via the following menu path: SPRO • SAP REFERENCE IMG • SAP GLOBAL TRADE SERVICES • GENERAL SETTINGS • LEGAL REGULATIONS • ACTIVATE LEGAL REGULATIONS AT COUNTRY/COUNTRY GROUP LEVEL.

Note that when you pick a combination of departure country and destination country, you need to list all of the possible combinations from where the transactions could be checked. With export transactions, the departure country is picked from the plant country key, and destination country from the partner country. With import transactions, the departure country is picked from the partner country and the destination from the receiving plant country key.

Within Figure 3.9 for the determination procedure activation, you can see the partner group assigned for import and export. These partner groups are mapped to these services and used for screening. You can group partners to be screened for a particular service within the group. The configurations to maintain the partner within the particular group are maintained under the configuration step: SPRO •

SAP Reference IMG • SAP Global Trade Services • General Settings • Partner Structure • Define Groups of Partners Functions. Here you list all of the partners you are interested in checking for embargo services. When you click on the configuration, it lists the entire partner group pre-delivered in the system. Select the partner group of interest, and click on the Assign Partner Function folder. This lists all of the partner function assigned to the partner group.

3.3.2 Activations Specific to Embargo Service Checks

Based on the determination procedure services assigned in the previous step, and the legal regulation activation maintained within SAP Global Trade Services • Legal Regulations • Activate Legal Regulations at Country/Country Group Level, you must activate the services for export and import checks. From the possible entries, pick the appropriate selection (see Figure 3.10). For embargo service checks on imports, we recommend 3: Check: Receipt/Import (Excluding Domestic). For imports, we recommend 3: Check: Dispatch/Export (Excluding Domestics).

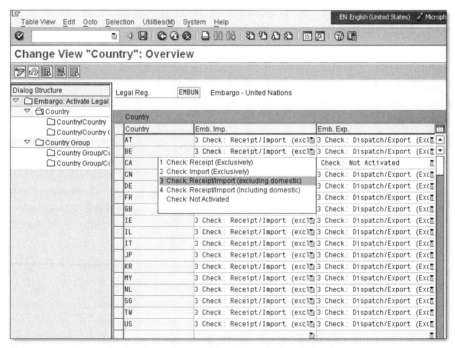

Figure 3.10 Determination Procedure and Legal Regulation Activation

3.3.3 Control Settings for Embargo Service Checks

The third step in the embargo service check is the control settings, which allow you to set up any settings that are specific to embargo checks, sanctioned party list, or legal control services. With embargo service checks, you map the partner group for import and export. If you want the system to send an email when documents are blocked, check the Sending of Mail Blck checkbox (see Figure 3.11).

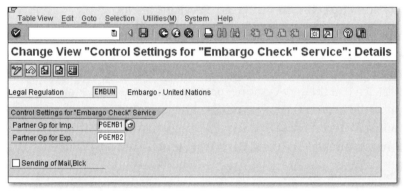

Figure 3.11 Legal Regulation Activation for Export/Import Services

3.4 Summary

In this chapter, we went through the baseline configurations that are fundamental to all modules. After that, we discussed the Compliance Management configuration settings that are used across all of the compliance services. Finally, we focused on the embargo services checks activation to understand the foundation of compliance settings. Within the embargo services, we went over the configuration setup, and in the next chapter, we will start with the data setup that is required to enable the embargo services. Understanding the baseline, foundation, and the embargo configuration setup will be valuable as we move to more complex functions within Compliance Management. In the next chapter, we will also look at the setup of the sanctioned party list from the configuration and the master data setup.

Every compliance setting has a two-fold setup — backend and frontend configuration — that completes the activation and enables the service. Now that you are familiar with embargo configuration, you will learn how to set up the embargo master data, apply it operationally, and move on to more complex setups. This chapter also discusses sanctioned party list (SPL) screening and the operational effectiveness of embargo, SPL, and tactical reporting.

4   Enabling Embargo and Sanctioned Part List Screening

With the background of the SAP BusinessObjects Global Trade Services baseline configuration, compliance foundation, and the embargo configuration set up, we will move on to the data set up that is required to enable the embargo. In this chapter, we will discuss the data setup that is required to enable embargo services. With every service activation, there is also an associated frontend data set up to enable the services from the business application. We will also go over the business process procedure (BPP), which ensures that the processes designed are effective. In this chapter, we address these two aspects of the embargo service activation, which will ensure that we have a complete solution implementation in place.

Sanctioned party list (SPL) activation makes use of the SAP BusinessObjects Global Trade Services baseline and the compliance foundations and concepts we went over with embargo. SPL extends its functionality and capability with content updates and screening of text. In this chapter, we will show you how to set up SPL from configuration and content. We will also review the business effectiveness with operational reporting and other functionality with SPL.

4.1   Embargo Applications

The process of exporting and importing goods involves outbound and inbound transactions that cross borders. For exports, which are beholden to the export country's regulations, you must check to make sure that the destination country is not on the embargo list. Similarly, for imports, which are beholden to the import country's regulations, you must check to make sure that the ship-from country is not on the embargo list. There are three different ways you can enable embargo country activation from the frontend setup:

▶ Embargo Countries – Global

▶ Legal Regulation and Country of Departure or Destination

▶ Legal Regulation and Specific to Country of Departure and Destination combination

In the following sections, we discuss each of these methods in more detail.

4.1.1   Embargo Country – Global

With this setup, you can list all countries that are under embargo for outbound and inbound transactions. (If you have only activated embargo legal regulations for exports, it will only check for embargo countries in outbound transactions. For more details on this, refer to Chapter 3, SAP BusinessObjects Global Trade Services Baseline Settings, where we discuss the configuration for embargo service activation.)

To maintain the setup for embargo countries, access the following menu path: SAP BusinessObjects Global Trade Services Area Menu /SAPSLL/Menu_Legal • Legal Control – Export (Figure 4.1). Under the Embargo section, click on Maintain Country-Specific Information, or use Transaction /SAPSLL/CNTRY. Then click Execute.

The steps to create embargo entries are as follows:

1. While you are in Transaction /SAPSLL/CNTRY, click on Execute (🔄). This brings up the Change Country-Specific Information screen.

2. Click on the Create icon (🗋) to maintain the countries.

3. After entering a country, double-click it. This moves the country into the time series with default valid-from and valid-to dates.

4. If you want to identify the country as an embargo country, select the country under the time series, and click on the Duplicate Row icon (🖂).

5. Check the Embargo checkbox, and click on the Save icon (🖫).

Figure 4.1 Embargo Country Maintenance

6. This list must include all of the countries with which you do business, with the countries identified for embargo listed as such.

4.1.2   Legal Regulation and Country of Destination or Departure

This functionality is used when you have a specific country or regulation for import or export, and you want to maintain an exclusive embargo list by legal regulation. For example, this might come in handy if you have a company and a subsidiary company with different embargo rules sharing the same SAP Business-

Objects Global Trade Services system. This functionality allows you to have different regulations both by country and by outbound or inbound transactions.

To maintain this setup, access the following menu path: SAP BusinessObjects Global Trade Services Area Menu (/SAPSLL/MENU_LEGAL) • Legal Control – Export or Import (Figure 4.2). Under the Embargo section, click on Legal Regulation/Country of Destination, or use Transaction /SAPSLL/CCCTRY. Then click Execute.

The steps to create the embargo entries are as follows:

1. While you are in Transaction /SAPSLL/CCCTRY, click on Execute (🌐). This brings up the Change Legal Control: Country-Specific Information screen.

2. Click on the Create icon (🗔) to maintain the countries by legal regulations.

3. After entering a country, double-click on the entry. This moves the country into the time series with default valid-from and valid-to dates.

4. If you want to identify the country as an embargo country, select the country under the time series, and click on the Duplicate Row icon (🗔).

5. Check the Embargo checkbox, and click on the Save icon (🖫).

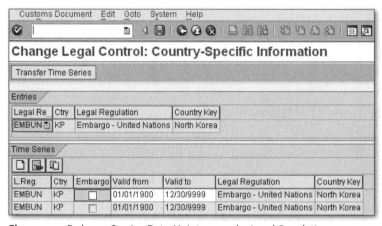

Figure 4.2 Embargo Service Data Maintenance by Legal Regulation

4.1.3 Legal Regulation and Specific to Country of Departure and Destination

This setup allows you to list embargo countries by the ship-from and ship-to legs. For example, a company might want to block transactions from the United States to Cuba but allow transactions from Canada to Cuba (as Canada doesn't have any restrictions on shipping to Cuba). With this functionality setup, you can list the legs that are prohibited.

To maintain this setup, access the following menu path: SAP BUSINESSOBJECTS GLOBAL TRADE SERVICES AREA MENU (/SAPSLL/MENU_LEGAL) • LEGAL CONTROL • EXPORT OR IMPORT (Figure 4.3). Under the Embargo section, click on Legal Regulation/Country of Dept/Destination, or use Transaction /SAPSLL/CEEMB. Then click Execute.

The steps to create the embargo entries are as follows:

1. While you are in Transaction /SAPSLL/CEEMB, click on Execute ( ). This brings up the Change Legal Control: Country-Specific Information screen.

2. Click on the Create icon ( ) to maintain the countries' legs by legal regulations.

3. After entering a country, double-click on the entry. This moves the country into the time series with default valid-from and valid-to dates.

4. If you want to identify the country as an embargo leg, select the country under the time series, and click on the Duplicate Row icon ( ).

5. Check the Embargo checkbox, and click on the Save icon ( ).

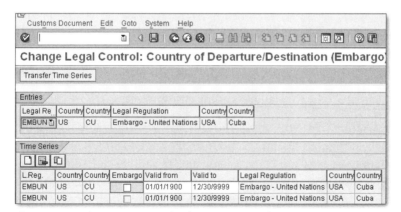

Figure 4.3 Embargo Activation by the Departure and Destination Country

4.2 Configuration of the Sanctioned Party List

In business transactions, you deal with business partners (such as customers, vendors, financial institutions, or individuals) who have various roles (e.g., sold-to, ship-to, end customer, or consignee, for exports; vendor and suppliers for imports). These business partners are screened in SAP BusinessObjects Global Trade Services against denied party lists, a process that is called *sanctioned party list screening*. When the business partners are created or changed in the feeder system, the addresses are transferred to SAP BusinessObjects Global Trade Services for screening. During the transaction processes, these business partner screening results are referenced. If, for example, an address is changed in a document, SPL screening would be performed at the document level.

Denied party lists are published by the government and regularly updated. SAP BusinessObjects Global Trade Services allows you to load this content as an XML file and use it for business partner screening. (There are companies who translate the government-published list into an XML file.) You can schedule a background job to get this updated file on a periodic basis.

The configuration of the SPL is slightly more complex than the configuration of embargo services. As you will recall, from Section 3.3.3, Control Settings for Embargo Service Checks, the three basic activation steps for embargo services are

1. Set the determination procedure for active regulations.

2. Activate legal regulations.

3. Set the control settings for legal regulations.

In addition to these steps, SPL settings have two more specific settings that are unique for its activation:

1. Activate business partner at the business partner function level.

2. Define the control procedure for address comparison.

In the following sections, we will apply the concept we understood with the embargo to the SPL configuration and extend it to SPL specific setup. We will see how SPL configuration differs from embargo and also the additional steps for content load. There are a few steps that are in addition to embargo and specific to the SPL screening; we will review them and then apply the compliance service activation concept and set up the configuration for content load.

4.2.1 Activating the Business Partner at the Business Partner Function Level

This involves setting up the application object control settings for business partners and their associated business partner functions. The control settings involve selecting the type of SPL block (default setting is titled 1 Process is Blocked – Service Removes the Block), the time of the SPL check (1 Synchronous or Asynchronous), and the business area it falls under (Logistics, Financial Accounting, or Human Resources).

The default SPL block setting means that the system screens the business partner, and, if it finds a block based on the system parameter settings, it blocks this business partner. Users can then review the results and manually release it or take appropriate action.

For the Time of SPL Check field, we recommend that you use Synchronous — except during conversion or volume transfer — when you should set it to Asynchronous. Then revert back to Synchronous for ongoing or regular transfers.

The Separation into Business Area field ensures that blocked business partner and associated transactions fall under the appropriate view for operational effectiveness and reporting.

Within the Activating Business Partner field, the default settings are pre-delivered for customers and vendors. You must ensure that the entries for other BP roles are maintained: contact person, employee (if you use an HR interface), bank, and so on.

If you want to restrict the control of review of business partners by company codes within your organization, check the Enhanced Authorization Check in Sanctioned Party List Areas box, and ensure that the security profile has the Foreign Trade Organization check in it.

Figure 4.4 displays the control settings for SPL. Here we defined the control functions that enable and control the key attributes for SPL services.

Figure 4.4 SPL Control Settings for Business Partners

4.2.2 Determination Procedure

The default determination procedure uses the country as key in determining the active legal regulation, which performs the service check. As explained in Chapter 3, determination procedures are used for determining the legal regulations. You can set the parameter for this determination, which can be country or a combination of country and country group, for example. For SPL, we recommend that you keep the standard delivered determination procedure unless there is a business need to have a different one.

4.2.3 Activate Legal Regulation

Similar to embargo service checks, you need to activate the SPL legal regulation. You have five different choices to pick from when doing this activation:

▶ Check: Dispatch (Exclusively)

▶ Check: Export (Exclusively)

▶ Check: Dispatch/Export (Excluding Domestic)

▶ Check: Dispatch/Export (Including Domestic)

▶ No Check (no SPL service activation)

As with Compliance Management, if you are obliged to screen your domestic partners as well, we recommend that you select option 4, Check: Dispatch/Export (Including Domestic). Also, ensure that you are activating for both imports and exports, per the requirement.

4.2.4   Address Comparison

Here you define the control procedure for address screening; in other words, you define the rules according to which the system performs sanctioned party list screening checks. These rules are used in performing the screening of the business partner address string against the denied party list.

Defining control procedures for address comparison is a two-step process:

1. Define the control procedure.
2. Detail the control for screening business partner addresses.

In the following sections, we discuss each of these steps in more detail.

Define the Control Procedure

Defining the control procedure involves selecting the language for screening (English) and the basis of comparison for the search term origin. For the search term origin, you can choose either the SPL entry or the business partner address (for index building and comparison). If you pick the SPL entry, the system uses the SPL entry as the basis for determining the percentage of match. For example, if there is an SPL entry with the name Dawood, and you have a business partner by the name of Dawod, your percentage would be the number of business partner characters that matches with the SPL entry — in this case, 5 — divided by the number of characters of the SPL entry — in this case, 6 — which would be 83%. This percentage calculation reverses if you select both Basis for Comparison String from Partner Address and Basis for Comparison Parallel from Sanctioned Party List/Address. This calculates the number of business partner characters that match with the SPL, which reverses the percentage calculation and takes into account the best-case scenarios.

Detail the Control for Screening Business Partner Addresses

In this step, you define the business partner address fields that are relevant for SPL screening, as well as what logical operator you want to assign to these selected fields: AND or OR. The OR operation is used when you want to search for a match that has one or more address elements. For example, if you have street, city, and country listed with OR operators, SPL searches will return results for any business partner address that has any one of these fields as a match. The AND operator, on the other hand, should be used if you want to capture individual address fields for match selection and result.

After the address object fields are identified for SPL screening and assigned an operator, you must configure the details behind the field selected. Follow these steps:

1. Check the Check Object box, if you want the Address field to be taken into consideration for SPL screening.

2. The Search Term Origin field defaults from the comparison procedure definition. If you prefer, you can pick a different selection for the address field. (Note, though, that we recommend keeping the default settings.)

3. Within the Linking Operator field, select the operator choice: OR or AND.

4. Within the Relational Operator field, you have two choices:

   ▸ A Comparison Index Contained in the Keyword from Address

   ▸ B Comparison Index and Keyword from Address Are Identical

   With the first option, the system searches for individual characters within the business partner addresses. With the second option, it considers only strings of characters. For closer hits, we recommended that you use B Comparison Index and Keyword from Address Are Identical.

5. Within the Minimum Field, you have Search Term and Originating Features percentage to be maintained for the search criteria. You must update the percentage of the search threshold. Search Term Percentage is calculated based on the number of character matches within the address as compared to the SPL content or address entry. Original Form looks for the complete form or word for a match. Take a case where you have a business partner named Dawod B Ibrahim and an SPL entry of Dawoad A Ibrahim. The system first searches the individual characters within the two business partner words (Dawod and Ibrahim), for Dawod, 5 out of 6 is a match, and for Ibrahim, it is a complete match. So the first round of percentage threshold is the search terms qualification: with Dawod it is 83.33% and with Ibrahim it is 100 %. There is no match for the middle name. So, if you had the search term less than 83.33, the search term would result in a success of match. Once the search term is successful, the system moves on to the Originating Form. If the search is successful, the original terms are matched against each individual word of the business partner with the SPL entry; in this case, the Dawod business partner address is matched

against the Dawoad SPL entry, and the Ibrahim business partner address is matched with the Ibrahim SPL entry. In other words, the business partner Originating Form name Dawod B Ibrahim has two of three words match against the SPL entry Dawoad A Ibrahim, so the percentage for the originating terms calculates to 66.66%. If you have percentage less than 66.66, then only this name will be found as a match.

6. Select Allow Multiple Matches for Origin if you want repeated words considered as individual entities. Without this selection, duplicate address entries will be considered as one. We recommend that you don't select this because it tends to raise the hit ratio and provide more false hits.

The Assign Address Fields lists all of the fields that you have selected to be used for SPL screening purposes. Figure 4.5 displays the configuration settings for comparison procedures with the list of fields and details behind each field. You can also see the list of fields that are listed for SPL screening. For example, the Name field object might be maintained in different fields within SAP ECC (Name1, Name2, etc.). You should list all of the fields you are interested in subjecting to SPL screening.

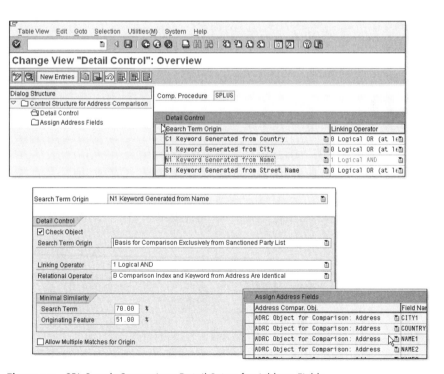

Figure 4.5 SPL Search Comparison Detail Setup for Address Fields

4.2.5 Control Settings

Control settings are defined for every service within SAP BusinessObjects Global Trade Services and are unique for each service. The control settings of SPL involve the setup of the following:

- List types
- Reference types
- Assigning time zone to deadline type
- Address activation

The configuration step for control settings can be found under SAP Reference IMG • SAP Global Trade Services • SAP Compliance Management • Sanctioned Party List Screening Services • Control Settings for Sanctioned Party List Screening Services, or via Transaction SPRO.

Figure 4.6 displays the control settings that influence the SPL screening and service checks.

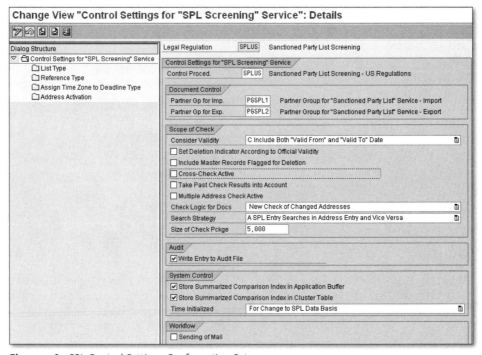

Figure 4.6 SPL Control Settings Configuration Setup

There are configurations that are associated with the control settings for SPL that are required for content maintenance. In the following sections, we discuss the add-on setup for SPL control settings and service activation, list types that allow you to add the denied party lists that you want to load, reference types, time zones, and the different business partner addresses you want to screen.

List Type

The denied party lists constitutes of the names and addresses of individuals, businesses, and entities who are banned from doing business with and are published by respective countries based on the restriction they want to impose for different national interest, terrorism or nuclear proliferation, and so on. These lists are published in different list and sublist categories, for example, DOS (State Department Statutorily Debarred Parties), DTO (State Dept, Designated Terrorist Organization), and so on. To allow the upload of content of the denied party list, you must define these list types in the system. Many of the list types are pre-delivered; contact the content provider to validate the lists and update the system with the missing list types.

Defining a list type involves the list type code, description, and minimum length of the index entries for the fields selected (Name, Street, City, etc.). The length of the character defined here is used to define the number of characters that will be used for a minimum hit. In other words, if you have defined 4, the search terms will only look for words that are four letters or more in length. We recommend that you keep the Name minimum index at 2 and the Street and City at 4, so that you don't get too many results.

Reference Type

The Reference Type field allows you to capture different names or aliases that represent the same person or entity. Some of the pre-delivered reference types are A.K.A. (also known as) and D.B.A. (doing business as).

Control Settings Details

The details-level configuration specific to the control settings for SPL involves the assignment of control procedures that are defined for address comparison (discussed earlier in Section 4.2.4, Address Comparison). With the document control, you must assign the partner group for import and the partner group for export.

(Partner groupings for export and import are maintained in the general settings, as we saw in Chapter 3.) Within the groups, list all business partners from the feeder system document for which you want to perform SPL screening.

Within Scope of Check, the following information needs to be updated:

1. **Validity**
   Keep the default selection, C: Include Both "Valid From" and "Valid To" Date.

2. **Check Logic for Docs**
   Keep the default setting, New Check of Changed Addresses. This ensures that the document partner addresses are screened when they are changed in the document. If the addresses are not changed, the system refers to the business partner master screen results.

3. **Search Strategy**
   Select the option A: SPL Entry Searches in Address and Vice Versa. This ensures that SPL screening is performed both (a) by selecting the entry in the SPL and finding a match in the business partner list; and (b) by taking a business partner address and performing the screening against the SPL.

4. **Size of Check Pckge**
   Keep this size based on the performance testing and sizing. For volume transfer, we normally recommend keeping the size lower (around 5000 to 10000).

5. **Audit**
   Check the Write Entry to Audit File box. This ensures that the SPL screening and release by system and manual are captured in the audit trail. During the initial transfer of a volume of business partners, we recommend that you turn it off, as it slows downs the business partner transfer.

6. **System Control**
   Select Store Summarized Comparison Index in Application Buffer and Store Summarized Comparison Index in Cluster Table. The first selection ensures that the SPL index build is stored in the application buffer, and the second one in the cluster table. SAP BusinessObjects Global Trade Services provides this feature of indexing for faster retrieval and text screening.

7. **Time Initiated**
   Select For Change to SPL Data Basis. This ensures that any update to denied partner list content will trigger SPL screening.

In addition to the previous list items, you must also check the following options:

- ▶ **Set Deletion Indicator According to Official Validity**
  This ensures that if you have a validity date assigned to the content, the SPL entry is marked for deletion and archive.

- ▶ **Include Master Records Flagged for Deletion**
  This allows you to include the SPL records that are marked for deletion.

- ▶ **Cross-Check Active**
  If checked, the SPL screening is performed against one another; in other words, Name would be screened against the Name field and other Address fields, such as Street, City, and so on.

- ▶ **Take Past Check Results into Account**
  This allows you to use past screening results for current searches. In other words, if, in the past, you had a hit against the name of Rajen, and the business user found it to be a false hit and released it, the system will remember this and not list the business partner as blocked.

- ▶ **Multiple Address Check Active**
  This allows you to perform SPL screening on multiple addresses, if it is maintained in SAP BusinessObjects Global Trade Services (main address, billing address, delivery address, etc.).

WorkFlow

SPL allows you to send a notification if documents are blocked due to SPL screening. To implement this, check the Sending of Mail check box under the Workflow section, as shown in Figure 4.6 and set up prerequisite steps. The prerequisite steps are part of the SAP BusinessObjects Global Trade Services frontend cockpit setup, which is accessed via Transaction /SAPSLL/MENU_LEGAL. Click on System Communication/Workflow under the System Administration section, and select WorkFlow. Then follow these two steps:

1. Maintain user groups. These help you group the users to whom you would like to send the notification.

2. Under Notification Control for Blocked Documents, maintain the foreign trade organization, legal regulation (SPLUS), and user groups you maintained in the previous step.

Comparison Terms

SPL master data requires that control settings be set up for the configured search terms. The master data setup can be accessed via the following menu path: SAP BusinessObjects Global Trade Services Area Menu (/SAPSLL/MENU_LEGAL) • SAP Compliance Management • Sanctioned Party List Screening • Master Data • Control Settings for Comparison Terms • General Settings.

One important master data setup for SPL is the maintenance of the business partner for the content load (business partner role as data provider). This can be maintained just as regular business partners are maintained, via SAP BusinessObjects Global Trade Services Area Menu (/SAPSLL/MENU_LEGAL) • SAP Compliance Management • Sanctioned Party List Screening • Master Data • Business Partner • Edit Business Partners. You must configure the control settings before you can load the sanctioned party list or denied party list content.

When you click on General Settings under Control Settings for Comparison Terms, there are subfolders that contain the following fields:

▶ **Delimiter**
Here you need to list all special characters, including numbers the content file might have; for example, hyphen (-), comma (,), quotes (""), and so on.

▶ **Excluded Terms**
Here you need to list all of the terms that you want to exclude from the SPL screening. There are a few terms that are common across all addresses, names, and so on, and excluding them will result in fewer false hits, for example, words such as "International," "Division," "PTE," and so on. SAP BusinessObjects Global Trade Services has some pre-delivered exclusions; you can review them and add to the list.

▶ **Alias Terms**
This allows you to screen alias names; in other words, if a person is known by a different name, and you want to use that name instead of the official name, you can maintain the alias. If you have a business partner named David who also goes by Dave, then maintaining the alias would mean that "Dave" would be used while searching the SPL.

▶ **Normalization**
Normalization allows you to replace certain characters or sets of characters with different characters for search purposes. For example, "psychology" could be replaced by "sychology," as they sound similar. If you maintain normalization

for "PSY" to "SY," the system replaces "PSY" with "SY" for the SPL search. It is recommended that the normalization setup is used once you have tried and understood the other settings, as having too many functional settings within control settings might make it difficult to interpret screening results.

▶ **TREX Destination**
With SAP BusinessObjects Global Trade Services 7.2, there is a SAP TREX function with SPL screening. If you plan to use it, you need to maintain the RFC destination for the comparison procedure.

Figure 4.7 displays the SPL frontend data set up, which will in turn enable the SPL services and business processes behind it.

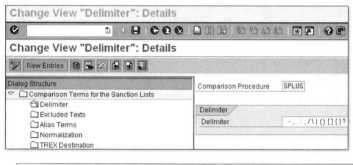

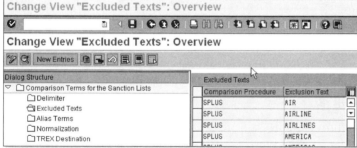

Figure 4.7 SPL Cockpit or Data Setup Within the Frontend

4.3   SPL Content Loading and Associated Processes

The following sections discuss the loading and associated processes — monitoring, indexing, and screening — of SPL content.

4.3.1 Loading

There are several different ways to load SPL content into SAP BusinessObjects Global Trade Services. One option is to manually maintain the SPL entries, which is an option that can be used to maintain internal, company-specific lists.

SAP BusinessObjects Global Trade Services also allows you to load content through an XML interface. To take advantage of this option, you must contract with a company that provides the initial load and periodic updates of the denied party list. You can then set up periodic jobs to load the updated information into the SAP BusinessObjects Global Trade Services system.

> **Note**
>
> You can set up a connection or ask the content provider to push the updated file into a particular location for you to pick up and upload into SAP BusinessObjects Global Trade Services. This could be based on a schedule or a trigger, such as if a new file is transferred into this particular directory.

You can also set up an SAP NetWeaver XI interface between your SAP BusinessObjects Global Trade Services system and the denied party list content provider. SAP BusinessObjects Global Trade Services is capable of automating this through an SAP NetWeaver XI interface.

In the following sections, we discuss the different reports, tools, and functionality within SPL screening and the operational effectiveness needed to make optimal use of it.

4.3.2 Monitoring

The Monitoring section has a list of reports that allow you to monitor the denied party list content that is loaded into the system. Following the content load, SAP BusinessObjects Global Trade Services allows you to monitor this content. You can view the content in different formats, such as an overview list (all of the address fields in one line) or a structured list (address fields separated by lines). Use the Display Overview List to look at the SPL in a list format and run the Display Structure List to display the SPL data in structure format, such as name, address, and so on. You can also display the SPL that is expiring by running the report Display Expiring Sanctioned Party List. Because the SPL content load can be very volume-intensive, and if you prefer, you can archive them. The report Display Archivable allows you to list the SPL entries that can be archived. SPL entry is very critical and sensitive information, so you can also track the changes to the databases with the report Display Change History.

4.3.3 Indexing

Comparing characters from a denied party list database to characters from a business partner database is extremely performance intensive. As such, SAP Business-Objects Global Trade Services provides a feature to build indexes based on these databases. SPL screening is accomplished using these indexes instead of raw characters, which improves performance.

To build these indexes, there are a few actions that need to be performed following the denied party list content load:

1. Generate comparison terms. This allows you to build the indexes for the SPL content. This option can be accessed via SAP BUSINESSOBJECTS GLOBAL TRADE SERVICES AREA MENU (/SAPSLL/MENU_LEGAL) • SAP COMPLIANCE MANAGEMENT • SANCTIONED PARTY LIST SCREENING • MASTER DATA • COMPARISON TERMS FOR SANCTIONED PARTY LISTS • GENERATE COMPARISON TERMS. Alternatively, you can use Transaction /SAPSLL/SPL_ST01. Enter the legal regulation, uncheck the Simulation Mode, and run it in the background.

2. After building the index, load it into the memory. Click on Aggregate Comparison Terms within Comparison Terms for Sanctioned Party Lists, or use Transaction /SAPSLL/SPL_ID01. Enter the legal regulation (e.g., SPLUS), and schedule it in the background. Alternatively, you can also run it online.

While you are in the master data tab under Comparison Terms for Business Partners, you have the option to build an index for business partners as well. This can be accessed via Transaction /SAPSLL/SPL_STBP. This allows you to build the index for the entire database or based on incremental load. For an ongoing run, select Changed Partner Addresses only.

> **Note**
>
> If you make any changes to the SPL configurations or control settings in the SAP BusinessObjects Global Trade Services SPL master data, we recommend that you reset the buffer. This function can be found under SAP BUSINESSOBJECTS GLOBAL TRADE SERVICES AREA MENU (/SAPSLL/MENU_LEGAL) • SAP COMPLIANCE MANAGEMENT • SANCTIONED PARTY LIST SCREENING • MASTER DATA. Under Customizing/Application Buffer, click on Reset Buffer, or use Transaction /SAPSLL/SPL_RESET. Then rebuild the SPL and business partner indexes. When you run the business partner index, select the option All Partner Addresses (Figure 4.8).

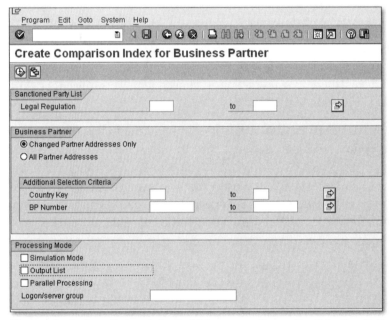

Figure 4.8 Business Partner Index Build Program or Transaction Selection Options

Resetting the buffer allows you to reset and reinitiate the indexes based on the configuration and SPL SAP BusinessObjects Global Trade Services frontend or cockpit settings. While running the transaction, check Initiate String Comparison and Initialize Legal Control, and execute the transaction or schedule it in the background. After this, you can arrange the SPL indexes and aggregate them. Similarly you can also build indexes on the business partner for quick retrieval, the concept is similar to your phone book or any book index at the end, where it allows you to quick search by sequencing of number or alphabetical characters.

4.3.4 Screenings

Business partners are created as master data in SAP ECC and then transferred to SAP BusinessObjects Global Trade Services. The screening of business partners is captured in the system with a code for future audit purposes. Table 4.1 explains the different screening scenarios available for business partners and documents.

SPL Screening Scenario	Description	Purpose
A1	Check Business Partner Address	Used in business partner screening when a business partner is initially transferred from the feeder system, or when the address of the business partner is changed in the feeder system and than transferred to SAP BusinessObjects Global Trade Services
B1	Periodically Check Business Partner Address	Allows you to re-screen a business partner with the existing SPL database.
C1	Business Partner Screening Against Delta Lists	Allows you to screen the existing list within SAP BusinessObjects Global Trade Services against the SPL delta file.
A2	Check Document Address	Used in document screening when documents are initially transferred or when the address is changed in the feeder system and transferred to SAP BusinessObjects Global Trade Services.
B2	Periodic Check Document Address	Used to re-screen the document partner with the existing SPL database.
C2	Check Document Address Against Delta Lists	Used when screening the existing documents within SAP BusinessObjects Global Trade Services against the SPL delta.

Table 4.1 SPL Screening Scenarios

Figure 4.9 displays the audit trail of business partner and document screening.

Display Audit Trail for Business Partner Address Check

BP	BP Number	Created by	Screening Date	L.Reg.	Scrn.Scen.	Name		City	Street
L.Reg. Seq.No.	Type Street			City			Ctry Name		
9000007250 12686		:00P12	10.11.2008 14:30:01	SPLUS	A1	XIAN AERO-ENGINE GROUP LTD		XIAN	
9000007250 12686			10.11.2008 15:02:56	SPLUS	B1	XIAN AERO-ENGINE GROUP LTD		XIAN	
SPLUS 1						CHENGDU	CN		
SPLUS 1							CHENGDU	CORPORATION	
SPLUS 1							XIAN	CO. LTD.	
SPLUS 1						XIAN	CN		
10006704 7174		:00P12	09.11.2008 19:45:37	SPLUS	A1	XIAN AERO-ENGINE GROUP LTD		XIAN	Xujiawan Beijiao
SPLUS 1						XIAN	CN		
SPLUS 1							XIAN	CO. LTD.	
SPLUS 1						CHENGDU	CN		
SPLUS 1							CHENGDU	GROUP CORPORATION	

Display Audit Trail for Document Address Check

DocumentNo Item Partner Ro	L.Reg.	Screening Date Created	Scrn.Scen.	SCR	UDR	Name	City Street	Country BP	BP Number Comm. S
L.Reg. Seq.No. Type Street City Ctry Name									
20004100	SPLUS	01.12.2008 04:13:39	A2			LAYTRON AG	Kuesnacht Faehnlibrunnenstrasse 3 CH	10003308 3824	
40005449	SPLUS	03.12.2008 06:48:45	A2			LAYTRON AG	Kuesnacht Faehnlibrunnenstrasse 3 CH	10003308 3824	

Figure 4.9 Audit Trail for Business Partners and Documents (A1 and A2)

There are three functional areas within the SPL: logistics, financial accounting, and human resources. All have the preceding screening scenarios. SAP BusinessObjects Global Trade Services also provides functionality to schedule these screenings in background and dialogue mode. As the screening jobs are performance-intensive and depending on your database size, we recommend that you run them as background jobs.

You can choose to perform synchronous or asynchronous screening on these business partners, but we recommend synchronous screening for regular business partner transfers, and asynchronous screening for volume transfers (such as during initial pre-go-live conversion). If you use synchronous screening, there is no need to set up any screening jobs. After initial load, you might get additional content as a new list or content additions to the original file, and these are called delta content loads. For delta content loads, however, you need to set up a delta-screening job for business partners and documents. Use C1 (business partners) and C2 (documents) for background delta-screening jobs.

These jobs should be scheduled in a partner sequence following the delta load of the SPL file, as explained here:

1. Run the SPL delta load file (Transaction /SAPSLL/SPL_UL01).

2. Build the index for SPL (Transaction /SAPSLL/SPL_ST01).

3. Load the SPL index.

4. Run the business partner index build while the SPL index is scheduled.

5. After both indexes are built, schedule the business partner delta screening (C1).

6. After the business partner delta screening is complete, schedule the document delta screening (C2).

SAP BusinessObjects Global Trade Services also allows you to run simulation screening against your existing business partners and documents; with SAP BusinessObjects Global Trade Services 7.2, you can run a simulation screening against an external file with business partner addresses in them. These simulation audits are captured within the system for future review and audit purposes.

4.3.5   Operational Effectiveness

There are a few tips and tricks that are important for operational effectiveness in SPL screening. In this section, we discuss these tips and tricks, introducing some new features and emphasizing some already-discussed features.

First, it is important to understand the business partner screening results. After the initial setup of the configuration rules, we recommend that you run the block partner report and understand the screening results. Plan on testing with results you expect to be blocked. You might have to do a trial and error with a combination of the configuration settings and the control settings within the SAP BusinessObjects Global Trade Services cockpit.

Indexes are important functions of the SPL screening. Plan on running the SPL index if one or more of the following happens:

▶ Change in the SPL database; new delta file loaded

▶ SPL configuration changes

▶ SPL control settings changes within the SAP BusinessObjects Global Trade Services cockpit

The reset of the buffer is important when one or more of the following happens:

▶ SPL configurations

▶ SPL control settings changes

4.4   Tactical Reporting

SAP BusinessObjects Global Trade Services provides effective tactical reporting, which is very useful for day-to-day operations. These reports allow you to review the blocks within SAP BusinessObjects Global Trade Services, analyze the reason for the blocks, and take appropriate action. For the SPL, you have one functional area in which to look at all of the export and import transactions. With embargo services, the report appears in two areas, export or import; for example, purchase orders appear in the import area, and sales orders in the export area. In this section, we review some of the reporting features and applications of embargo checks and SPL screening.

4.4.1   Reports on Embargo Business Partners and Documents

Embargo functionality can be found under Legal Control – Import or Export. This functionality is the same for both imports and exports, but we will use exports as an example. When you click on Legal Control – Export, you can see a list of functions within the Embargo section.

Release Block Document (Transaction/SAPSLL/EMB_BLRL_EXP) allows you to release documents that have business partners under embargo. If you have a scenario where you need to transact on a restrictive basis, this allows you to only release selective transactions. Similarly, Release Block Payments (Transaction /SAPSLL/FI_EMBRL_EXP) allows you to release block payment transactions selectively.

Display Release Documents (Transaction /SAPSLL/REL_DOC_EMBE) and Payment (Transaction /SAPSLL/REL_FI_EMBE) allow you to display the released documents and payments.

You can also display business partners under embargo. Figure 4.10 shows the report output of this transaction (Transaction /SAPSLL/EMB_BP_EXP), as well as the transaction that allows you to selectively release documents under embargo.

Display of Business Partners with Embargo Situation - Export

BP Number	c	L.Reg	Country of	Country of	Definitive From-Date	Definitive To-Date	Name	City	Street	Cty
14100	Country-Specific Information		KP		01.01.1900 00:00:00	31.12.9999 00:00:00	TECHNOLOGY CO LTD	KYUNGKI-DO	#1048-5 SINGIL-DONG DANWON-GU ANSAN SI	KP
39772	Country-Specific Information		KP		01.01.1900 00:00:00	31.12.9999 00:00:00	CAPITAL KOREN CO LIMITED	SEOUL	8F HANWHA BLDG 110 SOGONG-DONG JUNG-GU	KP
39147	Country-Specific Information		IR		01.01.1900 00:00:00	31.12.9999 00:00:00	Relocation Services Ltd	Co.Kildare	Portgloriam, Clain Road, Kilcock	IR
40306	Country-Specific Information		KP		01.01.1900 00:00:00	31.12.9999 00:00:00	DIAMOND IND CO LTD	OSAN CITY	520-2 WON DONG	KP
49546	Country-Specific Information		KP		01.01.1900 00:00:00	31.12.9999 00:00:00	SURPLUS GLOBAL INC	PYEONGTAEK-CITY	381 GAGOK-LI JINWI-MYEON	KP
52832	Country-Specific Information		KP		01.01.1900 00:00:00	31.12.9999 00:00:00	HWAN OH	SEOUL	23-804 HYANDAI APT	KP
55350	Country-Specific Information		KP		01.01.1900 00:00:00	31.12.9999 00:00:00	TECH CO LTD	YONGIN-CITY KYONGGI-DO	659-2 SEORI IDONG-MYEON CHEOIN-GU	KP

Legal Control: Release Blocked Export Documents (Embargo)

Ref. No.	Obj.Type	Log.System	CasDoc.No	Year	SPL	Embargo	Lic.	Restitutn	Lett.Cred.	Doc. Type	FT Org	Im/Ex	Created by	Created on	Changed by	Changed by	Time Stamp DPr
Item	Item	Cat	SPL	Embargo	Lic.	Restitutn	Lett.Cred.	Qualifier	Text	Product No	Number	Grouping	Legal Unit	Ctry of.PL DeptCtry Dest.	Ctry Bill.Ctry Trad.	Cntr-U-C Ctry Def. Date	

| 4502000757 BUS2012 | CLNT200 31626 | 2008 | | | | | | EXPORD | FTO_0028 2 | | 24.11.2008 14:02:41 | | 20.01.2009 15:28:47 | |
| 20 EXORD1 | | | | | | | 0190-14820 | | LU_5050 | US | US TW | US | | TW |

| 4502002921 BUS2012 | CLNT200 34998 | 2008 | | | | | | EXPORD | FTO_0028 2 | | 24.11.2008 14:18:00 | | 26.12.2008 04:33:31 |
| 50 EXORD1 | | | | | Blocking Reason: License 0015-03787 | | | LU_5050 | US | US SG | US | | SG |

4502016845 BUS2012	CLNT200 3462	2009						EXPORD	FTO_0078 2		19.01.2009 19:38:18		19.01.2009 19:38:18
10 EXORD1							0020-49785		LU_5050	US	US TW	US		TW
20 EXORD1							0200-02262		LU_5050	US	US TW	US		TW

| 40038762 LIKP | CLNT200 3463 | 2009 | | | | | | EXPDLV | FTO_0001 2 | | 19.01.2009 19:39:47 | | 19.01.2009 19:40:04 |

Figure 4.10 Reports Showing (a) Business Partners Under Embargo and (b) Release of Documents with Business Partners Under Embargo

4.4.2 Reports on SPL Screening of Business Partners

With SPL, import and export functions are under the same area. When you click on Sanctioned Party List Screening, the system defaults to the SPL Logistics tab. Within the Monitoring tab, there is a section for Business Partners and Documents. Within Business Partners, there are reports for Blocked Business Partners, Positive Lists, and Negative Lists. In this section, we discuss the most important of these reports, which is Blocked Business Partners.

This is a report that trade business uses most often. There are several options while running the report: Blocked Partner Only, All Checked Partners Without Positive and Negative List, and All Checked Partners with Positive and Negative List. The status displays different color codes: red represents blocked business partners, green represents not-blocked business partners, and yellow represents a soft block, where the business partner has not yet been screened. The report displays the status of the business partner based on the SAP BusinessObjects Global Trade Services system screened results. You can select a business partner and click on the Sanctioned Party List Screening icon (Sanctioned Party List Screening), which performs re-screening of the business partners and then displays the results, including the detail of the hits on the addresses. After receiving the screening results, you can click on the Detail Analysis icon to see more information about the results. Figure 4.11 shows a sample SPL screening result; the right-hand side provides the display of the SPL entry that was a match, and the bottom left-hand side displays the business partner address. While you are here, you have the following choices:

- Accept the screening results.
- Click on Release. (If the business partner is a false hit.)
- Click on Block. (If you want this business partner to be under Block status.)
- Click on Positive List or Negative List. (Explained next.)

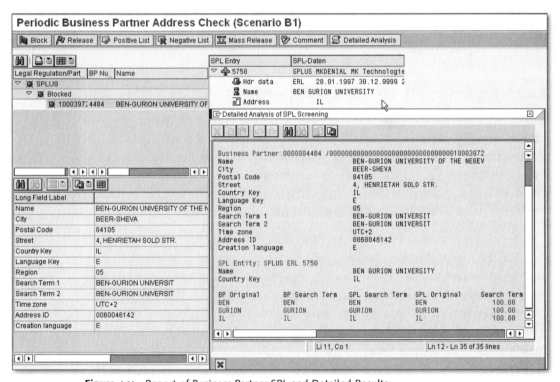

Figure 4.11 Report of Business Partner SPL and Detailed Results

When a user makes a decision to put a business partner under Block or Release, the system remembers that status, presuming there is no delta file match against that business partner and that there are no changes to the business partner address from the feeder system.

Positive and negative lists were introduced with SAP BusinessObjects Global Trade Services 7.0 and allow you to put a business partner under a positive or negative list as long as the address in the SAP ECC system hasn't changed. The business partner drops off the list if the address is changed in the feeder system because the original address has changed. This functionality is available with SAP BusinessObjects Global Trade Services 7.0 and 7.1. With SAP BusinessObjects Global Trade Services 7.2 and higher, you can decide to permanently keep the business partner in the positive or negative list, even if the original address is modified in the feeder system.

The positive list allows you to put business partners in a group that can be excluded from any delta screening and will have a status of Release, so that they are not blocked for any further document processing. The negative list, on the other hand, puts the business partner under a Block status, as the business partner is identified as blocked or negative, and for further document processing, these documents are blocked. With the release of SAP BusinessObjects Global Trade Services 7.2 and higher, you can permanently keep business partners on the list, even if the address is changed in the feeder's system.

If you place a business partner in the positive or negative list, and you then want to display this business partner, you must ensure that while running the Block Business Partner report, you make the appropriate selection to place the business partner in the right placeholder, Positive List, Negative List, Blocked, or Released. Alternatively, you can run the reports Display Positive List Business Partner (Transaction /SAPSLL/SPL_POSBPLO) or Display Negative List Business Partner (Transaction /SAPSLL/SPL_NEGBPLO).

Within the Logistics tab, under Periodic Screening, you have two functions: Check Positive List Business Partner Address (Transaction /SAPSLL/SPL_CHSB-1PLO) and Check Negative List Business Partner Address (Transaction /SAPSLL/SPL_CHSB1NLO). This allows you to re-screen the positive and negative lists so that you can review and decide which of the business partners you want to retain in the lists.

4.4.3 Reports on SPL Screening of Documents

Like the blocked business partner, it is possible to display the documents that blocked following the SPL screening. You can run SPL screening against the documents where the business partner address with the SPL entry appears, and if it finds a match, it will be reported in the blocked documents. Within the report, you can display the blocked document for both import and export transactions.

If you want to release the document without having to review the business partner, you can use the function Release Blocked Documents (Transaction /SAPSLL/ SPL_BLRL). Select the document, and click on the Release icon (🏴). When you release the document directly, the system provides a pop-up window where you can make comments on the release (see Figure 4.12). (A similar screen appears if you release a business partner without performing SPL screening.)

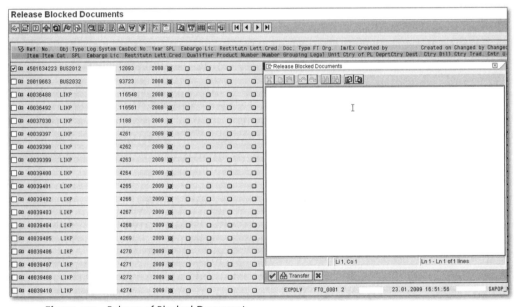

Figure 4.12 Release of Blocked Document

Display All Documents (Transaction /SAPSLL/SPL_CUHD) allows you to display all of the compliance documents that are transferred to SAP BusinessObjects Global Trade Services (blocked, not blocked, or technically incomplete, for both exports and imports).

Technically Incomplete Documents captures documents that are incomplete in SAP BusinessObjects Global Trade Services due to missing data (e.g., if a business partner is missing, or a legal unit is not mapped in SAP BusinessObjects Global Trade Services) (see Figure 4.13). SAP BusinessObjects Global Trade Services will only perform a screen after the documents are technically complete, and this report provides information on the missing data (for both imports and exports).

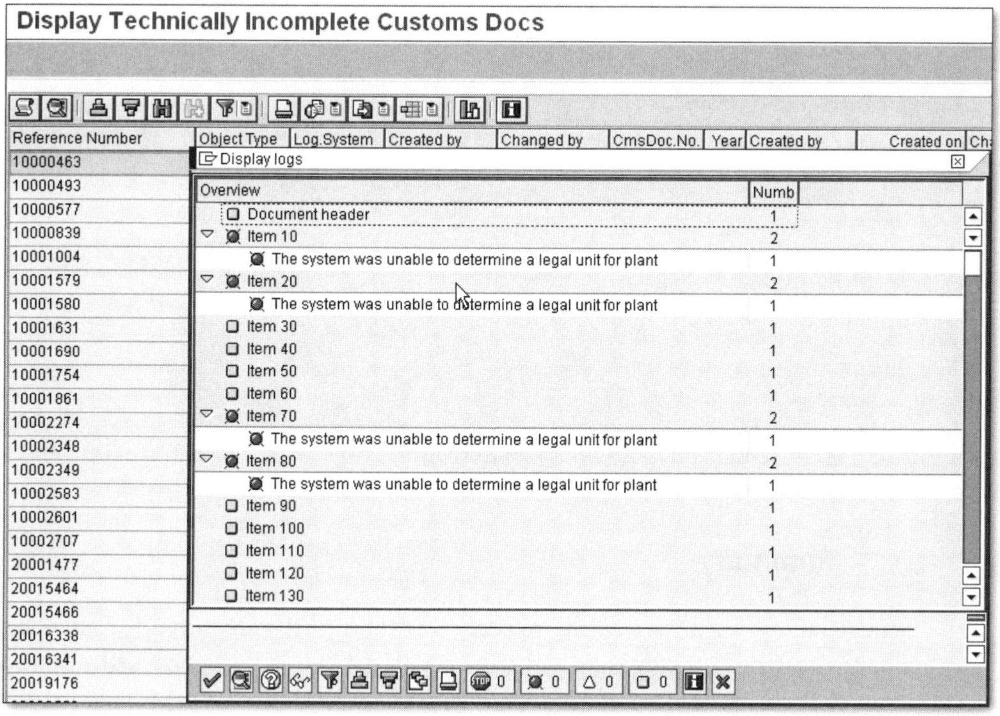

Figure 4.13 Technically Incomplete Documents

Finally, Re-Check Import/Export Documents allows you to re-determine or recheck the status of a document based on the latest information. If you release a business partner with documents blocked, you need to re-check the documents. When you run this report, enter the document number, and make sure that Save Log is checked, which ensures that the status is updated. If you want to see the results while online, select Display Log, which prompts you to re-check the results. Figure 4.14 shows the re-check document report screen.

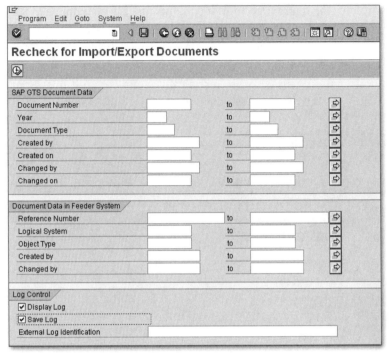

Figure 4.14 Report to Re-Check Compliance Documents

4.5 Summary

In this chapter, we discussed the master data setup that is required for enabling embargo service checking, and we then covered SPL configuration settings and master data setup. In the next chapter, we move on to another key piece of master data for legal control and trade processing: export and import legal control.

Products need to be classified for export and import trade processing. Compliance Management uses the product classifications to apply relevant controls and determine the license required to export or import a product. Customs Management uses product classification for export and importing reporting and declaration. Customs Management product classifications are used for determining importing tariffs, duties, or restrictions.

5   Classification

From a trade reporting and control point of view, products need to be classified. These classifications are used to identify different products for export and import purposes, and allow customs authorities to determine if any restrictions or controls need to be applied. *ECCNs,* which are part of the Commerce Control List, are issued by the Department of Commerce and are used to identify your product and determine if a license is needed to export it. The ECCN is an alphanumeric number that describes a product or type of item, so it can be identified for export by the customs authorities. Your company's product numbers or material numbers are internal to you company, and product classification is a standardized way to identify the products. ECCN also represents the control that might apply to the product for export processing. The *Harmonized Tariff System* (HTS) is an internationally agreed-upon commodity code and classification system for goods imported into any country. HTS codes are associated with the country of origin and indicate what import restrictions, tariffs, or duties are applied to products.

The *International Traffic in Arms Regulations* (ITAR) details the regulations governing the export of military- and defense-related products and technologies. It details the procedures, licenses and agreements, penalties, and administrative requirements relating to ITAR regulations. With ITAR regulations, the products are identified and classified with the *U.S. Munitions List* (USML). It is the responsibility of the exporter to properly classify the products shipped, as controlled to meet the compliance. This classification indicates whether the product requires a license or license exemption under special circumstances. Companies that deal with military equipment have to constantly deal with USML classification, but there are also companies that deal with civilian products that have dual applications, and need to classify and apply both ECCN and USML classifications to their products.

In the following sections, we will go over the design and application of the numbering scheme that represents the export and import classification numbers.

5.1 Numbering Schemes: Design and Application

Numbering schemes allow you to define the structure of your export and import classification numbers. It is important that you give some thought to their design because it will influence their application and use. There are various numbering scheme configurations that are pre-delivered and applicable to different functions with SAP BusinessObjects Global Trade Services, and the numbering scheme structure is modified based on the application. From a business application point of view, there are numbering schemes that are either meant for export or import, but in SAP BusinessObjects Global Trade Services, there are different numbering schemes based on the usage and application within the SAP BusinessObjects Global Trade Services module or functionality.

> **Note**
>
> Numbering schemes are defined within the general settings of SAP BusinessObjects Global Trade Services. Following the definition, these numbers are assignments to legal regulations, and based on the assignment, the license determination strategy is maintained. The license determination strategy allows you to maintain the license types, and the license type represents the export or import controls. For example, the ECCN assignment to the legal control applies to the compliance legal control — export or import. Similarly, the assignment of HTS codes applies to customs or transit processing legal regulations.

In the following sections, we will go over the different export and import numbers and their applications and functionality with SAP BusinessObjects Global Trade Services.

5.1.1 Export and Import Lists

ECCN is defined as a numbering scheme within SAP BusinessObjects Global Trade Services. While defining the number, you can decide the different levels you would like the structure to have; for example, the category, group and sub-category. Having different levels not only helps you organize the number but also the text and description for each level. In other words, if you want to search against a category or group, it is recommended that you maintain that as a structure level.

The pre-delivered structure of SAP BusinessObjects Global Trade Services is shown in the upper section of Figure 5.1. While defining the level, you have the option to configure the exact length or a range of length. Exact length will force users to maintain the exact length of the code. If you plan on getting ECCNs, you might want to check with your content provider for the structure they will be providing and maintain this structure accordingly.

In the following sections, we will go over the lists assignment to enable the import and export legal control.

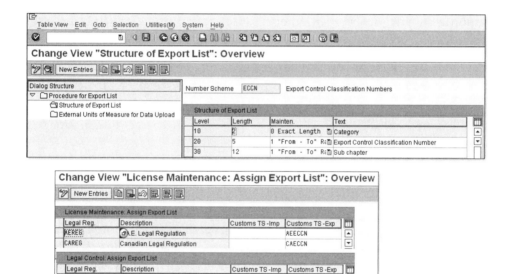

Figure 5.1 ECCN Structure Definition and Assignment

Export Lists Assignments

After the numbering scheme is defined, it needs to be assigned to the legal regulations for license maintenance and legal control. The legal control assignment allows you to assign the ECCN to specific legal regulations within a product. If you have a product shipped out of a specific country and have the export regulation active, the system will look for the classification assigned to this regulation. Assigning numbering schemes to license maintenance allows you to use the classification number for export license determination.

Within the assignment of the export list to the license maintenance and legal control, it's important that you only assign the export number and keep the Customs TS-Import blank, as shown in the bottom section of Figure 5.1. The menu path for the numbering scheme and assignment is SAP REFERENCE IMG • SAP GLOBAL TRADE SERVICES • GENERAL SETTINGS • NUMBERING SCHEMES.

Import Lists Assignments

Similar to export lists, you can maintain import classifications for import license determination. You have two options for this design: You can maintain a unique import numbering scheme for import license determination, or you can use the numbering scheme of the HTS for license determination purposes.

Note that to perform import license determination, you must have a legal regulation activated for imports. You can share the numbering scheme for more than one regulation; HTS is used for customs declaration and can also be used for import-compliance checking.

5.1.2   Harmonized Tariff Numbers and Commodity Codes

Import and export control makes use of the product classification to apply the legal control for goods that are being imported or exported. As mentioned earlier, international countries have come to an understanding on a common nomenclature, which promotes trade and facilitates the understanding of the classification numbers, the HTS. The first 6 digits of the numbers used in this system are always the same; beyond this, the numbers differ depending on the country. In fact, even the length of the number differs by country. For example, the United States, Canada, China, and Korea use 10-digit numbers, as do most of countries in the European Union (with the exception of Germany, which uses 11). Israel uses 8, Japan and Malaysia use 9, Singapore uses 8, and Taiwan uses 11. These codes help the importing countries identify the products being imported.

Exporting countries also use the classifications to record the goods exported for statistical purposes. The same numbers are used, but not all the digits are recorded. For example, the US harmonized tariff number Chapter 8426 (ships' derricks, cranes, including cable cranes, mobile) might be used for statistical purposes, even though the full number is 8426410005 (work trucks fitted with cranes).

When exporting from the United States, a product has to be reported to the US authorities with the classification number and value of the goods being exported. For US export reporting, the US government is only interested in knowing the classification number up to the first six digits of the tariff number, and the rest of the digits can be filled with zeros. The classification number used by the exporting country is called the *commodity code*. Commodity codes are also used by the European Union, within Intrastat and Extrastat reporting. These reports record the goods coming in and going out of the European Union.

The numbering scheme for harmonized tariff numbers and commodity codes are different from ECCNs, which we discussed earlier in this chapter. Harmonized Tariff System (HTS) numbers have a longer structure, with chapters, headings, subheadings, non-fully qualified numbers, and fully qualified numbers. There are also subfolders for additional functionality. Figure 5.2 displays the pre-delivered numbering scheme for Germany, which shows the structure and configuration settings within the folder management of customs products.

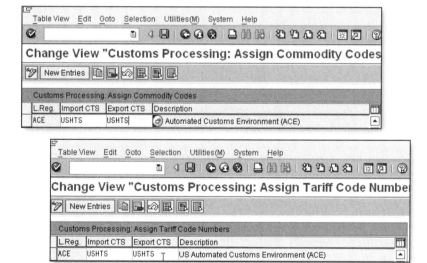

Figure 5.2 Harmonized Tariff System for Germany

With HTS, you also have associated dates of validity, so it is important that you configure that within the Maintenance of Customs Products folder by selecting the option listed as 1 Valid From and Valid To Date Can be Maintained. Within the External Units of Measure, you want to list all of the supplementary units of measure that are used in association with HTS. HTS numbers have their own units of measure, which are used for reporting purposes. The second part of Figure 5.2 displays this configuration assignment.

> **Note**
>
> Numbering schemes for commodity codes and HTS numbers are interchangeable and will appear in possible numbering schemes for assignment in Customs Management. They are used for export or import documentation and declarations.

In the following sections, we will go over the assignment of the numbering scheme for Customs Management and transit procedures.

Assignment

Similar to the legal control export and import list, we need to assign the numbering scheme defined as tariff number to customs and transit processing. Customers are moving toward using one numbering scheme for customs processing of exports (commodity codes) and imports (harmonized tariff codes), which eliminates the need to maintain the content and assignment of classification. To make use of this functionality, you must ensure that the same numbering scheme is assigned to exports and imports for legal regulation within HTS and commodity codes.

Figure 5.3 displays the typical case, with the one numbering scheme "USHTS" assigned as a commodity code and tariff code within customs processing.

> **Note**
>
> If you plan to use a harmonized tariff number to control an import license, than you need to ensure that the number is assigned to the legal regulation under SAP GTS • GENERAL SETTINGS • NUMBERING SCHEME • ASSIGN NUMBERING SCHEME OF TARIFF CODE NUMBER FOR LICENSE MAINTENANCE.

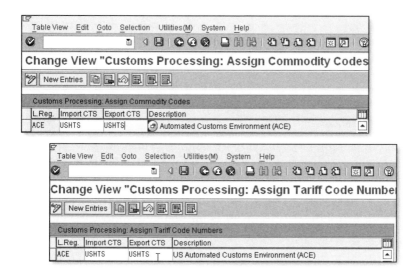

Figure 5.3 Assignment of Tariff Number and Commodity Code Within Customs Processing

End Uses

SAP BusinessObjects Global Trade Services 7.1 and higher provides the functionality to identify the end use for your product. These end uses are defined within SAP Global Trade Services • General Settings • Numbering Schemes • Define End Uses for Numbering Scheme of Tariff Code Numbers. Here you define the five-character end use code, with a description. Following the definition, you need to ensure that these end use codes are assigned to the tariff number definition within the folder End Use, as shown in Figure 5.2.

5.1.3   Other Numbering Schemes

Apart from the import and export numbering schemes, there are other numbering schemes that facilitate trade processing delivered with SAP BusinessObjects Global Trade Services 7.1 and higher. The menu path for these numbering schemes can be found under SAP Reference IMG • SAP Global Trade Services • General Settings • Numbering Scheme.

In the following sections, we will review additional numbering schemes that you could define other than the ones we reviewed so far for export, import, or tariff number, such as customs codes and other government agencies (OGA).

Customs Codes

In addition to product classifications, these are codes that are defined by authorities and used to identity shipped products. The structure definition is similar to the other numbering schemes.

Other Government Agencies

US customs authorities require identifying or assigning codes to your imported products to notify other government agencies that might be interested. The definition of the other government agencies (OGA) structure is similar to the other numbering schemes. Following the definition of the OGA numbering scheme, you must assign the codes with the tariff number definition under the Measure Types and the Coding Schemes folders, as shown in Figure 5.4.

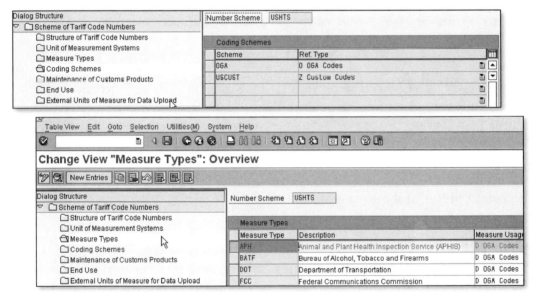

Figure 5.4 HTS Assignment to OGA Codes and Customs Codes

5.2 Product Content and Classification

SAP BusinessObjects Global Trade Services provides XML interface for content upload and manual updates. There are companies that provide the content in the

XML format specified by SAP BusinessObjects Global Trade Services, which you can then load directly using transactions or pre-delivered programs. In this section, we discuss the different options available for uploading or maintaining the content for the different numbering schemes we have defined and assigned.

Following content maintenance, the classification needs to be assigned to the product. There are various tools available to facilitate initial assignments, mass assignments, and reclassifications. In this section, we discuss some of the key functionalities and see what business process procedures work best for different business cases. We will go over the functionality to load the content manually, through XML files and associated functionality to facilitate the product classification and reclassification, when the regulations updates with the new number.

5.2.1 Content

The content load and maintenance for different numbering schemes are similar but sometimes use different transactions and programs. The content loads are separate for export, import and customs management commodity codes or tariffs. We will review the content load for export classification number; the same methodology applies to other numbering schemes. The method for the classification content load can be put into two broad categories:

- ▸ Manual
- ▸ Using an XML interface file

Classification for compliance (export control classification numbers or import control classification numbers) is manually maintained under SAP Compliance Management • Classification/Master Data. There are two sections, Export, on your right, and Import, on your left. To maintain export control classification numbers, click Maintain Export Classification Number. The system prompts you to enter the numbering scheme and then gives you the option to create or display. When you click on Create, it allows you to maintain the content manually.

Figure 5.5 displays the data selection for uploading content into SAP BusinessObjects Global Trade Services. To upload using an XML interface file, enter the data provider (business partner with the BP role SLLDAP selected), enter the numbering scheme (within Alternative Numbering Scheme), key in the path for HTS and the text XML file under Local or Application Server, check the Overwrite Text for Following Objects checkbox, and keep everything under General Control Parameters checked, except for Simulation Mode.

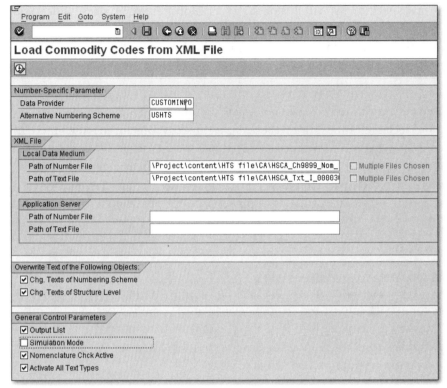

Figure 5.5 Content Loading Data Selection

When you maintain the classification, the screen proposes the options to maintain the different levels defined within the numbering scheme. Figure 5.6 displays the different folders and hierarchy within Content Maintenance.

5.2.2 Product Classification

As new products are created and transferred to SAP BusinessObjects Global Trade Services from the feeder system, products are researched and assigned appropriate classifications. SAP BusinessObjects Global Trade Services provides different functions and features to facilitate this process. The classification for products can be found under both Compliance Management and Customs Management. For Compliance Management, the menu path is SAP GLOBAL TRADE SERVICES • COMPLIANCE MANAGEMENT • CLASSIFICATION/MASTER DATA. For Customs Management, it's SAP GLOBAL TRADE SERVICES • CUSTOMS MANAGEMENT • CLASSIFICATION AND MASTER DATA.

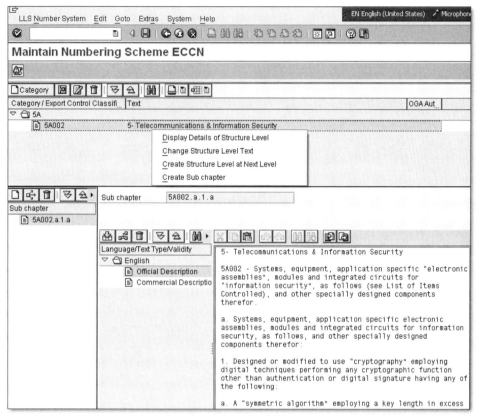

Figure 5.6 Export Control Classification Number with Structure and Hierarchy in Content Maintenance

In the following sections, we will go over classification tools that facilitate the product classification and reassignment of the classification when the classification changes. The reclassification allows you to assign a new number based on the regulation update from the government with a new number.

Worklist

Worklist is a classification tool that allows you to classify products for one numbering scheme, such as for compliance export classification or Customs Management HTS numbers (see Figure 5.7). It allows you to filter products that are due for classification based on the various selection options available (e.g., Newly Transferred to GTS, Created By, etc.).

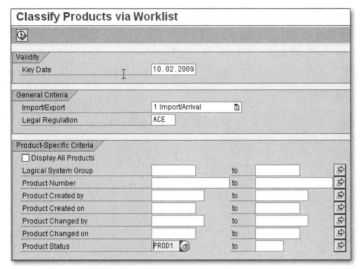

Figure 5.7 Data Selection Option for Product Classification Using Worklist

This function allows you to research the product based on its description and search and research classifications based on the different level descriptions maintained in the classification content. Following the search, you can use functions such as the clipboard to return to your search and assign the right classification. Worklist also allows you further filter while you are in the output report, and mass-assign classifications to lists of products.

Figure 5.8 displays the Worklist output and the various functions within the Worklist report. ⊞ takes you to the product details, ⊞ allows you to mass-assign the classification for selected products, ⊞ allows you to filter the list further, and so on.

Reclassification

Reclassification allows you to assign a new classification and replace an existing one. Different countries provide classification updates periodically based on the regulation change, and it is the responsibility of companies to reclassify the products that are affected.

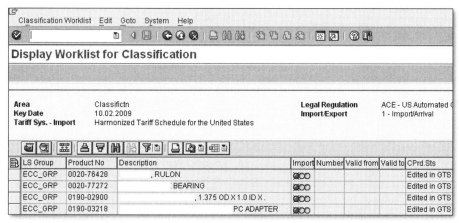

Figure 5.8 Worklist Functions and Features Facilitating Product Classification

You can plan reclassification for future dates, based on the validity of the new numbers. In other words, if you have a classification number expiring in the future, and a new number will need to be assigned, you don't have to wait until that date. You can run the reclassification with the new number validity start date in the future, and the new classification will become active on the validity date. Figure 5.9 displays two HTS codes that are updated with validity dates. In the figure, you can see two dates, Validity Dates, which are associated with the classification number validity dates (primarily used for the tariff codes). The classification period is the date the classification is valid from and to; in other words, it indicates which classification will be used for the product assignment within the document processing.

One View Product Classification

If a business wants to view all of the classifications in one view, you can review Legal Control Export and Import classification and Customs Management Commodity Code and Tariff Number or Preference determination numbering scheme and update respective numbers. Unlike Worklist, you must assign the classifications one product at a time; however, you can apply all of the classifications in one transaction (see Figure 5.9). You can use the search features to pull the right classification from the content database. With one transaction, you can get all of the views of the products, for example, the General Basic Data view, Classification Number for HTS and Commodity Codes, Legal Control for Export, and Import Control Number.

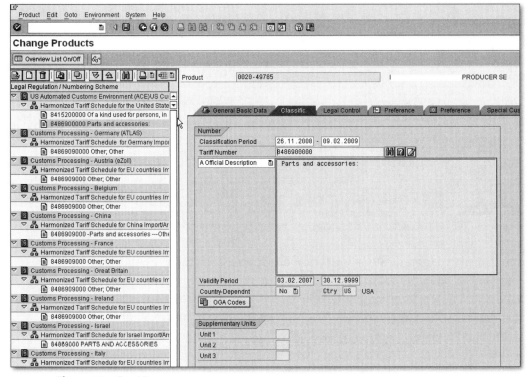

Figure 5.9 One View

Figure 5.9 also displays the supplementary units within the classification screen. These units are the units specific to HTS used for reporting purposes. For example, in the case of shipper export declarations, the reporting is based on HTS and not based on a company's product number. If you have a unit of measure for HTS that is different from the product unit of measure, it's important that you maintain it in SAP ECC or the feeder system, so that reports are in the HTS unit of measure. If maintained in the SAP ECC material master, with transfers from SAP ECC to SAP BusinessObjects Global Trade Services, this information flows to SAP BusinessObjects Global Trade Services. You can also maintain it within General Basic Data in SAP BusinessObjects Global Trade Services.

5.3   Summary

The definition of numbering schemes is important to content loads and structure because a good design helps you maintain the classification numbers and search for product classifications. In this chapter, we discussed how to maintain classifications manually and through an XML file, assignment to the different functionality, and ways that SAP BusinessObjects Global Trade Services provides functionality to facilitate product classification. We looked at the different numbering schemes that might apply to different functions with compliance, customs, and preferential processing. We reviewed different tools and functions that allow you to classify and reclassify a product when the regulations change.

In the next chapter, we move to the topic of legal control and license determination, which is one of the core functionalities within Compliance Management. ECCNs are used for legal control and license determination, and, with this chapter as a background, you will understand how these numbers help to perform export and import control.

Legal control is one of the most important components of Compliance Management, the other two being the embargo and SPL screening. This chapter deals with the system setup with legal control for the license determination for products involved in inbound or outbound transactions.

6   Legal Control: Export and Import

Legal control is the third and most important functionality within the compliance module and is the core of Compliance Management. The concept and fundamentals of this functionality is used across many other functions, for example, the letter of credit. The concept of legal control is the same for exporting and importing; it is only the different data elements and criteria that differentiate which service and functionality to check.

Within the configuration, the steps to enable export control and import control are similar, with the exception of the service activation and the numbering scheme assigned to the respective legal regulations. To avoid confusion, we recommend that you have separate regulations for exporting and importing, and also a different numbering scheme. The system uses the departure country regulation to check the control for export regulations and looks for the importing country regulations for import control.

For operational effectiveness and to distinguish import and export processes, SAP BusinessObjects Trade Services separates the SAP area menu for legal control into Import and Export sections. The data maintenance is separate, as is the monitoring of transactions.

In the following sections, we will go over the key configuration steps for building a foundation for legal control.

6.1   Export Legal Control Setup: Baseline Configuration

As with any other compliance service activation, legal control starts with the legal regulation definition within SAP GLOBAL TRADE SERVICES • LEGAL REGULATIONS •

DEFINE LEGAL REGULATIONS. Again, we recommend having separate regulations for imports and exports. While defining the regulation, use the Type of Legal Code as either (a) 00 Foreign Trade Laws (AWW, EAR), or (b) 03 Prohibitions and Restrictions. Within Import/Export, select (a) 1 Import/Arrival for Import Regulation, and (b) 2 Export/Dispatch for Export Regulation. Within the Original Country, key in the country of the export or import regulation.

While defining the legal regulations, you also have *deadline types*, which are valid-from and valid-to dates associated with the license determination check. Ensure that these are maintained within the Assign Deadline Types folder. Another key element to the legal regulation activation is the country group assignment.

Following the definition of the legal regulation, define the activation; in other words, define the countries against which this legal regulation will be active. Again, you have a choice to activate by country or country group. Using country groups for legal regulation activation makes it easier to add new countries to the master data, but it also makes it harder to keep track of what countries fall under what country groups.

This configuration also provides activation restrictions based on the ship-from and ship-to legs of the transaction. If you choose to use this option, please be aware that you need to maintain entries for all of the possible ship-from and ship-to countries for export regulation activation.

In the following sections, we will look at some of the configuration options for legal control activation by country group. Country group allows you to group countries that can be activated for ship-from and ship-to countries.

6.1.1 Country Group

The country group assignment has a dual purpose. First, it is used for legal regulation activation; and second, it is used for license type determination. If you want to make use of the country group for the legal regulation activation or license determination, you must assign the different country groups.

Using country groups for license type determinations can considerably reduce the determination table size. However, companies should be sure to evaluate their options because using a country group involves design decisions and ongoing business process procedures to interpret these country groups.

6.1.2 Item Category Activation and Depreciation Group

Export regulations call for licenses that are value- and quantity-restrictive; in other words, you get approval to ship only a limited quantity or value. Therefore, while you are in the general setting, you might want to review the pre-delivered depreciation group (SD0A01 for sales documents, MM0A01 for purchasing, etc.). Following the definition, follow the path SAP COMPLIANCE MANAGEMENT • GENERAL SETTINGS • DOCUMENT STRUCTURE • SELECT ACTIVATE ITEM CATEGORIES. Select the Activate Item Categories folder for Legal Control, select the item categories, and click on Details. In the Value Depreciation and Quantity Depreciation, select Allocation: Deduct from License, and enter the depreciation group maintained earlier within the depreciation group field.

Figure 6.1 displays this configuration screen. Check Adopt Legal Control Data from Preceding Item if you want the license information to be copied over from the preceding document.

Figure 6.1 Legal Control Activation for Item Category

As explained previously, the activation service works in combination with document types and item categories. As such, you must ensure that those mapped for relevant export checks are activated.

6.1.3 Numbering Schemes

The numbering scheme represents the product classification structure within SAP BusinessObjects Trade Services. As we saw in Chapter 5, there are a variety of numbering schemes. With regards to Compliance Management, you need to define the export list for the ECCN and assign it to legal control and license management.

> **Note**
>
> The legal control determines the assignment of classification to the product based on the legal regulations. Product classification is then used for license determination. With import legal control, you have the option to assign the Harmonized Tariff System (HTS) number or create a new numbering scheme, specific to the import control number. The advantage of using the HTS number is that the classification for import declaration can be used for the import license determination. To keep the controls separate, you might want to look at maintaining a separate classification number for imports.

Following the export list definition, the export list is assigned to license maintenance and legal control. For export control, you must ensure that the export list or export control classification number is assigned in the column Customs TS-Exp, to the appropriate legal regulation (Figure 6.2).

Figure 6.2 Assignment of Export and Import Number to License Maintenance

The menu path for this configuration is SAP REFERENCE IMG • SAP GLOBAL TRADE SERVICES • GENERAL SETTINGS • NUMBERING SCHEMES.

With legal control export, you need to assign the numbering scheme to the two configuration elements, license maintenance and legal control. Following are the two configuration steps:

▶ Assign numbering scheme of export list for license maintenance.

▶ Assign numbering scheme to export list for legal control.

The license maintenance allows you to maintain the license determination, and legal control enables you to determine the active legal regulation.

For legal control imports, you have a similar configuration setup within the GENERAL SETTINGS • NUMBERING SCHEME. If you want to use HTS for license maintenance, ensure that the tariff number is assigned to the legal regulation within the configuration step: NUMBERING SCHEME • ASSIGN NUMBERING SCHEME OF TARIFF CODE NUMBERS FOR LICENSE MAINTENANCE.

In the next section, we will go over the license types. License types represent the export and import control with products.

6.1.4 License Types

License types in SAP BusinessObjects Trade Services are representations of the control for export or import of goods. To understand the license type, let's first discuss some basics of export control. The ECCN is organized by category, group, and control. Some of the examples of the categories are as follows:

- ▶ 0: Nuclear Materials, Facilities and Equipment, and Misc.
- ▶ 1: Materials, Chemicals, "Microorganisms," and Toxins
- ▶ 2: Materials Processing
- ▶ 3: Electronics
- ▶ 4: Computers
- ▶ 5: Telecommunications and Info Security
- ▶ 6: Lasers and Sensors
- ▶ 7: Navigation and Avionics
- ▶ 8: Marine
- ▶ 9: Propulsion Systems, Space Vehicles, and Related Equipment

The second digit in the ECCN is group; the following are the different groups:

- ▶ A: Equipment, Assemblies, and Components
- ▶ B: Test, Inspection, and Production Equipment
- ▶ C: Materials
- ▶ D: Software
- ▶ E: Technology

The third digit represents the control for the product:

- ▶ 0: National Security Reasons (including Dual Use and International Munitions List) and Items on the NSG Dual Use Annex and Trigger List
- ▶ 1: Missile Technology Reasons
- ▶ 2: Nuclear Nonproliferation Reasons
- ▶ 3: Chemical and Biological Weapons Reasons
- ▶ 9: Anti-terrorism, Crime Control, Regional Stability, Short Supply, UN Sanctions, and so on

The preceding numbering scheme is formulated by the commercial control list for commercial goods control. There is an associated Country versus Control chart, which lists the countries in the y-axis and the reason for the control in the x-axis. Figure 6.3 displays a typical Country versus Control chart. License type translates these controls into different attributes within the license type definition for control checking.

Commerce Control List Overview and the Country Chart — Supplement No. 1 to Part 738 - page 1

Commerce Country Chart
Reason for Control

	Chemical & Biological Weapons			Nuclear Nonproliferation		National Security		Missile Tech	Regional Stability		Firearms Convention	Crime Control			Anti-Terrorism	
	CB 1	CB 2	CB 3	NP 1	NP 2	NS 1	NS 2	MT 1	RS 1	RS 2	FC 1	CC 1	CC 2	CC 3	AT 1	AT 2
Afghanistan	X	X	X	X		X	X	X	X	X		X		X		
Albania	X	X		X		X	X	X	X	X		X	X			
Algeria	X	X		X		X	X	X	X	X		X		X		
Andorra	X	X		X		X	X	X	X	X		X		X		
Angola	X	X		X		X	X	X	X	X		X		X		
Antigua & Barbuda	X	X		X		X	X	X	X	X	X	X		X		
Argentina	X					X	X	X	X	X	X	X		X		
Armenia	X	X	X	X		X	X	X	X	X		X	X			
Australia	X					X		X	X							
Austria	X					X		X	X	X		X		X		
Azerbaijan	X	X	X	X		X	X	X	X	X		X	X			
Bahamas, The	X	X		X		X	X	X	X	X	X	X		X		
Bahrain	X	X	X	X		X	X	X	X	X		X		X		

Figure 6.3 Commercial Control List and Country Chart for US Regulation EAR

> **Note**
>
> The US International Traffic in Arms Regulations (ITAR) stipulates that importer and exporters must follow certain standards to operate for defense-related materials and technologies. This involves a license based on the US Munitions List (USML). The same legal control and license determination concept applies to ITAR regulation, with the exception of agreements, which is unique to ITAR regulation. We will go over that in more detail in Section 6.4, ITAR and Agreements.

Figure 6.4 displays the different attributes that are available within the license types. With the license type definition, the appropriate object needs to be checked to ensure that the right control is used within the license type. In the next section, we will go over the control settings configuration setup for legal control.

Figure 6.4 License Type Definition Details and Attributes

6.1.5 Control Settings

Control settings for license determination allow you to configure legal control services settings and control parameters that influence the license determination. These settings are specific to the legal regulations, so if you have multiple regulations, such as one for commercial product importing (EAR), and another one for military product importing (ITAR), you must keep them separate.

Key configurations settings within the control settings are explained here:

▶ **Product Master Maintenance**
Here you have the option to enable the license determination for all of the products that qualify for legal control service checks, based on the legal regulation active for export or import determination. The other option is to only activate for selective products, using the option titled B: Only Specifically Selected Products are Relevant for Checks. With selective product options, the legal service only gets activated with the assignment of classification to the product.

Example

We once worked on a client implementation that imported products with restrictions. The configuration for this client was achieved by using the option of selectively checking the product for import license determination.

▶ **Control Grouping**
You can check this if you want to use country grouping for license determination. With legal control, you can use a country group for legal regulation determination or license type determination.

▶ **Peculiarity Code**
This is an additional code provided in case you want to have further granular control over the ECCN. For example, two products might have the same classification number but different applications or end uses; you could indicate this using this code.

▶ **Partner Group**
Here you need to assign two partner groupings: one based on the departure partner country, and another one on the destination partner country.

> **Note**
>
> For exporting, the partner group defined must be assigned to the destination country; for importing, the partner group must be assigned to the departure country. This is because the license determination uses the destination partner country to determine the export license, and the departure partner country to determine the import license.

▶ **License Type Determination Procedure**

Here you assign the determination procedure for license types. With legal control, you have two procedures that are in use, one for the legal regulation determination and another for the license type. The procedure for license type helps you build the license type determination table. The procedure definition is explained later, in Section 6.1.9, Determination Procedures: Legal Control and License Types.

▶ **Cascade Active within Approval Type Determination**

While building the license determination table, you might build it with different license types in sequence, starting with the least restrictive and ending with the most restrictive. To allow the system to search through the sequence of license types, you need to check this box.

▶ **Check Multiple Country Groups when Determining License Types**

You must check this box if you have one or more countries appearing in multiple country groups. This cues the system to look for a country in multiple country groups.

▶ **Sending of Mail**

Check this box if you want the system to trigger an email when a document is blocked due to legal control. There are associate settings for email notification setup that needs to done to enable this functionality. We will go over the email notification setup in Chapter 8, General Add-On Functionality and Features.

▶ **Manual Assignment Default**

Select the appropriate settings for license assignment. The recommended setting is B1: System, Manually Changed, Cannot be Changed by System. This means that the system will automatically assign a license, and, if manually changed, the system will not override the manual license assignment change.

▶ **Transfer Leg. Contr. Data**

When transferring legal control data license data, there are three possible options: 1 – Transfer License with Limited Check, 2 – Recheck License for New

Document, and 3 – Do Not Transfer License. We recommend that you use 2, as it allows you to recheck the document with the latest information. With the first option, when the legal control information is transferred from the subsequent document to preceding documents, it only checks for license validity.

▶ **Check External License No.**
Here you have to decide if you want the system to allow the use of the same external license number for a different license. We recommend that you pick the option titled A: Multiple Use of External Number Allowed. This will allow you to maintain the same external license number for multiple licenses. This helps when you have an old license that is expired because new licenses issued by the regulatory authority can be the same number.

> **Note**
>
> From a performance point of view, we recommend basing the creation and expiration of licenses based on the volume of documents assigned to them. This gives you greater control over the number of active licenses and their documents.

Figure 6.5 displays the control settings for legal regulations, statuses, and the details behind statuses definitions. The menu path for the control settings configuration is SAP REFERENCE IMG • SAP GLOBAL TRADE SERVICES • SAP COMPLIANCE MANAGEMENT • LEGAL CONTROL SERVICES • CONTROL SETTINGS FOR LEGAL CONTROL SERVICES.

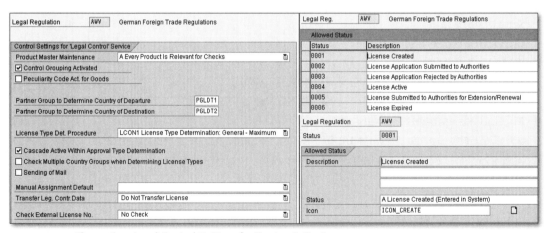

Figure 6.5 Legal Control Settings for Service Activation

6.1.6   Allowed Status

Statuses are another key setting associated with legal regulations. This setting allows you to list the different statuses that licenses have, which are then transferred to the license maintenance function. We recommend that you refer to the pre-delivered statuses because when you define a new regulation, it is important that the statuses are defined and assigned to it.

6.1.7   Time Zones

Assign the type of date (valid-from and valid-to) for the legal regulation with the time zone mapped to it. We recommend that the defined time zone is the same as all other time zone definitions, as well as the time zone of the SAP BusinessObjects Trade Services system. This will allow you to avoid discrepancies in the times captured for different activities within SAP BusinessObjects Trade Services.

6.1.8   Partner Groupings

Partner groupings are defined within the general settings of SAP BusinessObjects Trade Services, which lists all of the different groupings used by different services. As we discussed earlier, partner groupings list the different partners that are used for screening purposes. The license determination function validates the partner function sequence against the document partner function and uses that for license determination. For example, let's say that you have a partner group with the following sequence numbers: 10 - End Customer, 20 - Ship To, 30 - Sold To. If Ship To and Sold To appear in the document, the license determination first checks for End Customer. If it doesn't find it in the document, it moves on to the next sequence (Ship To), and uses the ship-to ID's country as the partner country for license determination. In the case of exports, it uses this country as the end destination country. If you did have an end customer, it would use that partner country key.

> **Note**
>
> Legal control also allows you to define and assign partner functions specific to a license type. If you use this function, it takes precedence over the partner group assigned to license determination in general.

Figure 6.6 displays the license type partner group functions exclusively used for license types.

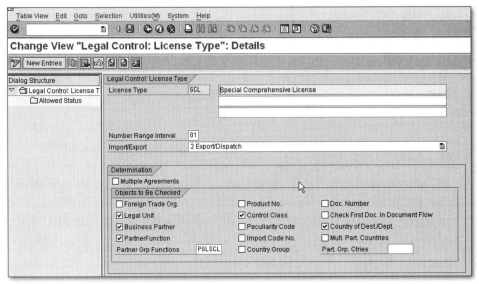

Figure 6.6 License Type Definitions with Details on Objects to Be Checked

6.1.9 Determination Procedures: Legal Control and License Types

The system uses determination procedures for determining active regulations, which might apply to any of the services within Compliance Management, such as the sanctioned party list, embargo, or legal control. Additionally, with legal control, there is a procedure for building the license determination table. In this process, you define the key determination strategies or criteria for license types. The SAP-delivered standard options for these include legal regulation, country, country group, control classification, and control classification group.

Within this determination procedure, you can build a sequence that starts restrictively and becomes more general; in other words, you can have the first sequence look for the combination of legal regulation, control class, and country group, and then have the next sequence look for only legal regulation and control class. We will look more closely at the building of license determination strategies in Section 6.3.2, Export/Import Data Setup.

Figure 6.7 shows the pre-delivered license determination procedure. The menu path for this configuration is SAP REFERENCE IMG • SAP GLOBAL TRADE SERVICES • SAP COMPLIANCE MANAGEMENT • LEGAL CONTROL SERVICES • DEFINE DETERMINATION PROCEDURE TO AUTOMATICALLY DETERMINE LICENSE TYPE.

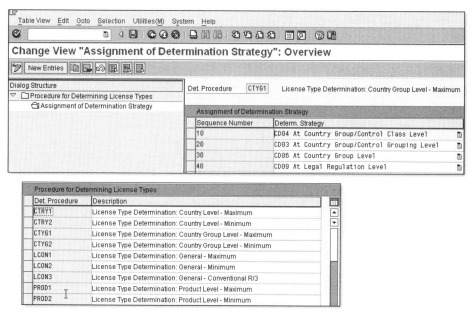

Figure 6.7 Assignment of the License Determination Procedure

6.1.10 Address Comparison for License Types

You can set up a procedure to identify the fields within a business partner that are key for license determination. The pre-delivered configurations list the name, street, city, and country, all of which you can assign to the license type definition. Figure 6.8 shows the fields that are attached to the procedure for checking, as well as the field assignment of the procedure to the license type definition.

The menu path for the configuration of license type determination is SAP REFERENCE IMG • SAP GLOBAL TRADE SERVICES • SAP COMPLIANCE MANAGEMENT • LEGAL CONTROL SERVICES • DEFINE CONTROL PROCEDURES FOR ADDRESS COMPARISON FOR LICENSE TYPES.

With this setting, the system checks for the valid license. If the business partner address is changed in the document and no longer matches the customer ID in the approved license, the system blocks the document. Now that you understand the export control activation for legal control, we will move to import control activation in next section.

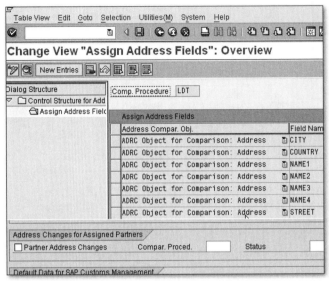

Figure 6.8 Address Comparison for License Determination

6.2 Legal Import Control

Import control allows you to configure your import checks the same way they are configured for export control, screening your inbound transactions and documents from the logistics system. With the activation of the compliance service, you have to choose to activate for imports at the same time you activate for exports. Figure 6.9 displays the import service activation for embargo services and sanctioned party lists. The legal control service activation is similar to other services; you need to ensure that the legal regulation is active for imports.

> **Note**
>
> We recommend that you activate the embargo services and sanctioned party lists for exports and imports; this way, you have only one regulation to manage across your company. With regards to legal control, however, it is better to have separate regulations for imports and exports because the service checks are very dependent on the associated data, which are different for import and export.

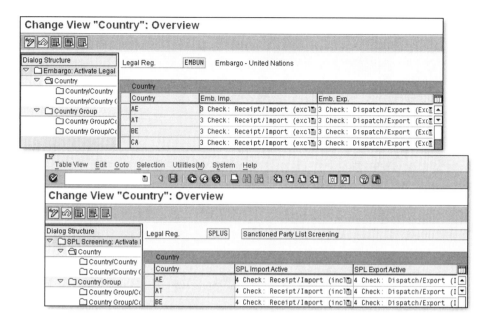

Figure 6.9 Embargo and SPL Setup for Import Control Activation

The key configuration steps to define import control are

1. Maintain a legal regulation that is specific for import control, separate from export control. Activate the legal regulation definition only for import or arrival. Figure 6.10 displays the legal regulation definition for import.

2. Activate legal regulation for the service. Activate only for imports, and, in the Legal Control Export screen, select the Check: Not Activated option. The bottom section of Figure 6.10 displays the activation of the import regulation.

3. Define the numbering scheme for the import list. If you plan on using the HTS number, ensure that it is assigned to the license maintenance and legal control.

6.2.1 Import Licenses

Similar to export license types, you must also maintain import license types, which allow you to configure the license attributes for import processes. These import licenses are unique for import purposes; you can choose to have any number of license types, based on the different import classifications and associated control you might have.

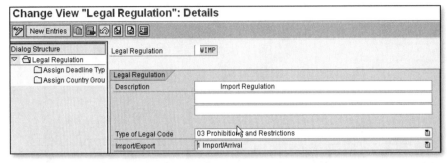

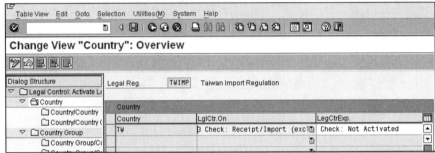

Figure 6.10 Import Regulation Activation

Like export control, you need to maintain the license determination table for import license type determination and also maintain the license based on the attributes you defined for the license type. We will go over license type determination table maintenance in Section 6.3.2, Export/Import Data Setup.

Import compliance checks are performed the same way as export compliance checks, when an inbound document (purchase orders, inbound deliveries, goods receipt, or invoice receipts) is created. These documents go through compliance checks, embargo checks, sanctioned party list screening, or license determination, based on the service activation for the countries. When a purchase document is created, it gets screened for embargos, and, if it includes a product from an embargoed country, the system blocks the document for review. Similarly, if you have a sanctioned party list activated, the document is screened. If a business partner is on that list, the system blocks the business partner for review and appropriate action.

With certain countries, a license is required to import goods. The import license can be used to only release transactions for which there is a license in the system, or to only release transactions if you are authorized to receive the products into the country.

6.3 Operational Effectiveness

SAP BusinessObjects Trade Services provides various tools, functions, and features for operational effectiveness. Export and import compliance checks involve performing trade compliance checks against the outbound and inbound transactions (such as sales orders, delivery notes, stock transport orders, vendor purchase orders, or inbound deliveries). Both export and import checks entail performing three trade compliance checks: screening the sanctioned party list, checking for embargos, and determining the proper licenses. The key difference between the export and import checks is the country key used for performing these checks. Export checks use the departing country's regulations, while import checks use the destination, or receiving, country's regulations.

Every business transaction that crosses a border, whether outbound or inbound, needs trade compliance checks. Compliance checks involve checking all of the business partners that are in the shipping document against the sanctioned party list to make sure that the country being shipped to is not under embargo and to determine whether the product being shipped needs a license or license exemption.

Say, for example, you have an outbound delivery. Before the delivery leaves, you have to check the business partners to whom the item has been sold or shipped to, the bill-to party, the freight forwarder, and the third-party shipper. You also have to perform a sanctioned party screening against all business partners, check the countries associated with the ship-to party or the ultimate consignee where the product will land, perform an embargo check against the country where the product is being shipped to, and determine the appropriate licenses against the ultimate consignee.

SAP BusinessObjects Trade Services can automate all of these checks to make the process faster and easier. You can configure the system to propose what licenses you'll need, and perform all your screening transactions and business partner checks against the denied party list. This leaves you time to look only at the exceptions, such as potential matches in the denied party list. Most importantly, your trade doesn't become bottlenecked with manually performed compliance checks that can be unpredictable and error-prone.

In the following sections, we will go over the legal control functions and transactions with legal control.

6.3.1 Legal Control and Operational Effectiveness

For operational effectiveness, the export and import controls are separated within Compliance Management. The data maintenance, tools, reports, and functions associated with export and import are under the screens Legal Control – Export and Legal Control – Import, respectively. When you click on Legal Control – Export or Import under Compliance, it will bring up the Compliance Management – Legal Control screen. This screen is broadly subdivided into nine sections. We will be discussing in the next sections the four critical functions that affect legal control for operational effectiveness.

Monitoring

This section lists all of the different reports that are available to manage and monitor your screened documents from different feeder systems. Blocked Document lists all of the documents that are blocked due to embargos, the sanctioned party list, missing classifications, licenses, and so on. Figure 6.11 displays the documents that are listed within typical blocked documents. The toolbar below the Legal Control: Display Block Export Documents allows you to perform functions (e.g., you can view the log of the block in detail, display the details behind the document, and recheck the document).

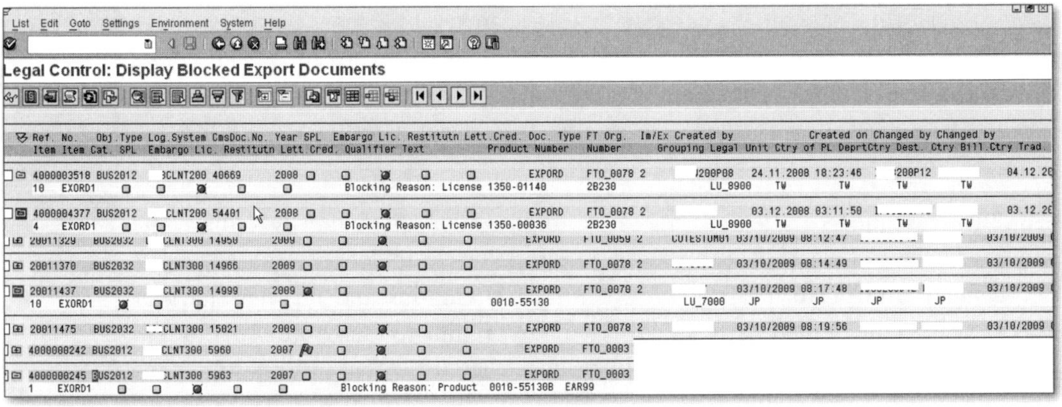

Figure 6.11 Block Document Report

Within the Monitoring tab, there is a transaction to view the technically incomplete documents. These reports provide you with the details of documents that have landed in SAP BusinessObjects Trade Services but are missing configurations or master data, which means that the system cannot perform any trade service checks. Additionally, the assigned document report lists all of the documents that are assigned to a license. You can also select Display Existing Document to list all of the documents that made it to SAP BusinessObjects Trade Services.

Recheck

The Recheck section provides a report or a program to recheck a document in SAP BusinessObjects Trade Services, so that it updates the document with the latest information. While running the recheck transaction (/SAPSLL/CUHD_MR_EXP or /SAPSLL/CUHD_MR_IMP), ensure that Save Log is checked. Checking it allows you to save the recheck log in the document, which is reported back when you display the log.

Legal Control Data

This functionality allows you to manually assign licenses to a document, or, alternatively, to change the system-assigned license. Use Transaction /SAPSLL/LCD_ CHANGE to assign a new license or to change the license assignment. With this transaction, you need to key in the feeder system reference number, logical system, and object type. When you click on execute, it will display all of the line items and possible licenses. You can select the line and the license, and click on Adopt License to assign the license.

Figure 6.12 displays the manual license assignment using the legal control change function.

Embargo

Embargo sections have reports and transactions associated with embargo screening. There is a report that allows you to review blocked transactions and selectively release them, if needed. You can also review business partners that are blocked due to embargos. In this section, you need to maintain the data for an embargoed country under the three different options:

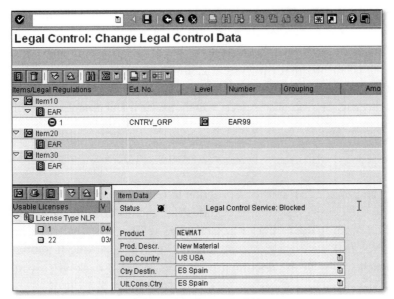

Figure 6.12 Legal Control: Manual Assignment of Licenses

1. **Maintain Country-Specific Information**
   When you maintain a country in this area, it blocks the business partner and transactions for import or export.

2. **Legal Regulation/Country of Destination**
   Here you specify the embargoed country specific to a legal regulation.

3. **Legal Regulation/Country of Dept./Destination**
   Here you specify the embargo block specific to a legal regulation and the departure or destination country.

6.3.2   Export/Import Data Setup

Export and import control involves data setups that are equally important as configurations and help you define your control and data for trade. These data setups go hand in hand with configurations and also involve setting up business data. They ensure that the necessary data to enable the controls are in place. Some of the key data setups related to legal control are as follows:

1. **ECCN or import list**
   Export control numbers are defined based on the Commercial Control List (CCL), which defines the controls associated with the classification numbers.

These numbers are individually assigned to products; alternatively, you can use the worklist to mass-assign the classification to a product. These classifications are associated with a legal regulation.

2. **Country group**

   If you decide to use the country group, you must maintain the country or countries that fall under the specific group.

3. **License determination**

   License determination strategy lists the determination sequence based on the key attributes selected in the license determination procedure for a partner regulation.

4. **Licenses**

   For every license type, you need to maintain the licenses in the system. It is important that these licenses are defined with valid-from and valid-to dates, and that they have an active status.

In the following sections, we will go over the license determination strategy. License determination is used for license type determination based on the legal regulation and classification.

License Determination

License determination is built based on the search the system would use to find the possible license types. Let's take an example of a license determination procedure with attributes such as legal regulation, country group, ECCN, and license types. For export, the system uses the departure country to determine the active legal regulation for legal control. It then uses all of the active legal regulations and the associated attributes to determine the license type. The country or country group in the procedure assignment is mapped against the destination country for export control based on the partner country; if you configure the system to use country groups, it searches for all country groups in which the partner country belongs and uses the country group in the search. Next, it determines the ECCN, which is derived from the classification assigned to the product for that exporting country regulation. These combinations are then used to find the possible license types. The search can go from the least control to the most control; in other words, if it can't find an appropriate license type in the first sequence, it moves to the next sequence. Figure 6.13 displays the typical license determination strategy table.

The transaction to maintain license determination is /SAPSLL/CD_MAINTAIN and can be accessed using the menu path SAP COMPLIANCE MANAGEMENT • LEGAL CONTROL – EXPORT OR IMPORT • MAINTAIN DETERMINATION STRATEGY.

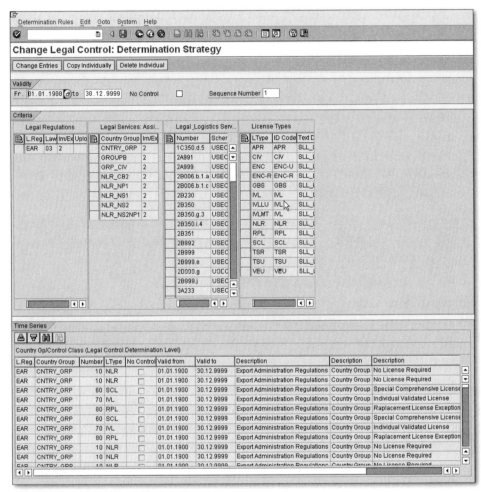

Figure 6.13 License Determination Table

Licenses

Based on the attributes defined in the license types, when you maintain the attributes, they will appear as defined in the configuration. The values maintained in the license are used for appropriate license assignment to the documents. Let's take an example of an individual validated license. If you have selected the attributes (value, quantity, product, classification number, country of departure or destination), license maintenance requires that you add the values associated with these selected attributes. The system then uses all of these key parameters in searching for the right license. Figure 6.14 displays the license maintained in the system for License Type IVL – Individual Validated License.

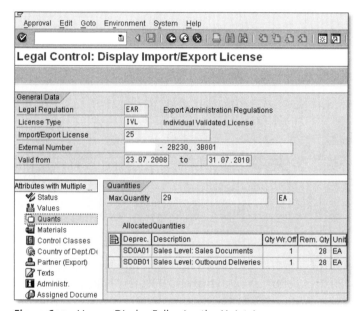

Figure 6.14 License Display Following the Maintain

6.3.3 Trade Reporting and Monitoring

There are several reports within Compliance Management specific to embargos, sanctioned party list screening, and legal control. For legal control export or import monitoring, the most frequently used reports are the blocked and assigned document reports. In the following sections, we discuss each of these in more detail.

Blocked

The block report reports blocked imports or exports. Here you can report the blocked document based on your organization (foreign trade organization or legal units), document creation, or block reasons; or with reference to the feeder system document number and type of document (delivery, sales order, purchase order, etc.).

The toolbar provides functionality and features to manage the trade block review and resolution. Figure 6.15 displays the report output with the first icon in the toolbar, which allows you to display the document and view more details. The next icon allows you to change the license assignment manually. The icon next to it allows you to change the product classification assignment, and the log icon displays the trade service check details. The icon showing the arrows allows you to recheck or re-determine the document, so that it gets the latest information from the system.

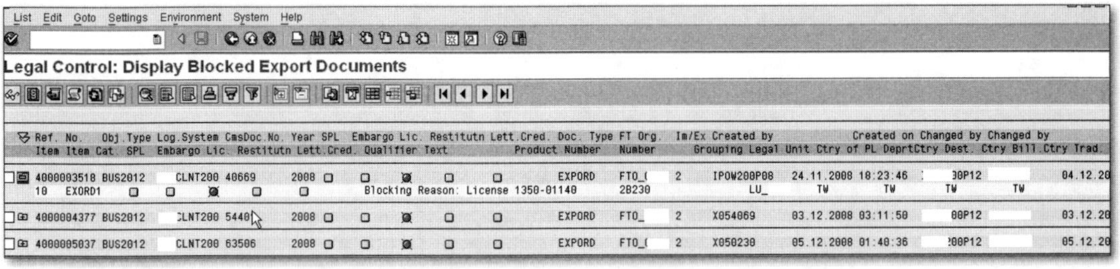

Figure 6.15 Blocked Document Report

You can configure the report layout for the most important information for quick review and disposition. Filtering allows you to filter the further selection of report output. You can also use the sorting to sort the list.

Assigned

The assigned report lists all of the documents that are assigned to a license. It provides the associated legal regulations, license types, and the country or country group. This report can be used for auditing purposes and allows you to review all of the details after the transaction has been completed. Figure 6.16 displays the assigned document report.

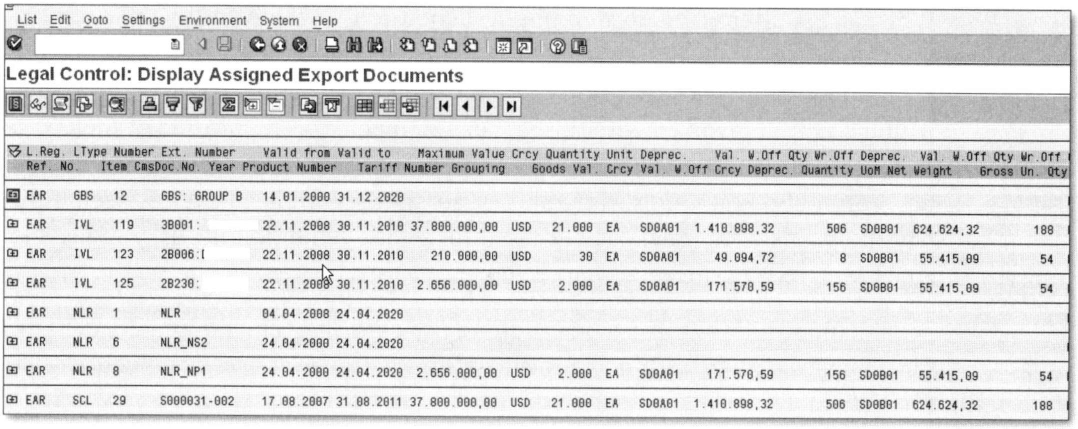

L.Reg. LType Number Ext. Number Valid from Valid to Maximum Value Crcy Quantity Unit Deprec. Val. W.Off Qty Wr.Off Deprec. Val. W.Off Qty Wr.Off
Ref. No. Item CmsDoc.No. Year Product Number Tariff Number Grouping Goods Val. Crcy Val. W.Off Crcy Deprec. Quantity UoM Net Weight Gross Un. Qty

EAR	GBS	12	GBS: GROUP B	14.01.2000	31.12.2020										
EAR	IVL	119	3B001:	22.11.2008	30.11.2010	37.800.000,00	USD	21.000	EA	SD0A01	1.410.898,32	506	SD0B01	624.624,32	188
EAR	IVL	123	2B006:[	22.11.2008	30.11.2010	210.000,00	USD	30	EA	SD0A01	49.094,72	8	SD0B01	55.415,09	54
EAR	IVL	125	2B230:	22.11.2008	30.11.2010	2.656.000,00	USD	2.000	EA	SD0A01	171.570,59	156	SD0B01	55.415,09	54
EAR	NLR	1	NLR	04.04.2008	24.04.2020										
EAR	NLR	6	NLR_NS2	24.04.2000	24.04.2020										
EAR	NLR	8	NLR_NP1	24.04.2000	24.04.2020	2.656.000,00	USD	2.000	EA	SD0A01	171.570,59	156	SD0B01	55.415,09	54
EAR	SCL	29	S000031-002	17.08.2007	31.08.2011	37.800.000,00	USD	21.000	EA	SD0A01	1.410.898,32	506	SD0B01	624.624,32	188

Figure 6.16 Assigned Document Report

6.4 ITAR and Agreements

The US International Traffic in Arms Regulations (ITAR) stipulates that US importers and exporters must follow certain standards to operate for defense-related material and technologies. Included in this is the requirement to obtain different licenses based on the US Munitions List (USML). The three main categories of licenses include hardware licenses, technical assistance agreements (TAA), and manufacture license agreements (MLA). Some cases call for multiple licenses across different processes.

In the following sections, we will go over the business process, configuration, and data setup for ITAR regulations and agreements.

6.4.1 Business Scenarios, Associated Configurations, and Data Setup

Imagine that a defense equipment manufacturing company wants to bid on a design for equipment or a control system to be used in a missile or fighter jet. Before it can even engage in the bid and share specific product information, the US State Department requires the exporter to apply for a technical assistance agreement (TAA) to facilitate the sharing of information. The TAA operates very much as a license does, and you can designate it for a specific product, USML, customer, country, and so on.

When an exporter wants to ship physical goods out of the country, the company needs to apply for an export license, such as a DSP-5 (for permanent export). The application for this license must reference the existing and valid TAA associated with the project involved with this sale or shipment. The application of the DSP-5 must take into account the attribute on the TAA such as dates, values, and quantities. For public exhibitions, trade shows, air shows, or related events, even if the physical goods were previously licensed for public exhibition needs, you need to apply for a DSP-73 (for temporary export).

For situations such as these, you can make use of the agreements and license type functionality features within SAP BusinessObjects Trade Services Compliance Legal Control.

6.4.2 Configurations Steps

The first step in the configuration is the definition of agreements. With SAP BusinessObjects Trade Services 7.1 and higher, SAP introduced Compliance Legal Control Agreements functionality. The company must start the information sharing with a design document in the form of a technical agreement. To do this, follow menu path SPRO • SAP GLOBAL TRADE SERVICE • COMPLIANCE MANAGEMENT • LEGAL CONTROL • DEFINE AGREEMENT. After you create an agreement, the system references it by the license type. While defining the agreement, in the Objects to be Checked section, select attributes within the transaction that you need to validate before assigning the agreement to the document or transaction.

In a typical case, you would select the Value Update and Quantity Update boxes in the Update section, and then select the appropriate choices from the dropdown lists. Make sure you define a depreciation group for use in the agreement quantity and value update. To do so, follow the menu path SPRO • SAP GLOBAL TRADE SERVICE • COMPLIANCE MANAGEMENT • LEGAL CONTROL • DEFINE DEPRECIATION GROUP. Create a name and description for the depreciation group, which helps to accumulate the value and quantity depreciation. After you define it, you need to assign it in the agreement definition. Figure 6.17 displays the agreement definition.

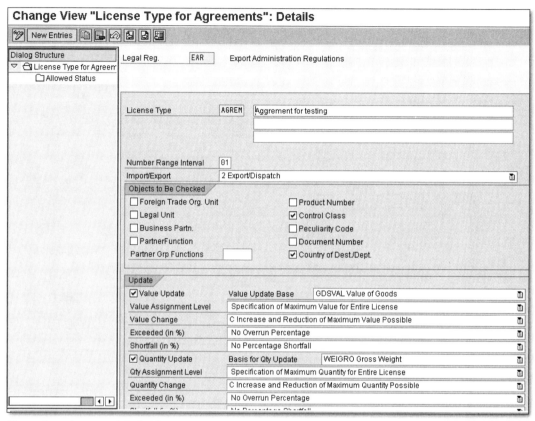

Figure 6.17 Agreement Definition

ITAR uses temporary and permanent licenses, and you might have to refer these licenses to the previous agreement. The license type defines the attributes you want to have in the license. While defining the license type, select the following to be updated: Object to be Checked, Value, and Quantity, respectively. Follow the menu path SPRO • SAP GLOBAL TRADE SERVICE • COMPLIANCE MANAGEMENT • LEGAL CONTROL • DEFINE LICENSE TYPE to display the license type definition. These definitions of attributes appear when you create licenses. Figure 6.18 displays the creation of a license type.

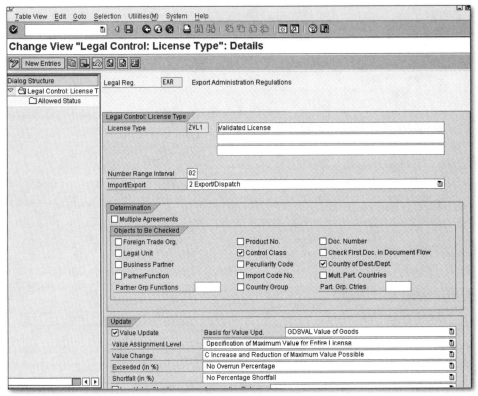

Figure 6.18 Creation of License Type

When you scroll down in the license type definition, you need to assign the agreement type to the license types. The screen prompts you to enter the new legal regulations and license type, and make necessary changes to other attributes. Under the Agreement tab, make sure you assign the Type of Agreement and Depreciation Group.

6.4.3 Data Setup

Following the agreement and license type definition, build the license type determination table. In the license determination, maintain the search logic for license type and agreement determination based on the determination procedure. For example, the license type is determined based on the departure country, destination country, grouping, and USML number. Follow menu path GTS COCKPIT • GTS COMPLIANCE MANAGEMENT • LEGAL CONTROL – EXPORT • DEFINE DETERMINATION STRATEGY. Build the table against the license type (ZVL1) and agreement (AGREM) based on the grouping for hardware and technical agreements for their respective classification numbers.

In the following sections, we will show how Agreements are defined and used in SAP BusinessObjects Trade Services systems. We will apply these concepts to the ITAR regulations.

Agreements

Follow menu path GTS COCKPIT • GTS COMPLIANCE MANAGEMENT • LEGAL CONTROL – EXPORT • MAINTAIN AGREEMENTS. Maintain the agreements based on the agreement defined in the configuration steps given in Section 6.4.2. Based on the attributes selected during configuration, the fields appear when you create or change agreements, for example, values, quantities, control classes, and countries of departure or destination. In the Agreement field, the system provides the internal number and external number, but you need to replace it and enter the actual agreement number. Enter dates in Valid From and Valid To for the period. Then maintain the values and quantity based on the approval issued from the US government. Within Control Classes, maintain the USML number, and within Country of Dept., maintain the country to which you're shipping the product.

Licenses

After you have the agreement in place, you can create licenses. When you create the license with the agreement assigned in the configuration, you must reference the agreement. You can create the license by following the menu path GTS COCKPIT • GTS COMPLIANCE MANAGEMENT • LEGAL CONTROL – EXPORT • MAINTAIN EXPORT LICENSES. Then enter the legal regulation and license type, and, from the dropdown list, select the agreement type and agreement number that you want to assign to the license. Figure 6.19 displays the agreement and license definition.

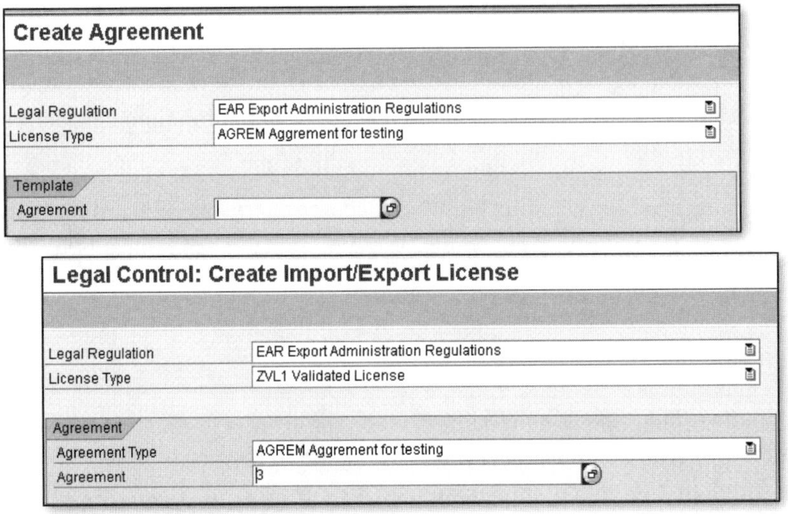

Figure 6.19 Agreement and License Definition

6.5 Summary

The legal control export and import functionalities are built on the same concept; thus, understanding exports helps you build imports. As you should see by now, legal control compliance setup uses many of the foundations you built with other compliance modules but also extends beyond them. For example, it makes use of the same service activation function, plus additional procedures to automate license determination. Similarly, license determination is based on license types, which represent the controls applied to particular products. Products are classified with these predefined classifications and translate to these controls based on the license determination table that has been built. And, just like other functions, legal control involves data setup along with configuration.

In the next chapter, we will move on to customs management. We will cover the concepts of baseline, foundation, and customs management-specific configuration; master data set up; and the business process associated with the operational use. We will go over the customs declaration with trade document print and communication setup for online submissions.

Following your compliance check, you are ready to ship and receive parts, which requires that you be ready with the trade declaration documents needed to export or import goods. Customs declarations are generated within Customs Management, where you can configure your system for print or online submission.

7   Customs Management: Application and Use

SAP BusinessObjects Global Trade Services Customs Management allows you to generate trade documentations for custom authorities declarations in either print or electronic form. You can print the trade forms and present them along with the goods being exported or if you prefer, you can mail or fax the documents ahead of time to the party importing the goods, be it your own company, broker, or customer. With electronic communication, the system converts the data into an intermediate document (an IDoc) and sends the IDoc output file (in text form) to middleware. Middleware acts as a translator to convert the IDoc file into the format in which the receiving system expects it.

In the United States, online communication to customs authorities is possible using Automated Export System (AES). AES is a standardized electronic export procedure from the US Customs and Border Protection (CBP) that helps companies manage their exports and connect with customs. Online customs declaration is mandatory for shipments of merchandise identified in the Commerce Control List (CCL) of the Export Administration Regulations (EAR) or the US Munitions List (USML) of the Internal Traffic in Arms Regulation (ITAR).

In this chapter, we will start with the foundation of Customs Management to get baseline configuration and move on to the configurations that are specific to Customs Management. We will review the communication setup for trade document print and online submissions. We will end the chapter with the Customs Management master data setup to enable the business process.

7.1   Foundations of Customs Management

With Compliance Management, we are concerned with screening and finding the appropriate approval to export, import, or validate goods, ensuring that the business partners we are dealing with are not on any denied lists. With Customs Management, however, the main objectives are the declarations and documentation, whether they are print, email, fax, or online. It is important to understand the basic concepts of this key functionality and how they are applied across different country regulations.

SAP BusinessObjects Global Trade Services Customs Management is broadly classified into two functionalities with similar configurations steps but different business applications: customs processing and transit procedures. *Customs processing* is used across all regulations, that is, when you have to generate documentation or declarations for exporting from or importing to any country. The *transit procedure*, however, is used mostly in Europe, to declare goods moving within the European Union. In the following sections, we discuss the different configurations of these two functionalities, as well as their applications and settings.

7.1.1   Legal Regulations

Similar to the different services in Compliance Management (sanctioned product list, embargo, and license determination), you must define a legal regulation for Customs Management. The steps for definition are similar to Compliance Management; following the definition of the regulation, you must list all of the countries to which the regulation applies. These configurations can be found under SAP REFERENCE IMG • SAP GLOBAL TRADE SERVICES • GENERAL SETTINGS • LEGAL REGULATIONS • DEFINE LEGAL REGULATION/ACTIVATE LEGAL REGULATIONS AT COUNTRY/COUNTRY GROUP LEVEL. When you define the legal regulation, ensure that you have the 01 Customs Processing code selected and that the relevant import and export codes are selected for the originating country of the legal regulation.

7.1.2   Numbering Schemes

For customs processing and transit processing, you must define numbering schemes, which allows you to assign classifications to products and is used for determination during customs declarations. There are different numbering schemes for export — called commodity codes — and import — called tariff codes. (Chapter

3, SAP BusinessObjects Global Trade Services Baseline Settings, discusses numbering scheme definitions and assignments in detail.)

The key point to remember is that you must define numbering schemes and then assign them to legal regulations. This configuration can be found under SAP REFERENCE IMG • SAP GLOBAL TRADE SERVICES • GENERAL SETTINGS • NUMBERING SCHEMES, and is achieved by following these steps:

1. Define the numbering scheme for commodity codes.

2. Assign the numbering scheme of the commodity codes for customs processing.

3. Define the numbering scheme for tariff codes.

4. Assign the numbering schemes of tariff codes for customs processing.

> **Note**
>
> SAP BusinessObjects Global Trade Services allows you to define two different numbering schemes for export and import. For export, you can define commodity code, and for import, the Harmonized Tariff System (HTS) number. Customers are moving toward having one numbering scheme to simplify the process and reduce the maintenance of one standard number that encompasses both the contents. If you want to use the HTS for export and import processing, define the Tariff Number to represent the Harmonized Tariff Number, and ensure that this numbering scheme is assigned to the export and import customs tariff number for Commodity Code and Tariff Code Numbers, respectively, for customs processing legal regulations.

7.1.3 Document Structures

The first step within the general settings is to configure the document structure. Start by identifying the document type specific to Customs Management. There are pre-delivered document types for customs processing and transit procedures, specific to export and import. These pre-delivered configurations give you an overview of the settings that are delivered; using them, you can make a copy and then create a new document type. The purpose of these document type definitions is to map the feeder system documents with the SAP BusinessObjects Global Trade Services document types, as well as the Customs Management functions associated with them.

The key configuration settings within document type definitions are as follows:

- **Import/Export Indicator**
  This defines the feeder system used for import or export declarations.

- **Number Range**
  This allows you to assign an internal number range for the customs declaration created. As transaction retrieval for review and reporting are done using the feeder system document, we generally recommend that you keep the same number ranges for Compliance Management and Customs Management. This will help you to better manage the number ranges for every year. However, if there is a definite need to distinguish Compliance Management documents from Customs Management documents, you can create separate number ranges for Customs Management.

- **Log Control**
  Here you define how the logs for document transfer are stored in SAP BusinessObjects Global Trade Services. This allows you to review the log of documents transferred in terms of success or failure. Within Document Transfer, select the option TD_MAP Movement Data: Document Replication Mapping (Live). With SAP BusinessObjects Global Trade Services 7.2, you can also perform a sanctioned product list check on Customs Management documents. Within Document Check, select the option Movement Data: Compliance Check Document (Live).

- **SAP Business Information Warehouse**
  If you want to send the Customs Management transaction to SAP NetWeaver BW, check the option titled Transfer to SAP NetWeaver Business Intelligence Active.

- **Control Data**
  Here you have configuration settings for access control, partner grouping, action profile, text determination, calculation profile, and item category. In the Access Control screen, we recommend that you select the Document Type and Legal Regulation combination. With Partner Grouping, select the grouping you have defined for export and import, as well as any other group you have defined for a specific business process. Grouping allows you to capture all of the partner types that you want to appear with this document transfer. Action Profile allows you to map the document to the communication technology used in SAP BusinessObjects Global Trade Services, called post-processing framework (PPF). (We will discuss the setup of this later in Section 7.3, Communication Setup: Post-Processing Framework.) If you have text determination customized for

Customs Management, assign it in Text Determination Procedure. Calculation Profile allows you to map the calculation profile for export or import purposes. The calculation profile consists of conditions where the values from the logistics systems are captured and duties are determined. Finally, within Item Category, assign the item category defined for Customs Management.

Figure 7.1 displays the typical settings for a customs document type. The configuration menu path can be accessed through SAP REFERENCE IMG • SAP CUSTOMS MANAGEMENT • GENERAL SETTINGS • DOCUMENT STRUCTURE • DEFINE DOCUMENT TYPES.

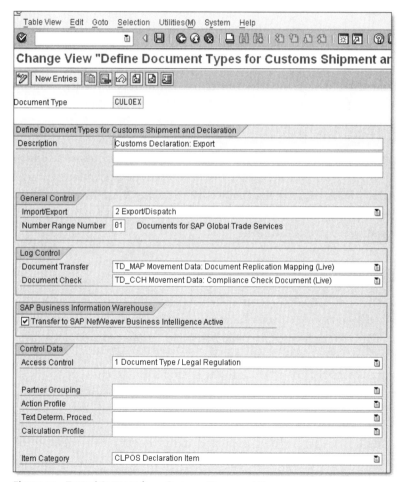

Figure 7.1 Typical Settings for a Customs Document Type

> **Note**
>
> Defined Customs Management document types needs to be activated for either customs processing or transit procedures. This is as simple as including the document types defined within these folders.

In the following sections, we will go over the Customs Management baseline supporting configurations within general settings and document type and item category activation.

Associated Configurations

There are two ways you can assign the Customs Management attributes, Action Profile, Partner Group, Tax Determination Procedure, and Calculation Profile: (1) by assigning directly to the customs document type, or (2) by assigning to the combination of legal regulation and document type. If you picked the legal regulation and document type combination while defining the document type, you must define the mapping within the configuration: SAP REFERENCE IMG • SAP CUSTOMS MANAGEMENT • GENERAL SETTINGS • DOCUMENT STRUCTURE • DEFINE CTRL SETT. A DOC. TYPE LEVEL AND LEGAL REG. LEVEL FOR CD/CS. Similarly, you must also map the determination procedure for the calculation profile to the document type and legal regulation under SAP REFERENCE IMG • SAP CUSTOMS MANAGEMENT • GENERAL SETTINGS • DOCUMENT STRUCTURE • DEFINE CONTROL DATA AT DOCUMENT TYPE LEVEL FOR CUSTOMS DOC. AND LEGAL REG.

Item Categories

While defining the item category, ensure the text determination procedure for items that needs to be assigned. If you want to transfer Customs Management document items to SAP NetWeaver BW, check the box titled Transfer to SAP NetWeaver Business Intelligence Active. As we saw earlier, in the document type definition, this item category is mapped or assigned to the customs document type.

Assignments

After defining the customs document type and item category, they need to be assigned to the feeder system document type and item category. Here, again, you have the option to assign to the logical system or logical system group. The configuration can be found under SAP REFERENCE IMG • SAP CUSTOMS MANAGEMENT

• GENERAL SETTINGS • DOCUMENT STRUCTURE • ASSIGNMENT OF DOCUMENT TYPES FROM FEEDER SYSTEM/ASSIGNMENT OF ITEM CATEGORIES FROM FEEDER SYSTEMS.

> **Note**
>
> If you have an inbound delivery note that should trigger a customs declaration for import, you might have to map the inbound delivery within the Assignment for Advanced Documents to Document Types from Feeder Systems.

7.1.4 Import Customs Declarations

The import cycle might start with your purchase order, which is followed by an inbound delivery note, goods receipt, and, finally, closed by an invoice receipt. These document types are triggered by the feeder system based on the plug-in configuration checked to transfer to SAP BusinessObjects Global Trade Services. Following the definition of the document type, you must map them to SAP BusinessObjects Global Trade Services. Purchase order document types are mapped to the customs declaration type called Import Order.

As explained in the preceding Note, you must assign the inbound delivery note to the SAP BusinessObjects Global Trade Services customs declaration document. The menu path can be accessed through SAP REFERENCE IMG • SAP CUSTOMS MANAGEMENT • GENERAL SETTINGS • DOCUMENT STRUCTURE • ASSIGNMENT FOR ADVANCED DOCUMENTS TO DOCUMENT TYPE FROM FEEDER SYSTEM. There are pre-delivered SAP BusinessObjects Global Trade Services customs document types for inbound delivery notes; you can assign one of these or create a new copy with reference to the standard document type.

In the following sections, we will discuss the configuration set up for duty corrections, inbound receipt, and dynamic field determination for declarations.

Duty Corrections

You are required to submit documents for duty correction with this configuration step. As such, you must define the customs document type: SAP REFERENCE IMG • SAP CUSTOMS MANAGEMENT • GENERAL SETTINGS • DOCUMENT STRUCTURE • DEFINE DOCUMENT TYPES FOR CUSTOMS DUTY CORRECTIONS. In Section 7.3.2, Post-Processing Framework, we discuss how to define duty rates and assign them to documents.

Receipts

Imports involve declaration against a vendor PO or vendor advance shipment notification. You can set up a document type so that it can be used to retrieve the import declaration; a purchase order, customs presentation number, or material reference number could be used in this regard. This configuration can be accessed via SAP Reference IMG • SAP Customs Management • General Settings • Document Structure • Define Determination of Prev. Doc. Type from Feeder System at Receipt.

Field Labels

Import declarations involve filing the declarations as per the customs authorities' specific filing format. With the customs declarations generic format provided by SAP BusinessObjects Global Trade Services, you can set up field labels that are used in the customs declaration, which are generated to dynamically, based on the customs or transit procedure. Figure 7.2 lists the procedure, the fields listed within the procedure, and the language and label determination for each field.

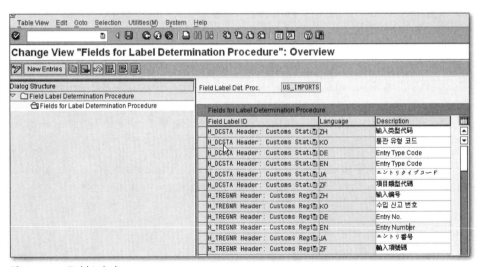

Figure 7.2　Field Labels

7.1.5　Customs Codes

The customs code list provides codes that are issued by different countries for communication with their respective customs authorities and is mostly used with the EDIFACT message exchanges for online submissions. The first step in this process is to define the procedure for custom code lists; we recommend that you have a procedure for each country. Define the code, and enter the description. The configuration can be accessed via SAP REFERENCE IMG • SAP CUSTOMS MANAGE-MENT • GENERAL SETTINGS • DOCUMENT STRUCTURE • CUSTOMS CODE LISTS • DEFINE PROCEDURES FOR CUSTOMS CODE LISTS.

After creating the definition, assign the procedure to legal regulations. These assignments represent different activities within the customs declaration and allow the customs authorities to identify certain pieces of information about importing or exporting goods; for example, mode of transport, duty type, customs status, and deferment types. Figure 7.3 displays the pre-delivered legal regulation, customs list object type, and procedure assigned.

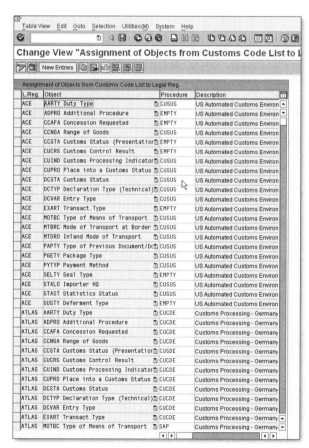

Figure 7.3 Assignment of Customs Code List to the Legal Regulation

After assigning the procedure to a legal regulation, you must maintain the customs code list for the legal regulation. This configuration step can be found under SAP REFERENCE IMG • SAP CUSTOMS MANAGEMENT • GENERAL SETTINGS • DOCUMENT STRUCTURE • CUSTOMS CODE LISTS • MAINTAIN CUSTOMS CODE LISTS. When you click on this configuration, it will prompt you to enter the legal regulation; after that, you must select the customs code list from the dropdown menu and click on Start Maintenance. In this screen, you can maintain the different codes and the associated descriptions. Figure 7.4 displays the code list for the Declaration Customs Code list type.

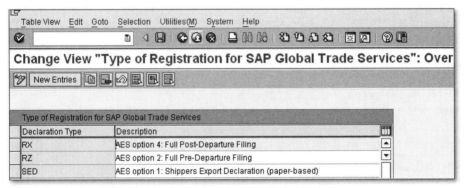

Figure 7.4 The Code List for the Declaration Customs Code List Type

7.1.6 Authorization

Some countries' customs processing has approval and release processes that involve setting up an authorization process. For example, to make an import declaration, there might be a prerequisite to provide some insurance document or bond. You can set up the different security types required for import clearance within SAP REFERENCE IMG • SAP CUSTOMS MANAGEMENT • GENERAL SETTINGS • DOCUMENT STRUCTURE • DEFINE SECURITY TYPES FOR CUSTOMS IMPORT PROCESSING. The concept of defining authorization is similar to the license type and license authorization in Compliance Management. Figure 7.5 displays some pre-delivered authorizations and their allowed statuses.

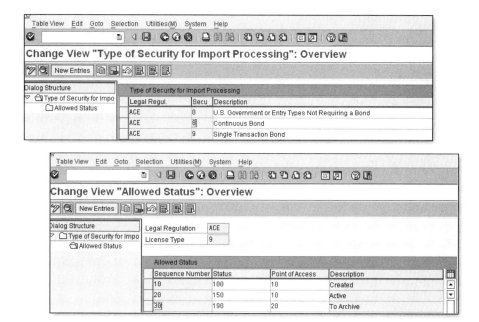

Figure 7.5 Pre-Delivered Authorizations and Allowed Statuses

Different countries might have authorization and release procedures requirements for export and import customs processing, which you can define with Customs Management. In Section 7.4, Cockpit Setup, we discuss the data setup requirement to enable these license activations and authorizations.

7.2   Configuring Customs Management

In the previous section, we discussed the configuration that applies to Customs Management and the transit procedure. Following the baseline configuration, in this section, we will go over the configurations that are specific to Customs Management; these configuration can be found under SAP REFERENCE IMG • SAP GLOBAL TRADE SERVICES • SAP CUSTOMS MANAGEMENT • "CUSTOMS PROCESSING" SERVICES.

This same concept can be applied to define the transit procedure. Similar to Compliance Management, Customs Management has a determination procedure that needs to be assigned for service activation. This setting is pre-delivered with the procedure to determine the regulation based on country key. If you need to have a different determination procedure, you can create a new one and assign it via SAP Reference IMG • SAP Global Trade Services • SAP Customs Management • "Customs Processing" Services • Assign Determination Procedure for Active Legal Regulations.

In the following sections, we discuss the activation of the customs processing services by legal regulations.

7.2.1 Activation

Activation is based on the country listed in SAP Reference IMG • SAP Global Trade Services • General Settings • Legal Regulations • Activate Legal Regulations at Country/Country Group Level, these countries will appear within the SAP Reference IMG • SAP Global Trade Services • SAP Customs Management • "Customs Processing" Service • Activate Legal Regulation. Here you must activate the legal regulation for import and/or export processing.

7.2.2 Control Settings

The control setting configuration step links the process template with the legal regulation. Here you assign the legal regulation to the process template, customs value currency, exchange rate type, and so on. The process template defines the message and sequence that is determined as part of the export or import process.

7.2.3 Preference Settings

If the company doesn't have a requirement to perform the preferential determination with trade regulations for products, you have the option of using a simpler solution of proposing the preferential treatment documents, Country of Origin, within the customs declaration without having to go through the implementation of Risk Management configuration. This configuration step can be accessed via SAP Reference IMG • SAP Global Trade Services • SAP Customs Management • "Customs Processing" Services • Define Proposal for Preference Document in Customs Declaration.

In this screen, you can configure to trigger preferential declaration documents based on the customs declaration. Select the Preferential Agreement that has been defined and activated, the country of origin of the product, the customs regulation, and the previous document type. Figure 7.6 displays the typical setting.

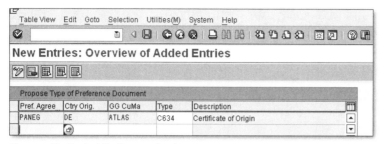

Figure 7.6 Typical Preference Settings

7.2.4 Customs Duty Setup

Customs declarations carry the cost of the goods and other associated values in the transaction transferred from the logistics transactions, proforma, or other billing documents. To ensure these values are transferred into the SAP BusinessObjects Global Trade Services customs declaration document for report and duty calculation, they need to be configured in Customs Management.

The first step in the customs duty configuration is to define the customs duty type. SAP BusinessObjects Global Trade Services has pre-delivered customs duty types, but if you want to create a new one, you can make a copy and edit it accordingly. Figure 7.7 displays the configuration setup with two different pre-delivered duty types. Duty Category allows you to identify the duty type with the value being captured, for example, transactional, anti-dumping, and so on. Distribution Type allows you to define the criteria for distributing the duty by value or weight. Maintenance Level allows you to define where the condition appears, whether in the header or line. Access w/Ctry has the option to select the duty type based on the product country of origin, departure country, or SAP standard. Select Pro-Rata Duty if you want only portions of the shipment to apply to the particular line item in the customs declarations.

After you define the duty types here, define them in the Customs Duty Framework. (In other words, list all of the duty types that are to appear in a customs declaration document.) This structure is defined under separate folders for import and export. The duty types are defined in sequence with assignment to the export or import regulation they belong to: Value Type, Amount Rule, and Exchange Rate. Figure 7.8 displays the configuration settings behind this setup.

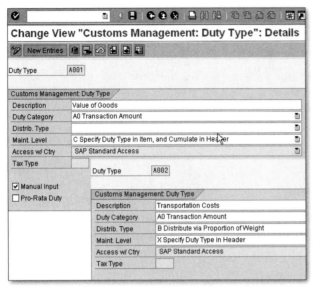

Figure 7.7 Configuration Setup with Two Different Pre-Delivered Duty Types

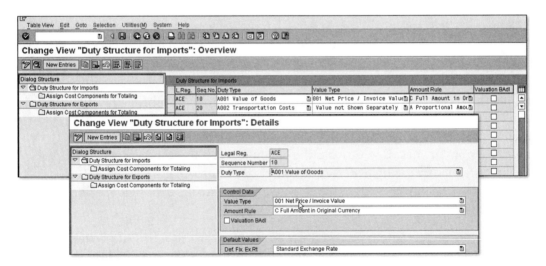

Figure 7.8 Duty Structure and Condition for Duty Type

To enable duty content to load into SAP BusinessObjects Global Trade Services, define all of the external duty types to the SAP BusinessObjects Global Trade Services customs processing duty type. Figure 7.9 displays the typical configuration settings.

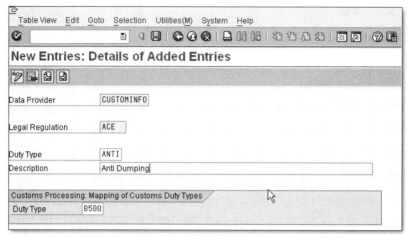

Figure 7.9 Assignment of Duty Type to Legal Regulation and Data Provider

7.3   Communication Setup: Post-Processing Framework

Customs Management in SAP Global Trade Services (SAP BusinessObjects Global Trade Services) is an SAP module used to standardize electronic communication processes, including customs declarations. Electronic communication in Customs Management takes place by printing messages or creating Electronic Data Interchange (EDI) messages. You can connect SAP BusinessObjects Global Trade Services to customs authorities all over the world to manage foreign trade activities. SAP BusinessObjects Global Trade Services can communicate and set up electronic customs processes with European, US, and Australian customs authorities, and address the different filing formats, data transmission requirements, and other features.

In the following sections, we discuss the online submission with the Automated Export Submission within Customs Management.

7.3.1   Automated Export Submission Scenario

As mentioned in the introduction of this chapter, AES allows electronic communication for exports leaving the United States. This electronically transmitted data replaces the requirement to file a paper Shipper's Export Declaration (SED). AES allows a US principal party in interest (USPPI) (i.e., the exporter) or its authorized agent to transmit commodity data. Commodity data includes commodity codes, which identify the materials or products as classified by the US Census Bureau (also called Schedule B) or the International Trade Commission (HTS number). HTS numbers are internationally agreed upon classification numbers for products traded internationally for import purposes.

Customs authorities provide two electronic filing options to report commodity data, called options 2 and 4:

▶ Option 2: Complete commodity data reporting prior to departure.

▶ Option 4: This option is only available to an approved USPPI. It allows an exportation to be made with no prior AES commodity data filing. You need to report complete commodity data as soon as you know it, and no later than 10 calendar days from the date of exportation. To use option 4, your company would have had to apply for filing by August 15, 2003, because new applications are not being accepted.

SAP BusinessObjects Global Trade Services can automatically create export documents that can be electronically sent to US customs using AES instead of an SED. Additionally, SAP BusinessObjects Global Trade Services can produce other documents that you can store or print, such as shipper letters of instruction or certificates of origin, if associated with the same process. Relevant documents for each business transaction are determined.

7.3.2 Post-Processing Framework

SAP BusinessObjects Global Trade Services uses post-processing framework (PPF) to determine documents to be printed or processed via EDI. PPF is a new technique that replaces output determination, formerly in Sales and Distribution (SD). You can adapt the standard PPF configuration according to users' needs. You can use either print or EDI messages with PPF; each message has an assigned PPF action.

For print or electronic communication with customs authorities, you define the technical prerequisite for the communications processes in addition to the process-specific settings by following these steps.

1. **Define the technical medium for messages for customer shipment.**
   Here you define the action definitions in an action profile. In the action profile, define all of the permitted actions and general conditions for the actions contained in the profile. For example, you can define the way in which the system performs the action (by method call or Smart Forms). Follow menu path SAP Reference IMG SAP BusinessObjects Global Trade Services • SAP Customs Management • General Settings • Communications Processes • Define Techn. Medium for Msgs (PPF Actions) f. Cust. Shipm. The different action definitions include general conditions and processing types (e.g., if the system executes actions by method call for EDI or Smart Forms). You can make use of standard delivered action profiles (US_CU_EX), which have as standard the following action definitions:

   ▶ US_CU_EX_CUSEX_M_UAES2 (Export Declaration Option 2 [US] for AES outbound IDoc generation)

   ▶ US_CU_EX_CUSEX_P_SED (SED print out)

   ▶ US_CU_EX_CUSEX_P_SLI (SLI print out)

2. **Define the action.**
   While you are in the Action Profile folder, you can click on the detail to see the details behind the action profile. Go to the action profile by double-clicking on the Action Profile folder and then Action Definition. Select Change and then the New Entries button. Double-click on the Processing Types folder while selecting your action definition. Then you need to choose your assignment. In this case, you have only a method call because this is the standard for EDI. Use the Default checkbox only if you create a new action template in the configuration. The system assigns the default processing to the new action template. Figure 7.10 displays the configuration setup for action profile and the processing type associated with it. Figure 7.11 displays the action definition associated with the action profile.

> **Note**
>
> The steps for document printing are similar to the AES communication setup, except for step 2 in the PPF. In the Action Definition (Permitted Processing Types of Action), select Form Name • Form Type • Format for form print.

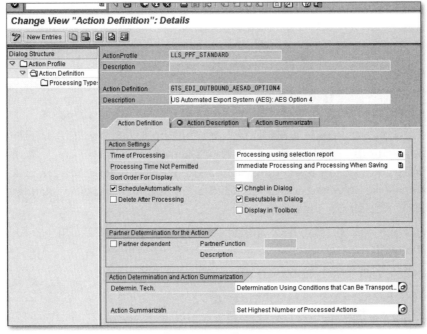

Figure 7.10 Configuration Setup for Action Profile

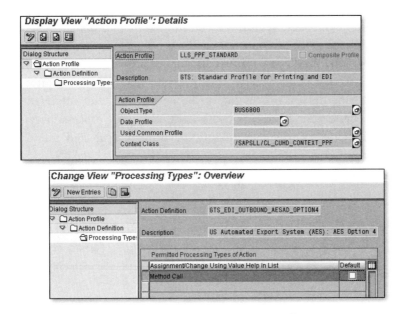

Figure 7.11 Action Definition Associated with Action Profile

7.3.3   Defining Condition and Output Parameters

The action profile displays the interface between the application and the PPF, giving a view of the application object type that shows only the settings that are of interest to the PPF. Using the settings provided in the action profile, the system evaluates the conditions that lead to the scheduling of actions (outputs) by the system.

Following the configuration step described earlier in Section 7.3.2, Post-Processing Framework, as a next step, you define the process templates based on the action profile and action definition configured. The action definition describes the content of an action independently of the processing type. At the action definition level, it specifies how the actions are found, which possibilities exist for the processing of actions, and whether they are set up to specific partners. The system assigns the action definitions and delivers them as defaults to action profiles. The action profiles in turn reflect the country and process combination. At this level, you can specify the details for action definitions and define additional conditions and parameters.

If you want to set up email communication, for instance, enter the recipient's email address as an action detail in this IMG activity. You can also add action definitions for the action profile here. We recommend that you copy the default settings from the action definitions, and then supplement them as required Ð for example, if you want to add new email recipients or change a processing time (immediate transit or initiated manually).

Follow the menu path GTS • CUSTOMS MANAGEMENT • GENERAL SETTINGS • COMMUNICATIONS PROCESSES • DEFINE CONDITIONS AND OUTPUT PARAMETERS FOR COMM. OF CUST.SH. Select the action profile, and double-click on it. The system lists the Action Definition on the right window. Click on the action profile, and go to the Processing Details tab to enter the number of pages to print out. Use the Receipt tab to enter the email addresses. Select the Start Condition tab to select the standard start condition, SLL_PPF_CUS_START_CONDITION. Then define the conditions and output parameters of the action profile. Schedule and start the conditions. Use the example of the conditions of an action profile given in the standard customizing.

Figure 7.12 displays the setup for conditions within the action profile.

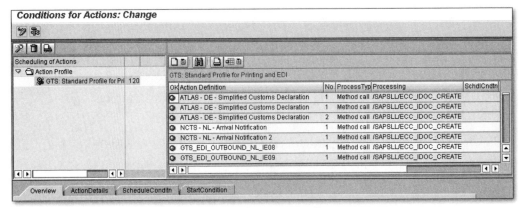

Figure 7.12 Setup for Conditions Within the Action Profile

7.3.4 Messages: Definition for Communication Process

Messages are like conditions that are assigned to the action definition, and you can use them for defining the process template and the message determination. Follow the menu path GTS • Customs Management • General Settings • Communications Processes • Define Messages for Communication Process. Select the standard message, and make a copy with reference to it. Change the Action Definition, and the system supplies the information shown in Customizing, as well as a standard set of messages for printing. You can use these standard messages, or copy one and edit it for your purposes.

7.3.5 Process Template

Following the configuration step defined in the previous section, as a next step, you define the communication processes with the customs authorities, structure them, and put each of the process steps into a logical sequence. This allows you to assign messages to each of the process steps and prepare the system so that users receive only process-relevant messages. Figure 7.13 displays the typical setup for the message type for online submission and print output.

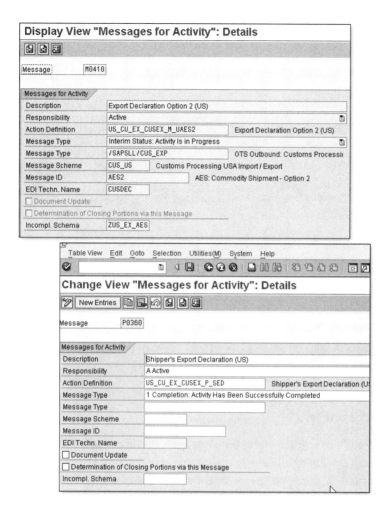

Figure 7.13 Message Type Typical Setup for Online Submission and Print Output

Follow the menu path GTS • CUSTOMS MANAGEMENT • GENERAL SETTINGS • COM-MUNICATIONS PROCESSES • DEFINE PROCEDURE FOR COMMUNICATION PROCESS. Define the process template to which you assign communication processes. Then assign the process template to a legal regulation. Within the process template, maintain the processes, process steps, and messages. Then maintain the sequence of messages, and choose a process to which you assign activities. Select Process Templ., and click on Process Activit. Then select the messages. Define the Activity Sequence for these messages. In the sequence you want, include the messages you have already defined in the earlier steps. While in this configuration, make sure to assign the activity or activities related to this process.

Figure 7.14 displays the setup for the typical process template.

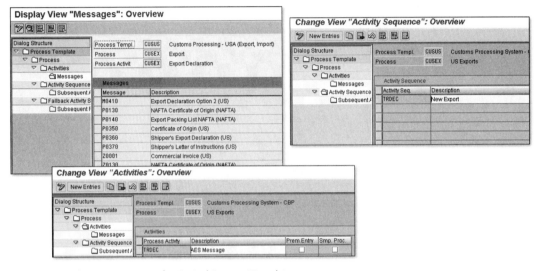

Figure 7.14 Setup for Typical Process Template

7.3.6 Message Parameters

For printed documents, you must maintain message determination and printer determination. If you are doing online submissions, than you need only set up the message determination. Within the message determination setup, the message with message determination selection is based on the following:

- Legal regulation
- Document type
- Departure group
- Destination group
- Country of departure
- Country of destination
- Mode of transport at border
- Less than or greater than net value specified

One typical determination setup, for Shipper's Export Declarations, is shown in Figure 7.15, using US customs regulation and a value greater than $2500.

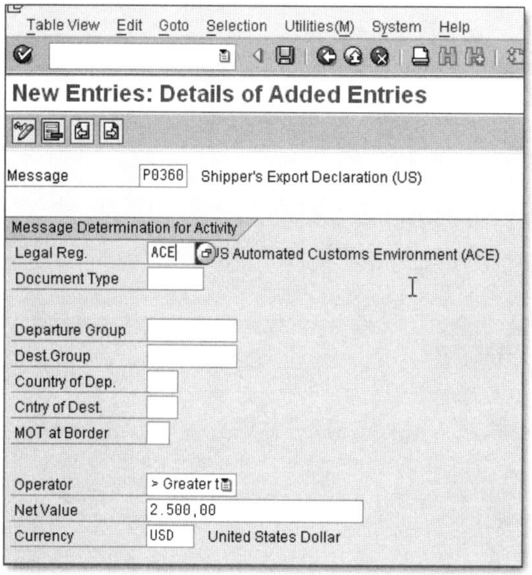

Figure 7.15 Example of a Determination Setup

Note

If you want to enable printer determination, you need to check the Printer Determination within the configuration step, SAP Reference IMG • SAP Global Trade Services • SAP Customs Management • Communication Processes • Define Conditions and Output Parameters for Comm. of Cust. Shipm. & Cust. Dcl. Figure 7.16 displays this configuration setting.

7.3.7 Middleware Communication Setup

If you use the online submission and EDIFACT communication with customs authorities, you must set up middleware communication. This involves some additional setup within the SAP BusinessObjects Global Trade Services system. In the following sections, we will discuss the configuration set up for the middleware interface.

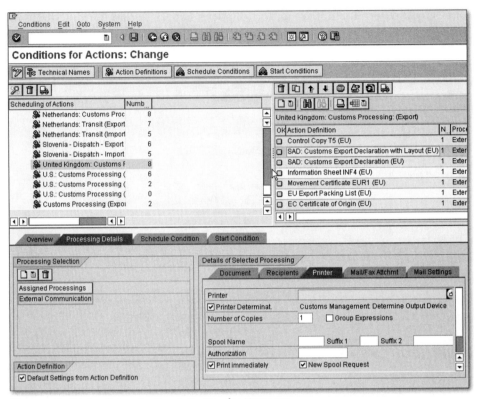

Figure 7.16 Printer Determination Activation for Messages

Remote Function Call Port

EDI communication to the AES involves the outbound IDoc/message. When you get a response from AES, you need to process it through the inbound IDoc. To send the outbound IDoc and to receive the inbound IDoc, you need to define ports. Set the receiver port for inbound to SAP BusinessObjects Global Trade Services from the Middleware or EDI converter. You also need a port for sending the outbound IDocs from SAP BusinessObjects Global Trade Services to the AES through the middleware. Set RFC destinations as usual for communication to these systems. Go to Transaction WEDI, expand the Administration folder, and click on Port Definition. Select Transactional RFC, and set up the port.

You must also create a file port for outbound IDocs. Figure 7.17 displays the configuration needed to define the inbound IDoc. While you are in the port creation, you can also create the file port by keeping your cursor on the folder file and clicking the Create icon. Enter the details of the directory where you want the file to be stored in the Directory field.

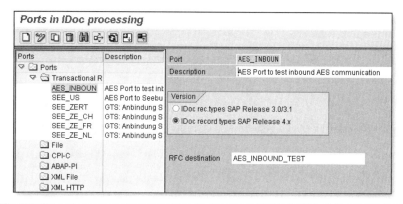

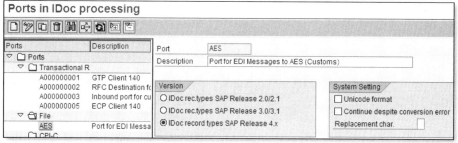

Figure 7.17 Configuration to Define Inbound IDocs

Partner Profile

For transmissions to the customs office, you must define a partner profile. While in Transaction WEDI, click on the Administration folder, go to the Partner Profile definition, and define the Partner Type as GP. This partner type is defined for each customs office (export/import) for outbound IDocs. Keep your cursor in the folder (Partner Type — GP), click on the Create icon, and fill in the details (Type — User; Agent — User ID; Language — EN; under Outbound Parameters, Message Type — /SAPSLL/CU-EXP; and under Inbound Parameters, Message Type — /SAPSLL/ CUS_INBOUND).

After that, define the partner type as LS to represent the SAP BusinessObjects Global Trade Services system, which sends this information and will receive the information back from the customs office. While in the partner profile definition, create partner type LS for inbound IDoc communication. Keep your cursor on the LS partner type, and click on Create. Fill in the details (Type – User; Agent – User ID; Language – EN; under Inbound Parameters, Message field - /SAPSLL/CUS_ INBOUND). Figure 7.18 displays the configuration setting for the partner profile.

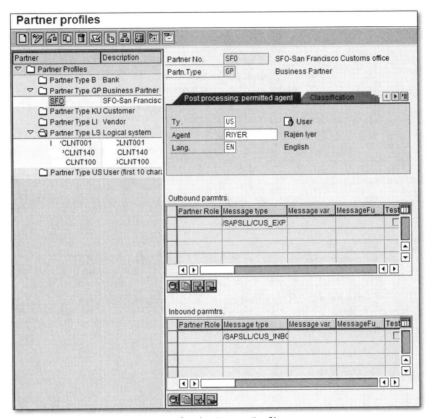

Figure 7.18 Configuration Settings for the Partner Profile

7.4 Cockpit Setup

SAP BusinessObjects Global Trade Services Customs Management has data within the cockpit that enables the business configuration setup. There are master data specific to Customs Management, which we will review, as well as classification tools to manage your content load for commodity codes, HTS numbers, and product classification. The transactions are monitored and managed within the screen titled Customs Processing – Import/Export for Customs Management and Transit under Transit/Presentation.

Customs processing for declaration and reporting transactions are found under SAP BusinessObjects Global Trade Services Area Menu • Customs Processing – Import/Export (or by using Transaction /SAPSLL/MENU_LEGAL). Within Customs Processing – Import / Export, you have functions within the four different tabs: Operative Cockpit, Monitoring, Monitoring of Logistics Processes, and Inventory Management.

There are other sections that are commonly shared by different functions:

▸ Document Processing

▸ Periodic Declaration

▸ Single Document Display

▸ Message and Print Processing

▸ Authorization

▸ Securities for Import

▸ Customs Value Calculation

The operative and monitoring functions both consist of reports that allow you to display the customs declaration. The key difference between these two functions is that the operative cockpit reports make use of the different statuses within the Customs Processing PPF in reporting, monitoring, and tracking. It can help you manage your worklist by listing documents that are already processed (printed), incomplete, or that need to be reprinted. Figure 7.19 displays the typical display outbound activity worklist with the process template configured in the SAP BusinessObjects Global Trade Services configuration. The operative cockpit will display only the active customs declaration, and monitoring will display even the documents that are canceled.

With document processing, you have the ability to create manual customs declarations (Figure 7.20). Select the foreign trade organization, and, within Enter Customs Declaration Manually, select Export and the subsequent action Export Declaration.

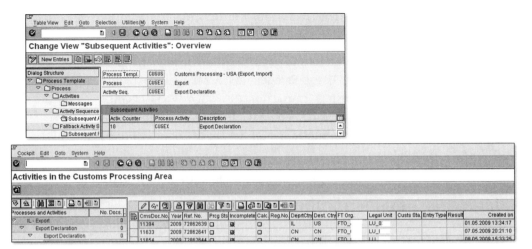

Figure 7.19 Typical Display Outbound Activity Worklist

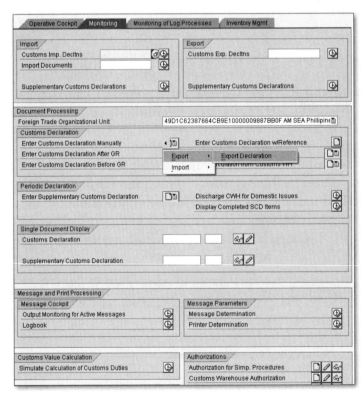

Figure 7.20 Manual Customs Declarations

In the next section, we will go over the functions and reports that are available for message view and execution.

7.4.1 Messages

There is another way to review customs processing declarations, based on the trade document that needs to be printed or submitted online. You can run the report called Output Monitoring for Active Messages, with statuses of Not Processed, Error, or Completed. This report can be found under the section Message Cockpit within the Customs Processing for Import/Export.

> **Note**
>
> If you have authorization or securities as part of the customs declaration process, you will have to maintain them within the SAP Customs Management: Customs Processing for Import/Export, under Authorization and Securities for Import Processing. These are logged as license maintenance, as seen with SAP COMPLIANCE MANAGEMENT • LEGAL CONTROL.

7.4.2 Classifications

Within SAP CUSTOMS MANAGEMENT • CLASSIFICATION, there is functionality to load the classification content from an XML file or manually maintain individual entries. Product classification can be updated with different reports. Using the worklist, individual products can be reclassified. Worklist allows you to review product lists that are in SAP BusinessObjects Global Trade Services for clarification and also allows you to use functionality such as search, clipboard, and mass-assign to facilitate the classification process.

Additionally, there are reports such as Display Tariff Number Data Sheet, which allows you to display the details data sheet against individual classification numbers or the content you have maintained in the system. Display Product Catalog can provide you with a report of all of the products that have been classified. Figure 7.21 display an output of this report.

Prod. Catalog for Applied Materials Inc. / Santa Clara CA 95054-3299

Tarif Code Numbers (ECT, HS) Key Date: 08.05.2009

Number	Numbering Scheme Name	Supp. Unit	Product Number	Product Master Short Text	LS Group	BUn	Valid from	Valid to
2501000000	Harmonized Tariff Schedule for the United States	TO	0190-00856		ECC_GRP	EA	10.11.2008	31.12.9999
			0190-00856B		ECC_GRP		10.11.2008	31.12.9999
2710112500		ST	5070-90007		ECC_GRP		10.11.2008	31.12.9999
2710119000		KG	5070-00084		ECC_GRP		10.11.2008	31.12.9999
2710193080		ST	5070-01003		ECC_GRP		10.11.2008	31.12.9999
			5070-01037		ECC_GRP		10.11.2008	31.12.9999
			417705		ECC_GRP		26.11.2008	31.12.9999
			0137-0034-000		ECC_GRP		10.11.2008	31.12.9999
			10081976		ECC_GRP		04.12.2008	31.12.9999
			5070-00063		ECC_GRP	LB	10.11.2008	31.12.9999
2710193500		KG	5070-01016		ECC_GRP	EA	10.11.2008	31.12.9999
2710194000			0190-71139		ECC_GRP		05.12.2008	31.12.9999
			0190-71132		ECC_GRP		26.11.2008	31.12.9999
			5070-01062		ECC_GRP		10.11.2008	31.12.9999
			0190-08054		ECC_GRP		10.11.2008	31.12.9999
			5070-01076		ECC_GRP		10.11.2008	31.12.9999
			5070-90012		ECC_GRP		10.11.2008	31.12.9999
			4205		ECC_GRP		26.11.2008	31.12.9999
			5070-00009		ECC_GRP		10.11.2008	31.12.9999
			5070-00007		ECC_GRP		10.11.2008	31.12.9999
			P26768		ECC_GRP		10.11.2008	31.12.9999
			5070-00045		ECC_GRP		10.11.2008	31.12.9999
			5070-01077		ECC_GRP		10.11.2008	31.12.9999
2710194590		ST	0138-0057-000		ECC_GRP		10.11.2008	31.12.9999
2804300000		KM3	0820-01040		ECC_GRP		10.11.2008	31.12.9999
			0820-01040B		ECC_GRP		10.11.2008	31.12.9999
2811221000		KG	0242-04150B		ECC_GRP		10.11.2008	31.12.9999
			0242-04150		ECC_GRP		10.11.2008	31.12.9999
2814100000		TO	5040-01012		ECC_GRP		10.11.2008	31.12.9999
			5040-01012B		ECC_GRP		10.11.2008	31.12.9999
2815120000		KG	0190-06084		ECC_GRP		10.11.2008	31.12.9999
2817000000			5030-90000		ECC_GRP		10.11.2008	31.12.9999
			5030-01003		ECC_GRP		10.11.2008	31.12.9999
2833250000			0190-00854		ECC_GRP		10.11.2008	31.12.9999
2853000095			5090-01003		ECC_GRP		10.11.2008	31.12.9999

Figure 7.21 Display Product Catalog: Sample Report

7.4.3 Master Data

As part of Customs Management, there are certain master data that are to be maintained. Customs office is one important piece of master data that is required as part of the online submission setup. You can maintain the customs office in the SAP BusinessObjects Global Trade Services customs master data. The customs office represents the office from which the goods leave and the declaration of the submission type. From the customs offices, companies receive authorization or approval for specific procedures, which helps the receiving entity to validate that approval. Customs office codes are reported along with the customs declaration to indicate the customs office that the goods are shipped out from. To configure this setting, follow the menu PATH GTS AREA MENU • SAP CUSTOMS MANAGEMENT • MASTER DATA • CUSTOMS OFFICES • EDIT CUSTOMS OFFICES (or use Transaction BP).

In the Maintain Business Partner screen, click on the Organization icon. Enter the business partner number, select the role as Customs Office, enter the name and address, and save the entry. Figure 7.22 shows the customs office maintain screen with display mode.

After you maintain the business partners to represent the customs office, you must assign the customs office number. The customs authorities have designated numbers, which you must use while transmitting to AES through US Customs. Follow the menu path GTS AREA MENU • GTS CUSTOMS MANAGEMENT • MASTER DATA • CUSTOMS OFFICES • EDIT CUSTOMS OFFICE NUMBERS. Select your legal regulation, enter the customs office number, and click on the Execute icon. This brings you to the Display Customs Office Numbers screen (see Figure 7.22). Click on the Change icon. Now the office number for partner (OFN) is editable, and you can enter the customs office number in the OFN field.

Figure 7.22 Business Partner Definition

7.4.4 Identification Numbers

You should maintain the trade identification number for your customer and vendor because this information might have to be printed in the trade documents. This can be updated using the transaction code under SAP CUSTOMS MANAGEMENT

• MASTER DATA • EDIT TRADER IDENTIFICATION NUMBER. Similarly, you can also maintain the business identification number for your foreign trade organization and legal units; for example, the VAT number, EIN number, and so on. These transactions are available under SAP CUSTOMS MANAGEMENT • MASTER DATA • ENTERPRISE ORGANIZATION.

7.5 Summary

Customs Management is a part of SAP BusinessObjects Global Trade Services that helps you to prepare your customs documentation following your compliance service checks, either using standard printouts or by making use of standardized electronic communication processes. Electronic communication in Customs Management takes place by printing messages or creating Electronic Data Interchange (EDI) messages. You can connect SAP BusinessObjects Global Trade Services to customs authorities all over the world to manage foreign trade transactions and activities. SAP BusinessObjects Global Trade Services can communicate and set up electronic customs processes with European, US, Asian, and Australian customs authorities, and can address the different filing formats, data transmission requirements, and other features.

After reading this chapter, you should be familiar with the foundation of Customs Management and understand the different configuration settings required for setup, including the SAP BusinessObjects Global Trade Services cockpit setup to support the configuration and enable business processes. You should also know the key configurations for printing trade documents and for online submissions, as well as the associated middleware and other setups required for automated electronics submissions.

In the next chapter, we will go over some of the add-ons and additional functionalities that you can enable. The next chapter helps you enhance Compliance Management and Customs Management functionality.

8 General Add-On Functionality and Features

Now that you are familiar with the SAP BusinessObjects Global Trade Services Compliance Management and Customs Management, we will consider some very useful and important functionality that enhance or support Compliance Management and Customs Management. These functionalities can be very important in meeting critical requirements, for example, text determination that carries text and notes information from your SAP ERP and logistics system to SAP BusinessObjects Global Trade Services.

The standard SAP to SAP BusinessObjects Global Trade Services interface transfers minimal material information. To help facilitate classification, you may need to bring additional material attributes into SAP BusinessObjects Global Trade Services, which might provide more details or might help with segregating the material flowing into SAP BusinessObjects Global Trade Services. This can be achieved through a combination of configuration and technical changes, which is one of the useful add-on functionalities offered by SAP BusinessObjects Global Trade Services.

Email notifications and workflows are another new functionality introduced with SAP BusinessObjects Global Trade Services 7.1. This allows you to create an email with notification of blocked business partners or documents, or information about embargos and license blocks and then forward it to the appropriate business individual or group.

In this chapter, we discuss how to set up the text items and procedure for capturing information from the feeder system. If you want to bring in additional information from the product master from the SAP ERP system, you need to configure the customs product. We will look at how to configure the system for capturing additional information from the feeder system. Email notification allows you to send the notification to individuals or groups. And case management allows you to manage blocked business partners, where it needs to be escalated for appropriate approvals for releases. We will go over the email notification and case management. Documents transferred from the SAP ECC system might not be complete, and you can make use of default data determination. We will look at the functionality behind the default data determination and the associated configuration. We will also go over the configuration setup to build the interface with your SAP ECC Human Resource Management (SAP HRM) system.

8.1   Text Determination

Text determination allows you to capture free-form information from SAP Business-Objects Global Trade Services, whether it was manually entered or carried over from the feeder system. This text information can be used to take specific actions or simply to be printed in trade documents. Texts are captured within different documents in Customs Management, such as licenses or products, with different objects. For customs documents, text control is a two-step process: defining the text ID specific to text objects, and assigning it to the procedure.

Text information is captured within objects that are associated with text IDs. Text IDs are identification or code assigned to the text, so that the system can retrieve the information based on the identification. The object for customs declaration is SLL_CUHD_C. There are pre-delivered text types with this object, but you can also create custom text types if required. The configuration step is accessed THROUGH SAP REFERENCE IMG • SAP GLOBAL TRADE SERVICES • GENERAL SETTINGS • TEXT CONTROL • DEFINE TEXT IDS FOR FOREIGN TRADE-SPECIFIC DOCUMENTS. Select Text Objects and IDs, and click on Change to add text IDs to the object. If you select the text object SLL_CUHD_C and double-click, you will see a display of existing text IDs. Click on the Create icon to create a new one.

Following the text ID definition, you need to assign it to the text determination procedure. There are some pre-delivered text IDs assigned to text determination procedures; you must add newly created IDs to this list. This configuration step can be accessed through: SAP REFERENCE IMG • SAP GLOBAL TRADE SERVICES • GENERAL SETTINGS • TEXT CONTROL • DEFINE TEXT DETERMINATION PROCEDURES FOR CUSTOMS SHIPMENTS AND DECLARATIONS.

Following the assignment of the text ID to the procedure, assign the text determination procedure to the relevant document type or item category. This configuration is accessed via SAP REFERENCE IMG • SAP GLOBAL TRADE SERVICES •
SAP CUSTOMS MANAGEMENT • GENERAL SETTINGS • DOCUMENT STRUCTURE • DEFINE
DOCUMENT TYPE AND DEFINE ITEM CATEGORY.

Figure 8.1 shows a text ID assigned to a text object and, in the second section, a
text ID assigned to a text determination procedure.

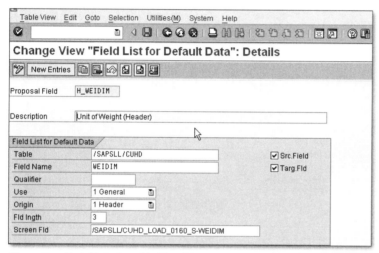

Figure 8.1   Text ID Assigned to Text Object; Text ID Assigned to Text Determination Procedure

In the following sections, we will discuss the configuration steps that are needed
to define the license text and the set up that will help you assign it to the appropriate business object.

8.1.1   License Text

Text IDs specific to license types are assigned to the object SLL_LCLIC, and the
defined text ID should be assigned to a procedure via SAP REFERENCE IMG • SAP
GLOBAL TRADE SERVICES • GENERAL SETTINGS • TEXT CONTROL • DEFINE TEXT DETER-
MINATION PROCEDURE FOR LICENSE TYPES. The pre-delivered text determination procedure for licenses is SLL_LCLIC1. If you have any custom text IDs, ensure that
they are assigned to the text object and then to the text determination procedure.
The text determination procedure is then assigned to the license type. The configuration for assigning the license determination to license type can be found under

SAP Reference IMG • SAP Global Trade Services • SAP Compliance Management • "Legal Control" Services • Define License Types.

Figure 8.2 shows a text determination procedure assigned to a license type definition.

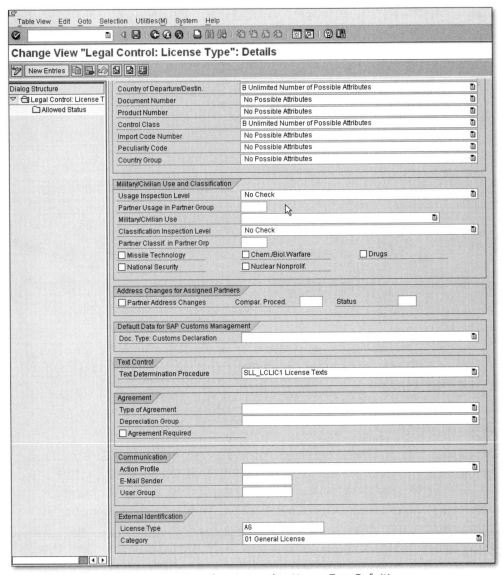

Figure 8.2 Text Determination Procedure Assigned to License Type Definition

8.1.2 Product Text

The object for product text is SLL_PR. Following the text ID assignment to the object, assign the text IDs to the text determination procedure. This configuration step can be accessed via SAP REFERENCE IMG • SAP GLOBAL TRADE SERVICES • GENERAL SETTINGS • TEXT CONTROL • DEFINE TEXT DETERM. PROCEDURES FOR COMMENTS FOR PRODUCT CLASSIFICATION. After defining the text determination procedure, assign the text determination procedure to legal regulations and scheme via SAP REFERENCE IMG • SAP GLOBAL TRADE SERVICES • GENERAL SETTINGS • CUSTOMS PRODUCTS • CONFIGURE TEXT DETERMINATION PROCEDURE FOR CLASSIFICATION COMMENTS. Figure 8.3 shows a text ID assigned to a text determination procedure and a text determination procedure assigned to a legal regulation and scheme.

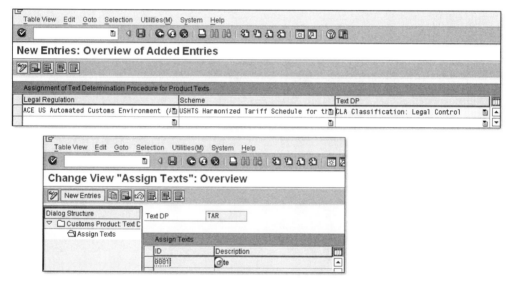

Figure 8.3 Text ID Assigned to Text Determination Procedure; Text Determination Procedure Assigned to Legal Regulation and Scheme

8.2 Customs Product

The standard interface of SAP BusinessObjects Global Trade Services and SAP ECC transfers the following information from the material master:

▸ Feeder system product number

▸ Item description

- Base unit of measure

- Gross weight

- Net weight

- Document unit of measure conversion

However, additional product attributes are often needed to facilitate classification. To configure this, start with the definition of the product attributes from the feeder system. First, gather the technical name, description, and parameter values. Maintain the key attribute, description, and key check function. If you want to validate against a pre-set value, select the dropdown option titled 1 Existence Check (Against Value Table). Figure 8.4 displays the configuration selection options and step definition.

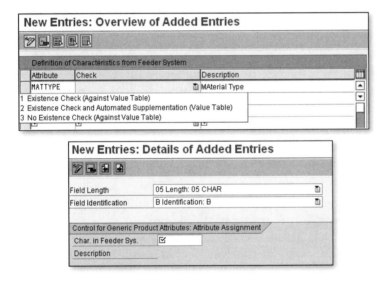

Figure 8.4 Configuration Selection Options and Step Definition

The SAP ECC field identified in the previous step needs to be assigned to the appropriate field length and field identification available in SAP BusinessObjects Global Trade Services. The field length should be picked from the available field lengths, which are 1, 2, or 40 characters. The field identification allows you to tag a unique key with these fields. This configuration step is accessed via SAP REFERENCE IMG • SAP GLOBAL TRADE SERVICES • GENERAL SETTINGS • CUSTOMS PRODUCTS

• DEFINE PRODUCT CHARACTERISTICS FROM FEEDER SYSTEM AND ASSIGN FIELD ATTRIBUTE TO PRODUCT CHARACTERISTICS FROM THE FEEDER SYS.

Based on the possible field lengths you have picked for your field attribute, you need to maintain the possible attribute values for the attribute defined in the earlier steps. There is a list of configuration steps for different attributes, and you have to pick one based on the attribute character size you picked for the definition (Length 01, 40, etc.).

> **Note**
>
> The preceding configuration step brings the selection value into the SAP BusinessObjects Global Trade Services Attribute and Selection screen. To transfer the product attribute from SAP ECC to SAP BusinessObjects Global Trade Services, you need to make use of the BADI. Refer to the user exit EXIT_SAPLSLL_LEG_PRR3_004 for capturing this value from SAP ECC and bringing it in to SAP BusinessObjects Global Trade Services as part of the change point transfer.

8.3 Case Management and Email Notification

Case management provides you with the option to define procedures for routing blocked business partners, blocked documents, embargo checks, or license determinations to the appropriate individual or group for review and action. This helps the spread of authority, responsibility, and information flow from the system to individuals or groups.

A *case* (as in, "case management") represents a defined hierarchy route model based on authorization rendered to a defined person in charge. You can decide how to route cases, and, if any additional information is required, include attachments. A case can provide the process structure and relevant information for decision making and audit purposes.

In the following sections, we will discuss the record management that allows you to capture the information to prepare a case, which is presented to the appropriate individual for review and action.

8.3.1 Record Management

The Case Management functionality within SAP BusinessObjects Global Trade Services utilizes the records and case management functionality within the cross-application component. This can be configured via SAP REFERENCE IMG • CROSS-APPLICATION COMPONENTS • GENERAL APPLICATION FUNCTIONS • RECORDS AND CASE MANAGEMENT.

Define the activity and activity function for the process route via SAP REFERENCE IMG • CROSS-APPLICATION COMPONENTS • GENERAL APPLICATION FUNCTIONS • RECORDS AND CASE MANAGEMENT • CASE • PROCESS ROUTE • DEFINE ACTIVITIES AND ACTIVITY FUNCTIONS FOR PROCESS ROUTE. Here you need to define the activity, task number, and the object to which the activity and task type belong. For each activity, you must also maintain the activity function. Figure 8.5 shows the configuration settings for activity functions.

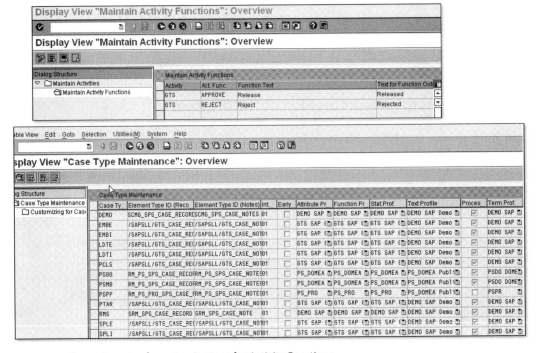

Figure 8.5 Configuration Settings for Activity Functions

In the following sections, we discuss the case type that helps you describe the different cases that needs to be considered for escalation and review by different individuals or authorities in the organization.

Case Type

The case type describes the process to which the business case belongs, in terms of the structure of information flow. You must define the case type, description, the process to which it belongs, the area ID (for SAP BusinessObjects Global Trade Services, it is /SAPSLL/SAP BusinessObjects Global Trade Services), and so on. This is pre-delivered with SAP BusinessObjects Global Trade Services 7.1 and higher. The lower section of Figure 8.5 shows these configuration settings.

Case Management

After configuring the cross-application component, you must configure a few settings within the SAP BusinessObjects Global Trade Services general settings. Define the data-supplying procedure for the object being integrated into case management. Default procedures are currently maintained within the pre-delivered configurations for business partners, customs documents, and products. Figure 8.6 displays the default procedure, default rules, and the accesses within. This configuration can be accessed via SAP Reference IMG • SAP Global Trade Services • General Settings • Case Management • Define Default Data for Case Management.

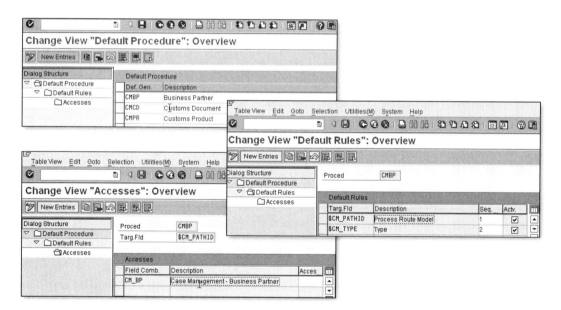

Figure 8.6 Default Settings

As a last step, activate case management. Select the object, and check Case Management, as shown in Figure 8.7.

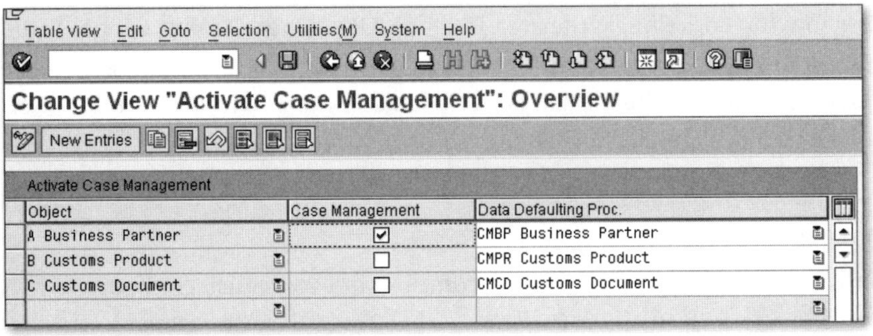

Figure 8.7 Activate Case Management

SAP BusinessObjects Global Trade Services System Communication/Workflow Setup

Within the SAP BusinessObjects Global Trade Services cockpit, set up the attributes for default data rules. Follow the menu path SAP BUSINESSOBJECTS GLOBAL TRADE SERVICES AREA MENU • SYSTEM COMMUNICATION/WORKFLOW • DEFINE ATTRIBUTES OF DEFAULT DATA RULES. Key in the procedure for defaulting data, and click Execute. Here you will have to enter values for the process route model and type that apply to the procedure data selected (e.g., business partner). For process routes, enter the foreign trade organization, business partner, and process route model. For case type, enter the foreign trade organization, business partner (customer or vendor), and type. The field to maintain differs depending on the procedure data selected; for example, with a customs document, you will have to maintain the document type, goods direction, foreign trade organization, process route model, and case type. With a customs product, you will have to pick the service (Customs Management, Compliance Management, or Risk Management), legal regulation, numbering scheme, and case type. Figure 8.8 shows the default data maintenance for default procedures.

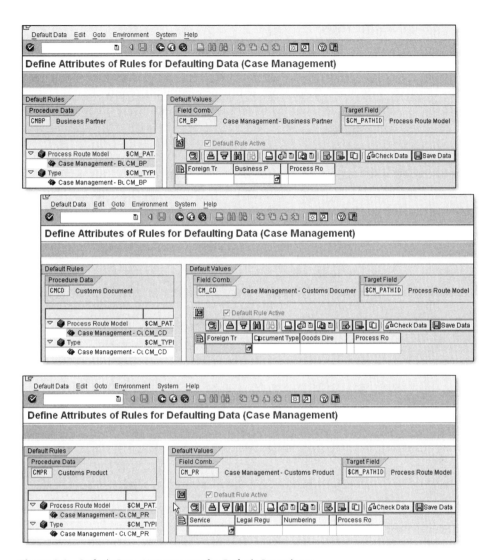

Figure 8.8 Default Data Maintenance for Default Procedures

> **Note**
>
> After these configurations are set up, the reports for blocked business partners, documents, or products, will have a Create icon that allows you to create a case. After creating a case, you can have the group responsible for the case review it (it will appear in their inboxes).

8.3.2 Email Notification

Case management helps you manage the routing of information to the appropriate authority, as well as any follow-on actions (such as to release or retain the block on a business partner, document, etc.). Some businesses might require that an email be sent to a group of people whenever there is a blocked business partner, document, license, or embargo.

To enable email functionality, check Sending of Mail under the Workflow section within the control setting definitions for Embargo, Legal Control, and Sanctioned Party List Screening. If you are looking for an SPL block report, check the Sending of Mail within the control setting for the legal regulation – SPL. Figure 8.9 displays the configuration settings for embargo services.

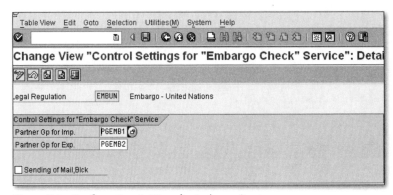

Figure 8.9 Configuration Settings for Embargo Services

There are a few settings within the SAP BusinessObjects Global Trade Services cockpit that enable email functionality:

▶ **Maintain User Groups**
Here you need to maintain the user group that will receive the email notification for blocked business partners.

▶ **Maintain Foreign Trade Organization, Document Type, and User Group**
This is relevant if you want notification for incomplete and blocked documents. The settings for this can be found under SAP BUSINESSOBJECTS GLOBAL TRADE SERVICES AREA MENU • SYSTEM COMMUNICATION/WORKFLOW:

  ▶ Notification Control for Incomplete Documents

  ▶ Notification Control for Blocked Documents

8.4   Default Data and Incompletion Checks

In this section, we discuss the add-on functionality within SAP BusinessObjects Global Trade Services Customs Management, which can be used to enhance and support the Customs Management implementation. Two of these add-on functionalities are default data determination and incompleteness checks, both of which we discuss in more detail in the following sections.

8.4.1   Default Data

Having default data available for SAP BusinessObjects Global Trade Services customs declarations is a functionality available in SAP BusinessObjects Global Trade Services Customs Management. If, for example, dates are not transferred from the SAP ECC feeder system, you can have SAP BusinessObjects Global Trade Services provide default dates. In the following sections, we discuss some of the configurations for using default data.

Date Fields

You can define default data for date fields via SAP REFERENCE IMG • SAP GLOBAL TRADE SERVICES • SAP CUSTOMS MANAGEMENT • PROCEDURES FOR DEFAULTING DATA • DEFINE DEFAULT DATA FOR DATE FIELDS. Define the procedure and default rules for the procedure, and then define the target date fields within the default rules. Maintain the Target and Screen fields in the SAP BusinessObjects Global Trade Services customs declaration document, as well as the lead time (if applicable) and time difference. Finally, click on Activate to activate the default data field. Figure 8.10 displays the configuration setup for the date fields.

Default Data by Business Partner

With default data for business partners, you can define procedures and rules that automatically fill in the business partner fields at the document header level. In the default rules, use the Target field to specify the business partner function that will be used as a default, and fill in the associated screen field. Check on the Active checkbox. The lower section of Figure 8.10 shows the configuration setting and procedure for business partner defaults.

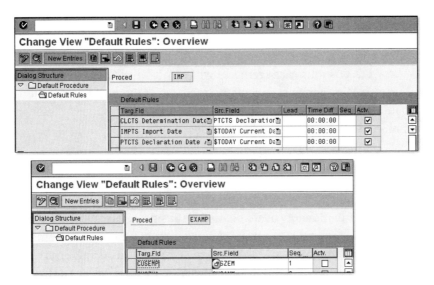

Figure 8.10 Configuration Setup for Date Fields

Extend Field List for Data Proposal

With this configuration setting, you can list the data you would like the customs document to supply, if it is not already transferred or populated, such as the proposal field, table, field name, qualifier, screen field, target field (indicator should be checked), use (general, partner, or text), origin (header), and field length. Figure 8.11 shows the configuration details for this step.

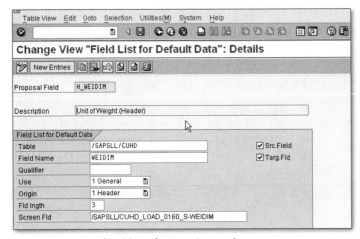

Figure 8.11 Extend Field List for Data Proposal

Define Procedure

With this functionality, you can define a procedure that includes the default data for document fields or messages. Define a general procedure, description, and output determination for a document or message. This configuration step can be found under SAP Reference IMG • SAP Global Trade Services • SAP Customs Management • Procedures for Defaulting Data • Define Data For Document Fields, Messages, and Documents.

After you define the procedure, click on the Field Combination folder to define the field combination, which allows you to have multiple fields with default data. The field defined in the Extended Data fields for the data proposal is listed here in fields one through five.

Within Default Rules, list all of the Target fields with default data; accesses are associated with individual Target fields. Figure 8.12 shows the details behind this configuration setting.

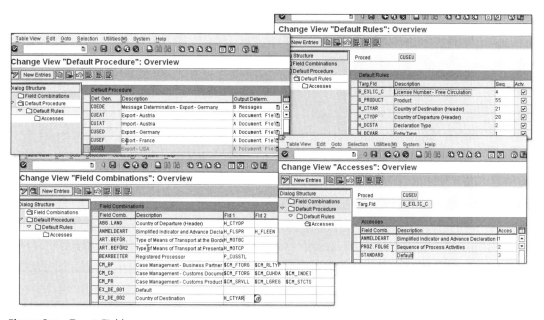

Figure 8.12 Target Fields

Finally, assign the procedure to the legal regulation. You can assign the Default Date fields defined, the Default Partner data fields defined, and the procedure for lists of fields by legal regulation, document type, and process.

With the procedure definition, you must also maintain the actual data within SAP BUSINESSOBJECTS GLOBAL TRADE SERVICES AREA MENU • SAP CUSTOMS MANAGEMENT • MASTER DATA • DOCUMENT DEFAULT DATA • DEFINE ATTRIBUTES OF DEFAULT DATA RULES.

8.4.2 Incompletion Checks

Incompletion check is a very powerful functionality within SAP BusinessObjects Global Trade Services Customs Management. The configuration can be accessed via SAP REFERENCE IMG • SAP CUSTOMS MANAGEMENT • GENERAL SETTINGS • CONTROL INCOMPLETENESS CHECKS IN CUSTOMS SHIPMENTS AND CUSTOMS DECLARATIONS. In this step, define the incompletion procedure, the function module that is invoked, and the fields that need to be checked. The function modules are pre-delivered, so, while defining the fields to check, you must pick from a dropdown list. Along with the fields themselves, you can also specify field length, field type (character, alphanumeric), field category (required), and length qualifier (less than or greater than the value specified). Figure 8.13 shows one of the pre-delivered configurations with the procedure to check for US automated export submissions.

Following the procedure definition, you must assign the procedure to the appropriate message under SAP REFERENCE IMG • SAP GLOBAL TRADE SERVICES • SAP CUSTOMS MANAGEMENT • GENERAL SETTINGS • COMMUNICATION PROCESSES • DEFINE MESSAGES FOR COMMUNICATION PROCESSES. The lower section of Figure 8.13 displays the assignment of the procedure to the message. When attempting to print the SAP BusinessObjects Global Trade Services customs declaration document, the incompletion check is run and lists the fields that are not populated. After the fields are populated, the system can process the message (i.e., either print it out or make an online submission).

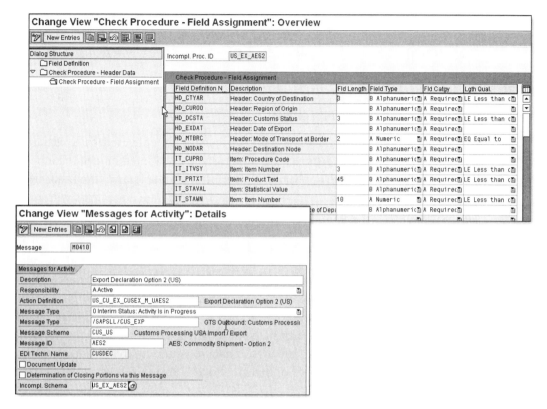

Figure 8.13 Incompletion Checks

8.5 Application Integrations: HR, FI, and EH&S

Primarily, sanctioned party list screening is used to screen business partners (e.g., customers, vendors, or financial entities) against the denied party list. However, you can also use SAP BusinessObjects Global Trade Services 7.0 (or higher) in combination with other SAP services. For example, you can perform sanctioned party list screening against your SAP ERP HCM employee data, or, with E-Recruiting implemented in SAP ERP HCM, you can interface with the SAP BusinessObjects Global Trade Services system to screen individuals who are being considered for hire. Similarly, you can also screen your financial entities and institutions.

In the following sections, we discuss the configurations for setting up communication between SAP BusinessObjects Global Trade Services and other systems. We will go over the detailed steps in building the interfaces with the SAP ERP HR system with SAP BusinessObjects Global Trade Services for SPL screening. The same concept can be applied to the SAP FI interface. We will review the key differences in the interfaces building with SAP HR and SAP FI. We will also go over the interface with SAP EH&S.

8.5.1 SAP ERP HCM Integration

Application Linking and Enabling (ALE) is technology delivered by SAP that is used for transferring data between SAP systems in a distributed model. It connects distributed systems though applications, distribution models, and communication (synchronous and non-synchronous), and uses intermediate documents with message types for defining data that needs to be transferred between systems.

This integration scenario provides the functionality to distribute SAP ERP HCM data into SAP BusinessObjects Global Trade Services. The data distributed provides the basis for the business partner in SAP BusinessObjects Global Trade Services and is also used for sanctioned party list screening. SAP ALE is the method by which the SAP ERP HCM data are distributed to the SAP BusinessObjects Global Trade Services system. To take advantage of the integration, you must implement the SAP ERP HCM module with the master data of your employees. You also need SAP Web Application Server 6.40 or higher, and SAP BusinessObjects Global Trade Services 7.0 or higher.

In this section, we explain the steps involved in linking SAP ERP HCM and SAP BusinessObjects Global Trade Services.

1. **Define the logical system.**

The logical system represents the feeder system sending the data and the receiving system that receives the data. Use Transaction SALE or Transaction SPRO, and then follow this menu path: SAP IMPLEMENTATION GUIDE • SAP NETWEAVER • APPLICATION SERVER • IDOC INTERFACE/APPLICATION LINK ENABLING (ALE) • BASIC SETTING • LOGICAL SYSTEMS • DEFINE LOGICAL SYSTEM. In this step, define the logical systems designated for the SAP ERP HCM systems within the SAP technical landscape.

2. **Assign the logical system to the client.**

Assign a client to each logical system designated for SAP ERP HCM within the SAP technical landscape. Use Transaction SALE or Transaction SPRO, and follow this menu path: SAP IMPLEMENTATION GUIDE • SAP NETWEAVER • APPLICATION SERVER

• IDOC INTERFACE/APPLICATION LINK ENABLING (ALE) • BASIC SETTING • LOGICAL SYSTEMS • ASSIGN LOGICAL SYSTEM TO CLIENT. Table 8.1 displays some sample configurations, including a prototype and development environment systems.

3. Maintain sending and receiving remote function call (RFC) connections.

Assign a client to each logical system designated for SAP BusinessObjects Global Trade Services systems within the SAP technical landscape. Use Transaction SALE, and follow this menu path: IDOC INTERFACE/APPLICATION LINK ENABLING (ALE) • COMMUNICATION • CREATE RFC CONNECTIONS. Here you define the source system (SAP ERP and the target system (SAP BusinessObjects Global Trade Services). You can create the RFC connection under the ABAP connections. Click on the Create icon ⬚, and the system prompts you to enter the RFC destination, selection of connection type, description, technical settings, and logon details. In Technical Settings, maintain the target host, system number, and IP address of the server. In Logon Details, maintain the user ID and which source system you use to log on to the target system. Figure 8.14 shows the configuration settings for RFC connections.

Figure 8.14 Configuration Settings for RFC Connections

4. **Define the RFC destination.**

Define the RFC destination from the SAP ERP HCM system to the SAP Business-Objects Global Trade Services system. Double-click on ABAP connection ECD-CLNT050 to see the details of the definition. While defining the RFC connection, select the connection type as 3 (ABAP Connection). You can enter the description to represent the system. Further, specify the host within the Target Host field under Technical Settings. The source system connects to the target system with a logon user, and you need to define the RFC connection, and the logon properties and the security for this user.

5. **Determine the RFC destinations for method calls.**

Assign RFC destinations to source logical systems by keeping the cursor on the logical system (e.g. ECDCLNT050) and clicking on the icon titled Standard BAPI destination. The system then asks you to enter the destination system (e.g., GTD-CLNT050). You can display the RFC destinations assigned to each logical system by using Transaction SALE, and following this menu path: IDOC INTERFACE/APPLICATION LINK ENABLING (ALE) • COMMUNICATION • DETERMINE RFC DESTINATIONS FOR METHOD CALLS. Here you can define the standard delivered message types and the associated function modules. The message type identifies the data that needs to be transferred to the target system Ð for example, from the master data, you are interested in the name and address but not the date of birth, salary, and other data. The function module enables the transfer of data. Note that the logical system and the RFC destination must be the same, and that Basis has to define the port for the connection to work. Figure 8.15 displays the method call for data transfer from SAP ERP HR to SAP BusinessObjects Global Trade Services.

With these steps complete, you still must set up ALE and activate the BAdIs. We discuss these two processes in more detail in the following sections.

Set Up ALE in SAP ERP HCM

ALE setup involves identifying the sender and receiver system as a partner, similar to the setup of an EDI with one SAP system to another subsystem. Follow these steps:

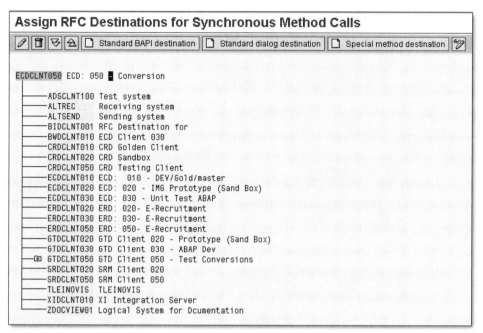

Figure 8.15 Method Call for Data Transfer From SAP ERP HR to SAP BusinessObjects Global Trade Services

1. **Set up the port for partner profiles.**

SAP ERP HCM and SAP BusinessObjects Global Trade Services are the logical systems. In this step, you define the port for the Partner Type LS (logical system). Similar to EDI, the ALE model needs to identify or recognize the target system as a logical partner. The partner profile helps you define the target system as a partner with whom you are exchanging data. For the agent, use service user WF-BATCH. To define the sender, use Transaction WE20, and follow this menu path: PARTNER PROFILES • PARTNER TYPE LS LOGICAL SYSTEM. While defining the partner profile for the source system, assign the port, which the system uses for data transfer. Then define the basic message type for capturing the data for data transfer. (The message type enables you to identity the data that needs to be transferred to the target system.) Figure 8.16 displays the partner profile definition for the sender and outbound receiving port, and the basis type definition for data transfer.

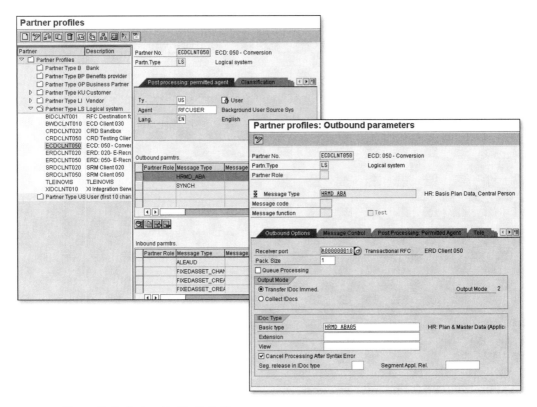

Figure 8.16 Partner Profile Definition

You must also define the receiving system, which, in this case, is the SAP Business-Objects Global Trade Services receiver SAP BusinessObjects Global Trade Services-CLNT050. Define the partner type as logical to represent these systems. Under the outbound and inbound parameters, define the message types for sending and receiving data. Here you can see a definition for the E-Recruiting SAP ERP HCM partner profile setup. Within the message type for outbound settings under Partner Profile, you need to define the receiver port (identification for receiver) and the packet size of the data transmitted. If you want to be able to delete or cancel the data after transmission, check the box Cancel Processing After Syntax Error. Figure 8.17 displays the partner profile definition details for source and target logical systems, and the associated message type definition settings.

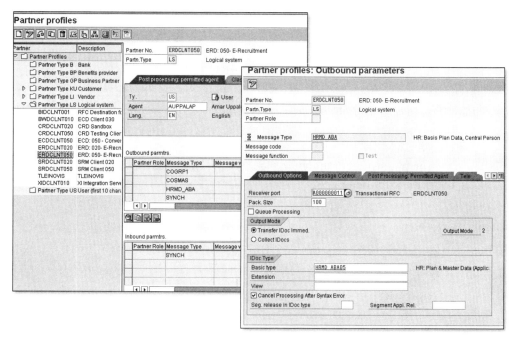

Figure 8.17 Partner Profile Definition Details

2. Create the distribution model

In this step, create a new distribution model for the SAP ERP HCM system ALE. A distribution model describes the sending and receiving of information to logical systems for data transfer, with an application layer, distribution service, and communication. Use Transaction SALE, and follow this menu path: IDOC INTERFACE/APPLICATION LINK ENABLING (ALE) • MODELING AND IMPLEMENTING BUSINESS PROCESSES>MAINTAIN DISTRIBUTION MODEL AND DISTRIBUTION VIEW • MODEL VIEWS. Click on the Edit icon and then on the Create Model View button.

While you are in the Model view, update the message type and the BAPI. The BAPI helps you to choose the pre-delivered business application interface for setting up the communication service between the two systems. Filtering allows you to filter any sensitive data from being transferred to the target system, for example, the employee's salary, compensation, and date of birth. Click on the Add Message Type button, which produces the pop-up screen; then enter the Model View, Sender, and Receiver that you maintained earlier. Enter the Message Type "HRMD_ABA". Click on the green check mark icon, and you can see that the message type is added.

3. **Create a filter to select and properly distribute data into the SAP ERP HCM system.**

The purpose of this step is to filter out any sensitive information from the data being transferred to SAP BusinessObjects Global Trade Services (e.g., date of birth or payroll information). Expand the model view, and double-click on No Data Filter Set, as displayed in Figure 8.18. Enter "E-Recruit" as the model view, "ECD-CLNT050" as the sender, "SAP BusinessObjects Global Trade ServicesCLNT050" as the receiver, and "HRMD_ABA" as the message type. After you perform this step, you see the tree structure shown in Figure 8.18. These are the settings that are used for the connection template.

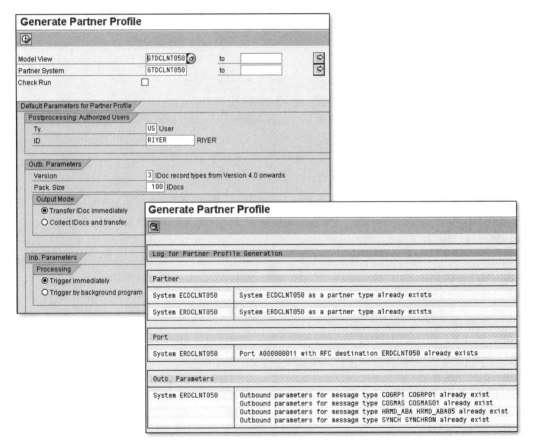

Figure 8.18 Tree Structure

4. Filter Group

Keep the cursor on Data Filter Active, and double-click on it to create different filter groups. The filter group allows you to group the data filter for transfer data into the receiving system. The SAP ERP HCM system has many infotypes that gather information based on a specific structure, and you can filter the data to be specific to these infotypes. For example, infotype 1000 determines the existence of an organization, and 1001 contains information about the relationship between objects. Using the example of an infotype, you need to choose the relevant infotypes 0105 (communication) and 0006 (address) for SAP BusinessObjects Global Trade Services screening. You might also want to select the employment status, so that you only transfer newly hired or current employees, and not those who have left the organization.

> **Note**
>
> There are two setups for the Employment Status filter. The full ALE that establishes a baseline of active employees in the SAP ERP HCM system uses employment status 3 (active). Then set the following ALE to employment status 3 (active) and the next to 0 (withdrawn) to capture the changes in status.

5. Generate the partner profiles

Define the partner profiles of outbound and inbound messages identified for a given distribution model. Use Transaction SALE, and follow this menu path: IDOC INTERFACE/APPLICATION LINK ENABLING (ALE) • MODELING AND IMPLEMENTING BUSINESS PROCESSES • MAINTAIN DISTRIBUTION MODEL AND DISTRIBUTION VIEW • MODEL VIEWS. In the screen that appears, select ENVIRONMENT • GENERATE PARTNER PROFILES to bring up the report shown in the bottom section of Figure 8.18.

6. Distribute the distribution model view

Distribute the model that you created in the logical system into the receiving system, so that you don't have to maintain the distribution system in the receiving system. Use Transaction SALE, and follow the menu path: IDOC INTERFACE/APPLICATION LINK ENABLING (ALE) • MODELING AND IMPLEMENTING BUSINESS PROCESSES • MAINTAIN DISTRIBUTION MODEL AND DISTRIBUTION VIEW • MODEL VIEWS. Select the model view created, and select EDIT • MODEL • VIEW • DISTRIBUTE.

7. View the model distributed into the target SAP BusinessObjects Global Trade Services system

The model view should now be visible in the SAP BusinessObjects Global Trade Services system. To verify this, use Transaction SALE, and follow this menu path: MODELING AND IMPLEMENTING BUSINESS PROCESSES • MAINTAIN DISTRIBUTION MODEL AND DISTRIBUTION VIEW. Here you should see the model you created in the source system and the mirror or replica of it created in the receiving system, with the sender logical system as SAP ERP and the receiver logical system as SAP BusinessObjects Global Trade Services.

8. Set up the partner profile inbound parameter

Similar to the setup of the sending logical system, set up the partner profile for receiving the data. Use Transaction WE20, and then select PARTNER PROFILE • PARTNER TYPE LS LOGICAL SYSTEM. Select the SAP BusinessObjects Global Trade Services system in the list Partner Type LS.

9. Create the SAP ERP HCM logical system in SAP BusinessObjects Global Trade Services

Define the source or feeder system (outbound) logical system in the target system. In this case, within SAP BusinessObjects Global Trade Services, you need to define the source logical system, which is the SAP ECC system, as outbound, and then define the SAP BusinessObjects Global Trade Services system as inbound. Because you use the ALE model as a standard interface with a subsystem — which can be an SAP system or an external system with EDI communication — the terms source and feeder are interchangeably used. SAP represents every system as a logical entity and for ALE communication; the data are received with inbound intermediate documents (IDocs) and sent out through outbound IDocs.

> **Note**
>
> For testing purposes, the Processing by Function Module section may be set to Trigger by Background Program. This holds all incoming IDocs in the SAP ERP HCM system for manual processing. This is useful for testing purposes. You can change this parameter back to Trigger Immediately after you complete testing.

The message type defined within the partner profile for the sender system allows you to maintain the inbound parameters. The message type definition allows the system to recognize the data sent by the sender and process code for processing the information.

10. **Activate the BAdI**

To activate the BAdI, use Transaction SE18, and follow this menu path: SAP MENU • ABAP WORKBENCH>UTILITIES • BUSINESS ADD-INS • DEFINITION. If there are multiple implementations of the BAdI definition HRALE00SPLIT_INBOUND, it may be necessary to define the implementation RPM_CP_HRALE as the active implementation.

Select UTILITIES • ADJUSTMENT • MULTIPLE ACTIVE IMPLEMENTATIONS. Select the definition HRALE00SPLIT_INBOUND. Verify that the implementation RPM_CP_HRALE is the active implementation. If it is not, deactivate the currently active implementation, and then activate RPM_CP_HRALE as the active implementation. Click on the Activate Implementation icon to produce a pop-up window. The system asks if you want to activate the BAdI; click on Yes to do so.

BAdI Activation

The BAdI HRALE00SPLIT_INBOUND is standard and allows exclusive handling of object P (person) within the E-Recruiting application. Based on the message type selection, the system generates the IDocs in the receiving system. IDoc segments are collections of fields within the message type. Transaction BD53 shows standard or default fields within the message type HRMD_ABA05. Text highlighted in green represents the selection of fields; pink fields are the default fields.

By keeping your cursor on the segment and going to EDIT • SELECT, you can select the IDoc segment. Default segments within the message type are then passed to method HRRCF_CAND_FROM_EE_ALE, which extracts relevant data and creates the candidate, the user, and the organizational assignment (if necessary). The IDoc represents the message type segment and field for the data element.

This BAdI deletes all S-to-P (position-to-person) relationships from the inbound IDoc. The object P does not exist in E-Recruiting; thus, the central person (CP) must be assigned to the position (S). With the IDoc inbound review and verification, you complete the final steps in the setup. This step validates the data that are identified for transfer. These segments and fields are pre-delivered. You wouldn't have a requirement to add or change any of the pre-delivered fields.

8.5.2 SAP FI Integration

The integration for SAP FI is similar to SAP HR. In the following sections, we discuss what needs to be done in both SAP ECC and SAP BusinessObjects Global Trade Services.

SAP ECC Configuration

Activate the function module within the SAP ECC feeder system: SAP REFERENCE IMG • CROSS APPLICATION COMPONENTS • SAP BUSINESS PARTNER • DATA DISTRIBUTION • ACTIVATE FUNCTION MODULE. Figure 8.19 displays the configuration that needs to be checked: Event – BPOUT Business Partner Outbound, Object – BUPA Business Partner, Item – 300000 and Function Module - BUPA_OUTBOUND_ALE_MAIN.

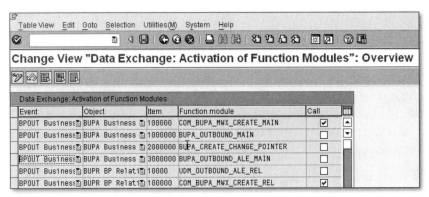

Figure 8.19 SAP FI Integration Configuration

You must also maintain the distribution model. Within the partner profile, use the message type BUPA_INBOUND_MAIN_SAVE_M with the basic type BUPA_INBOUND_MAIN_SAVE_M01.

Within SAP ECC, activate the BAdI with the implementation name /SAPSLL/BP_MAINTAIN, using Transaction SE19.

SAP BusinessObjects Global Trade Services Configuration

There are also several configuration steps within SAP BusinessObjects Global Trade Services. First, define the business partner role in SAP BusinessObjects Global Trade Services via SAP REFERENCE IMG • CROSS APPLICATION COMPONENTS • SAP

Business Partner • Basic Settings • Business Partner Roles • Define BP Roles. Define a role MKK – Contract Partner.

Following the business partner role definition, go to SAP Reference IMG • SAP Compliance Management • Sanctioned Party List Screening Services • Activate Business Partner at Business Partner Role Level. Key in the application objection "BUPA", the type of SPL block as 1 Process is Blocked – Service Removes the Block, the time of SPL check as 1 Synchronous – When Document is Updated, and within the Business Areas select C0 Finance Accounting.

Finally, activate the view in SAP BusinessObjects Global Trade Services for the business partner role MKK defined. Using Transaction BUSD, select the business partner role, go to the folder BP View, and add the application SLL (Legal and Logistics). Click on Call Only.

8.5.3 SAP EH&S Integration

Environment, Health and Safety is a module within the SAP ECC system that supports activities within the areas of safety, health, and environmental protection, and applies to a number of industries (chemical, pharmaceuticals, oil and gas, consumer products, high tech, automobile, etc.). SAP EH&S allows you to manage dangerous goods, substances, agents, waste, and the packaging associated with them. There are different sub-modules or components within SAP EH&S; for example, Product Safety helps manage hazardous substances by generating material safety sheets, creating labels, and so on.

SAP EH&S can be interfaced with SAP BusinessObjects Global Trade Services Compliance Management for any goods movement in or out of the company premises. This functionality is available in SAP BusinessObjects Global Trade Services 7.2 and higher. Let's use a purchase order as an example. On the SAP ECC side, you must activate SAP EH&S for the purchase order document type. In this case, the function module that gets invoked is the /SAPSLL/CD_PO_EHS_CHECK_RFC_R3. SAP EH&S maintains the information for the material procured in the purchase order and checks for the threshold limit and the notification status of the substances. SAP EH&S substance volume tracking sends a status message to the SAP BusinessObjects Global Trade Services system. If the status from SAP ECC is negative, the document is blocked; if positive, it is released. If you review a blocked document report in SAP BusinessObjects Global Trade Services, you will see that the document was blocked due to a hazardous substance check.

In the following sections, we discuss the configurations required in SAP ECC and SAP BusinessObjects Global Trade Services for setting up an interface with SAP EH&S.

SAP ECC Configuration

To enable the SAP EH&S functionality checking within SAP BusinessObjects Global Trade Services, there are specific settings that must be configured within SAP ECC (other than turning on the document for SAP BusinessObjects Global Trade Services service check). First, define the regulatory list: SAP REFERENCE IMG • ENVIRONMENT, HEALTH & SAFETY • BASIC DATA AND TOOLS • SPECIFICATION MANAGEMENT • SPECIFICATION MASTER • SPECIFIC REGULATORY LIST.

Then perform a series of configuration steps within SAP REFERENCE IMG • ENVIRONMENT, HEALTH & SAFETY • PRODUCT SAFETY • SUBSTANCE VOLUME TRACKING:

▶ **Specify Scenarios**
Here you define the scenarios or scenario categories for Substance Volume Tracking. As a first step, define the scenarios with the scenarios category. Then maintain values for Specific Data Determination per Regulation and Scenario, where the regulation is mapped to the scenario, material determination, and substance determination. Under the folder titled Function Modules per Scenario Category, maintain the function for confirming the data and transfer of logistics data. Figure 8.20 displays the configuration setup for this step.

▶ **Specify Selection Criteria for Volume Tracking**
Here you specify the data selection criteria, which helps restrict the information that is monitored and tracked. Maintain the regulation, the scenario it maps to, the table that you want to restrict, field, sequence number, and the lower and upper limit of the field value being checked. The second half of Figure 8.20 displays this configuration setting.

▶ **Specific Quantity Limits and Reactions on Overall Status**
Here you can specify the quantity limits that apply in individual regulations for substances that are monitored. Within the folder Relative Quantity Limit Values, you can specify different levels with message types: Information, Warning, or Error. Figure 8.21 displays the configuration settings for this step.

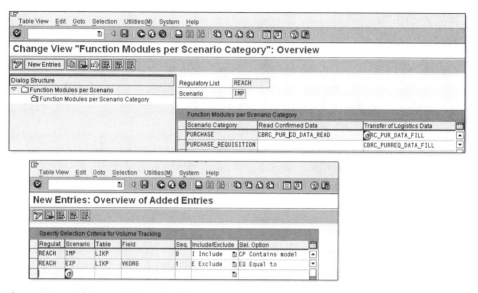

Figure 8.20 Substance Volume Tracking

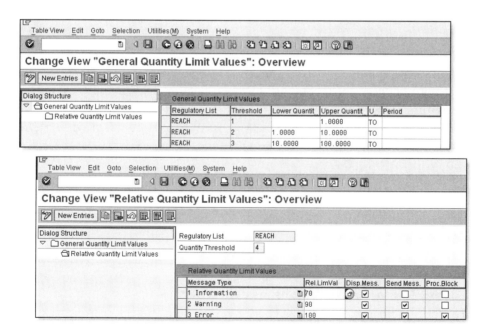

Figure 8.21 Specific Quantity Limits and Reactions on Overall Status

▶ **Setup Online Checks**
Here you need to set up online checks for substance volume tracking to see if the quantity limits are exceeded for transactions, purchase orders, sales orders, and so on. Maintain the entries for Regulation, Scenario, Scenario Category, Relevance Check, Volume Determination, Limit Value Check, Block Follow-on Document, Message Collection, and Message Output by Email.

▶ **Specify Data Transfer (Property Tree)**
Here you specify how the system transfers a quantity of a substance to be tracked to the property tree, which can be tracked for a particular period (e.g., a year). Maintain the entries for Regulatory List, Data Determination, and Data Assignment.

▶ **Specify Regulatory Lists**
Here you define the regulatory body that enforces the environment, health, and safety, and as a company, you need to be compliant to these regulatory body regulations. Follow this path: SAP REFERENCE IMG • ENVIRONMENT, HEALTH & SAFETY • BASIC DATA AND TOOLS • SPECIFICATION MANAGEMENT • SPECIFICATION MASTER • SPECIFIC REGULATORY LIST.

SAP BusinessObjects Global Trade Services Configuration

You must also perform certain configuration steps within SAP BusinessObjects Global Trade Services. First, you must have a regulation defined and activated for the countries for which you want this check to be performed. Then perform the following steps within SAP REFERENCE IMG • SAP GLOBAL TRADE SERVICES • SAP COMPLIANCE MANAGEMENT • HAZARDOUS SUBSTANCE CHECK SERVICES.

▶ **Assign determination procedure for active legal regulation**
There is a pre-delivered configuration for a hazardous substance check, which is based on country key.

▶ **Activate legal regulation**
You can activate the legal regulation for a hazardous substance check based on the country for export and or import.

▶ **Control data for hazardous substance check service**
For the legal regulation defined, check the Haz. Subst. Check Active checkbox, with the partner group assigned for country of departure and destination.

▶ **Define alternative RFC destination for SAP ERP EH&S**
This is optional. If you have a separate system for SAP EH&S, you can specify here the RFC destination of the SAP ECC system where the SAP EH&S is configured.

8.6   Summary

This chapter discussed the add-on functionalities and features available in SAP BusinessObjects Global Trade Services to enhance your Compliance Management and generic trade functions with text determination, use custom products to help facilitate classification, set up email functionality to send information about blocked business partners and documents, define a case and manage the workflow for handling your review and approval of blocked business partners, use default data determination to complete documents or data that needs to completed manually, use the incomplete check to validate key data prior to printing or online submission, and interface with SAP ERP HR and FI for sanctioned party list screening and with SAP ERP EH&S to manage hazardous and dangerous goods. All of these add-ons can help you improve the efficacy of your business processes.

In the next chapter, we move on to preference treatment and processing. Preference processing can help manage your risk and make use of trade agreement between countries.

Enabling preference processing when you are dealing with exports and imports between trade agreement countries helps you save on duty taxes.

9 Preference Processing or Preferential Treatment

SAP Risk Management consists of three main functionalities: preference processing, letters of credit, and restitution. Preference processing, which is the subject of this chapter, is one of the most important. It helps exporters fulfill all of the legal requirements for customs tariff preferences and show that their goods are eligible for preferential treatment. This enables their customers to import these goods either duty-free or at a reduced rate. By providing evidence of eligibility for preferential treatment, exporters gain significant competitive advantages. Duties apply to goods imported into a country and are generally either a percentage of the price of the product, or a fixed rate tied to the Harmonized Tariff System (HTS) and the country of origin.

Duty and restriction applies to goods imported into a country. Countries promote goods movement for products with countries with whom they have trade agreements. Duty rates and preference rules apply to a HTS number, which comes from the numbering system used by the international trade community as a common understanding for importing and exporting. A duty rate could be a percentage of the price of the part or a fixed rate, tied to the HTS and the country of origin. The country of origin is also delivered as data by content providers along with corresponding HTS codes.

In the following sections, we discuss the configuration steps to set up preference processing that can be applied to your business.

9.1   Preferential Treatment and Determination Configuration

Preferential processing can be found under the SAP BusinessObjects Global Trade Services Risk Management. Preferential processing helps exporters fulfill all of the legal requirements for customs tariff preferences and show that their goods are eligible for preferential or special treatment. This also enables your customer to import these goods either duty-free or at a reduced rate of import duty. By providing evidence of eligibility of preferential treatment, exporters gain significant competitive advantages.

Preference processing involves maintaining the following:

- Vendor declarations
- Materials or bills of material (BOM)
- The result of the threshold value for preferential treatment
- The threshold value of the product as compared to its ex-works price (i.e., the price quoted by the seller for delivery to the predefined location — for example, up to the buyer's door and there onwards, it is the buyer's responsibility)

If you have a BOM, the preferential status is set for the main component in the product master. The system determines the results and saves them for each main component. On the sales document, you can compare the determined threshold value with the ex-works price, and determine the preference situation for the current delivery. The ex-works price must be greater than or equal to the threshold value. If the system determines a positive preference status, it allows you to print a preferential statement. Vendor Declarations Management, a part of preference processing, provides functionality for requesting vendor declarations and sending reminders. You can request vendor declarations via email, XML, or supplier self-service. You need to update these vendor declarations into the system, and the system then allows you to aggregate them. The system also allows you to issue vendor declarations for the customer's purposes, or revoke them.

For declaration to customs, you must classify the goods according to a numbering schema. The numbering schema for the European Union is called *combined nomenclature*, and you declare imported and exported goods based on the subheading of nomenclatures under which they fall. This determines which rate of customs duty applies and how the goods are treated for statistical purposes. SAP BusinessObjects Global Trade Services Risk Management provides functionality to configure for the North America Free Trade Agreement (NAFTA) and the EU Trade Agreement. Preference processing assumes prerequisite steps are being completed in a feeder system for sales, purchasing, and so on. Note that one of the prerequisites of a SAP BusinessObjects Global Trade Services Risk Management implementation is that you also need to implement the Compliance Management or Customs Management functionalities within SAP BusinessObjects Global Trade Services. As with preferential treatment, you need to have the corresponding master transactional data from Compliance Management or Customs Management.

In the following sections, we will discuss the configurations required for both the feeder system and SAP BusinessObjects Global Trade Services.

9.1.1   Feeder System or SAP ERP Setup

Logistics and transactions data are captured within the SAP ERP system, and you need to set up the interfaces and associated configuration to enable the functionality. To set up preference processing for your feeder system, follow these steps:

1. **Set up communication from SAP ERP to SAP BusinessObjects Global Trade Services**

You need to set up the communication between the feeder system (e.g., SAP ERP) and SAP BusinessObjects Global Trade Services for transferring master data (e.g., customer, vendor, materials, and BOM). The system communication between SAP ERP and SAP BusinessObjects Global Trade Services uses Application Link Enabling (ALE) for master data transfer and remote function calls (RFCs) for transactions. Set up both SAP ERP and SAP BusinessObjects Global Trade Services as logical systems. Then set up system communication in SAP ERP and SAP BusinessObjects Global Trade Services. To set up the communication on the SAP ERP side, use Transaction /SAPSLL/MENU_LEGALR3. Go to the Basic Settings tab and in the System Connection to SAP BusinessObjects Global Trade Services section, where you can perform all of the listed processes:

▶ Define Logical System

▶ Assign Logical System

▶ Maintain RFC Destination for RFC Calls

▶ Maintain RFC Destinations for Method Calls

▶ Maintain ALE Distribution Model

Figure 9.1 displays the SAP feeder setups within the SAP BusinessObjects Global Trade Services area menu within the SAP ERP system.

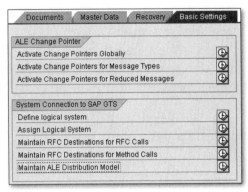

Figure 9.1 SAP Feeder Setups

2. **Set up document transfer in SAP ERP**

In SAP ERP, configure the documents and transactions that need to be transferred. This enables the different services checks in SAP BusinessObjects Global Trade Services when the documents are transferred. You can find the configuration by following menu path SPRO • Sales and Distribution • Foreign Trade/Customs • SAP Global Trade Services – Plug-In • Control Data for Transfer to SAP Global Trade Services • Configure Control Settings for Document Transfer. Figure 9.2 shows an example with application SD0A. You can find documents in the following applications:

▶ **MM0A:** Receipt/Import: Purchasing Document

▶ **MM0B:** Inbound/Import: Inbound Delivery Note

▶ **MM0C:** Receipt/Import: Material Document

▶ **SD0A:** Dispatch/Export: Sales Document

▶ **SD0B:** Dispatch/Export: Outbound Delivery Document

▶ **SD0C:** Dispatch/Export: Billing Document

Figure 9.2 provides the details behind the configuration setup for the control settings in the SAP ERP plug-in for transferring documents.

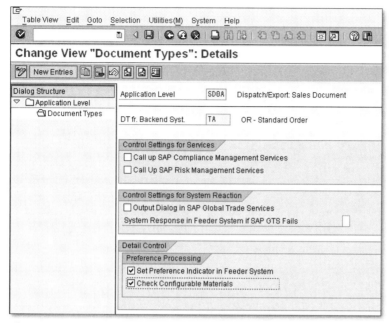

Figure 9.2 Control Settings in the SAP ERP Plug-In for Transferring Documents

3. **Maintain Billing of Material (BOM) transfer settings**

Maintain the settings for BOM transfers from SAP ERP at three levels: global, country, and plant. You must always begin by setting the control parameter at the global level because the system uses the data you select at the global level to propose the data at the country and plant level. First, select the BOM category as static or configurable. The BOM application is, for example, production or sales. You select either the cross-plant preference model or plant-specific preference model. Then select the rule set required for the preference agreement (e.g., EU or NAFTA). Select the type of BOM explosion you want, which is either top-down or bottom-up. Companies might use multiple versions of BOMs. If you do, in the alternative BOM, you can enter the name of any alternative BOMs for transfer to the SAP BusinessObjects Global Trade Services system. In the Exclusion of Material Types section, you can select the type of materials from your feeder system that you want to exclude from the transfer. This option might be used for materials that are not part of the core product, and that you don't want used as part of the preferential determination calculation (e.g., packaging materials). Figure 9.3 displays the control settings for BOM transfer to SAP BusinessObjects Global Trade Services from the feeder system.

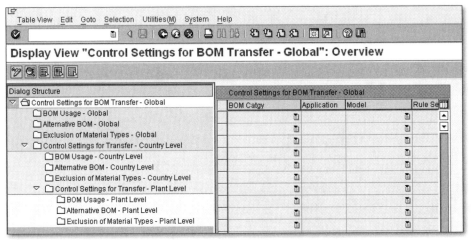

Figure 9.3 Control Settings for BOM Transfers

4. Define a worklist for vendor-based long-term vendor declarations

The structure of the worklist for vendor-based long-term vendor declarations in SAP BusinessObjects Global Trade Services is based on your settings for the transfer of purchasing documents and material documents. In this IMG activity, you can filter out the documents for the worklist structure that are relevant for this process.

Requesting and sending reminders for vendor-based long-term vendor declarations only makes sense for vendors located in the same preference zone. You can record the combinations of your country and other companies in your preference zone in this activity. The system only creates entries in the worklist for vendor-based long-term vendor declarations for documents whose business partners are located in the countries you entered in this activity. The system compares your entry for the vendor country in this IMG activity with the entry from the vendor master record, or from the process in Materials Management (partner with the vendor partner role). If you do not configure any settings in this IMG activity, the system creates an entry in the worklist for every document of a document type and application level for which you have configured the preference processing service and structure of the worklist for vendor-based long-term vendor declarations.

To configure these settings, follow IMG menu path SALES AND DISTRIBUTION • SAP GLOBAL TRADE SERVICES – PLUG-IN • PREFERENCE: DEFINE WORKLIST FOR VENDOR-BASED LONG-TERM VENDOR DECLARATIONS. Enter the country where your organization is located. In the Country Organization column, enter the organization value, and in the Worklist Country column, enter the country information. You need to define the countries for the vendors whose documents you want the system to use to structure the worklist for vendor-based long-term vendor declarations. Figure 9.4 displays the worklist structure definition for vendor-based long-term declarations.

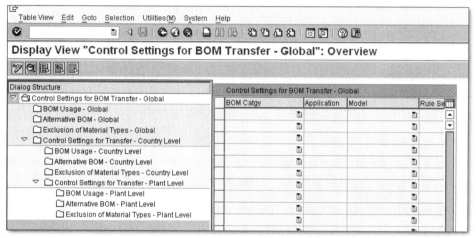

Figure 9.4 Worklist Structure for Vendor-Based Long-Term Declarations

9.1.2 SAP BusinessObjects Global Trade Services Configuration

SAP BusinessObjects Global Trade Services is installed in a separate client. After installing it, maintain the system time zones. Then synchronize settings between the feeder system and SAP BusinessObjects Global Trade Services, including the unit of measure, the ISO codes for the units of measure, country codes, country-specific settings, and currencies.

The units of measure play a key role in the material base unit, both when you transfer products and while using the transaction for item quantity or weight. Country-specific settings are used as part of the address with your partner in the transactions. Currencies play the role for determining the value conversion from one currency to another and the converted value for a specific transaction.

In the following sections, we discuss the basic setup within the SAP BusinessObjects Global Trade Services system to receive the information from the SAP ERP system and baseline configuration to set up the preferential processing in the SAP BusinessObjects Global Trade Services system.

Basic Setup

Basic setup involves setting up the baseline and foundational configuration, establishing the communication, organizational parameter, product, and declarations. In this section, we will go over these critical configuration steps.

1. **Set up communication in SAP BusinessObjects Global Trade Services.**

Follow IMG menu path SAP NETWEAVER • GENERAL SETTINGS, and, below that, use the Set Countries, Currencies, and Check Units of Measurement options to adjust these settings. Then set up system communication in SAP BusinessObjects Global Trade Services (similar to the communication setup you did with SAP ERP). These setups enable the connection; you can set up configurations specific to the modules later.

To set up the system communication, use Transaction SPRO, and follow this menu path: SAP GLOBAL TRADE SERVICES• SYSTEM COMMUNICATION • SYSTEM CONNECTION TO FEEDER SYSTEM. From there, perform the following functions:

▶ Define logical system for feeder system

▶ Assign logical system

▶ Define group for logical system

▶ Assign logical system to a group of logical systems

Identify SAP BusinessObjects Global Trade Services as a logical system, and assign the client to the logical system. The logical system group allows you to group the feeder system and SAP BusinessObjects Global Trade Services so that they can share the same common data and configuration elements.

2. **Set up number ranges**

For master data and the transactional data that are transferred from SAP ERP or R/3 to SAP BusinessObjects Global Trade Services, SAP BusinessObjects Global Trade Services assigns an internal number. You need to create number ranges for business partners and products as a prerequisite. Then create both internal and external number ranges for business partners. Use internal business partner numbers for mapping the business partner that is transferred from SAP ERP. Use external number ranges for creating organizational data in SAP BusinessObjects

Global Trade Services. You also need number ranges for the customs documents, which are created for Compliance Management or Customs Management. Specific to preferential treatment, you need to configure the following number ranges:

▶ **Vendor declarations**
The vendor declaration number range is year dependent and client independent. You need to create three number ranges: one for vendor-based long-term vendor declarations, another for long-term vendor declarations for the customers' purposes, and the last for the revocation of long-term vendor declarations for the customers' purposes.

▶ **Preference models**
You need to create number ranges for different preference models, including plant-based and cross-plant models, as well as the preference model for the configuration of bills of product.

▶ **Bills of product**
Also called BOM, the component under the final product helps determine the preference condition. The country of origin and the tariff system influence the final product HTS number and the country of origin determination.

> **Note**
>
> Because number ranges are year-specific, we recommend creating the number ranges for future years.

3. **Define and assign organizational parameters**

You need to map SAP ERP organizational parameters in SAP BusinessObjects Global Trade Services. For example, map the SAP ERP company code to the SAP BusinessObjects Global Trade Services foreign trade organization, and the SAP ERP plant to the SAP BusinessObjects Global Trade Services legal unit. You can create the foreign trade organization and legal unit by using Transaction SPRO and following this menu path: SAP GLOBAL TRADE SERVICES • GENERAL SETTINGS • ORGANIZATIONAL STRUCTURE. Then select Define Foreign Trade Organization, Define Legal Units, and Assignment of Organizational Units from Feeder System to Foreign Trade Org.

Be careful to pick the right business partner role while creating the foreign trade organization or legal unit. The company code in SAP ERP represents the entity that financially owns the goods or services, and the plant represents the physical location from where the products are shipped or received. Another important organizational unit for preference processing is the administrative unit. An administrative unit is responsible for all transactions within the preference program or determination. Choose the partner role SLLMGR, and maintain the address data. Use Transaction SPRO, and follow this menu path: SAP RISK MANAGEMENT • PREFERENCE PROCESSING SERVICES • DEFINE ADMINISTRATIVE UNITS FOR VENDOR DECLARATIONS.

4. **Define the country group**

Country groups simplify the process of making license determination settings. This is an option if you have countries with similar or the same legal regulations. You can find this configuration under Transaction SPRO and then by following this menu path: SAP GLOBAL TRADE SERVICES• GENERAL SETTINGS • LEGAL REGULATIONS • DEFINE COUNTRY GROUP. After this configuration, you can maintain or assign countries to the corresponding country group in the SAP BusinessObjects Global Trade Services cockpit. Use Transaction /SAPSLL/MENU_LEGAL, and follow this menu path: GTS AREA MENU: PREFERENCE PROCESSING SERVICE • MASTER DATA • PREFERENCE ZONES • ASSIGN COUNTY TO COUNTRY GROUP. Figure 9.5 displays the country assignments to the country group.

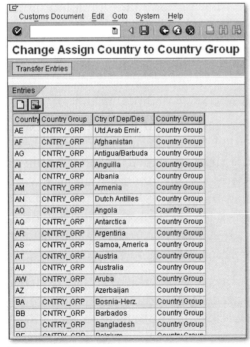

Figure 9.5 Country Assignments to Country Group

5. Define and activate a legal regulation

Define legal regulations to represent the preference law of a particular country. Assign the legal regulation to the corresponding country groups of import and export. Then upload the preference rules with reference to the legal regulation. Following the definition of the regulation, you need to activate it. You can find the configuration to do this by using Transaction SPRO and then following this menu path: SAP GLOBAL TRADE SERVICES• GENERAL SETTINGS • LEGAL REGULATIONS • DEFINE LEGAL REGULATION. The type of legal code determines the kind of regulation and its functionality. Define if the regulation applies to both import and export, or just export. Every regulation must have an original country. After you define it, activate it. When you need to list the country or country group, this regulation is active. Figure 9.6 displays the configuration for legal regulation definition and activation.

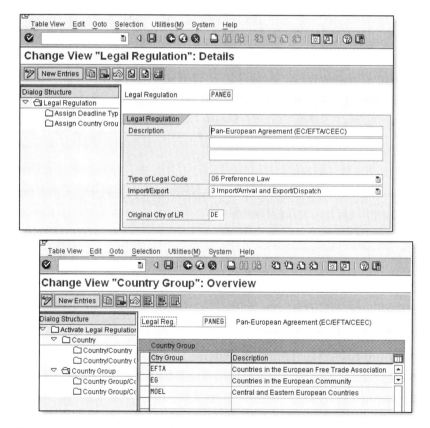

Figure 9.6 Legal Regulation Definition and Activation

Generic Settings for Risk Management

Follow these steps to configure the generic settings for Risk Management:

1. Activate the document type and item category

Activate the document types for which you want to display preference statements in SAP BusinessObjects Global Trade Services. You can make a provisional preference statement for a product based on order data and a binding preference statement based on sales documents, such as a billing document. For preference processing, activate the document types for billing documents and sales documents. As mentioned earlier, the document is already activated for Compliance Management and Customs Management, and the services for preference determination are activated by the document type. To perform this configuration, use Transaction SPRO, and follow this menu path: SAP RISK MANAGEMENT • PREFERENCE PROCESSING SERVICE • ACTIVATION • ACTIVATE DOCUMENT TYPES.

2. Map the earlier defined SAP ERP document types to SAP BusinessObjects Global Trade Services customs document types

You can do this in Compliance Management via GENERAL SETTINGS • DOCUMENT STRUCTURE. Similar to the order types, you also need to activate the item categories for preference processing. Use Transaction SPRO, and follow this menu path: SAP RISK MANAGEMENT • PREFERENCE PROCESSING SERVICE • ACTIVATION • ACTIVATE ITEM CATEGORY. Figure 9.7 displays the preference processing activation for document types.

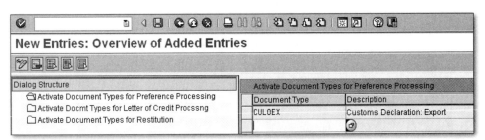

Figure 9.7 Preference Processing Activation for Document Types

3. Define an organizational structure attributes.

We need to update the organization with the preferential specific settings. Update the attributes of the administrative unit with the names and IDs.

4. Define the model

Preferential processing is a determination process, where the system uses different model for aggregating the vendor declarations and the influence it has on the final determination of country of origin and product tariff. There are two model to choose from. You can also define one of two models:

▸ **Plant-based preference model**
In the plant-based model, you define the parameters for aggregating vendor declarations and for regulating plant-based preference determination. These parameters include the feeder system and the plant from the feeder system for which you want to perform preference determination.

▸ **Cross-plant preference model**
In the cross-plant model, specify the parameters for aggregating vendor declarations and for regulating cross-plant preference determination. These parameters include the feeder system and the plant group from the feeder system for which you want to perform preference determination. If you want to aggregate the BOM as a basis for preference determination for different plants, use cross-plant preference determination. If you aggregate the vendor declaration statements for goods from three different plants, and only goods from two of these plants are eligible for preferential treatment according to the vendor declarations, none of the goods are assigned the preference indicator, so they will be determined as eligible for preference. All of the plants in a plant group must belong to a group of feeder systems.

You can only group plants from different countries in one group if they have a common legal regulation. For example, due to the European Union being a customs union, you can combine plants from different countries within the European Union in one plant group. In the free trade zone of NAFTA, for example, you can only group plants from one country in a plant group.

5. Activate the preference agreement

The pre-delivered configuration has the determination procedure LEPRE as the country group activation. You don't have to change the pre-delivered setting. You can see this screen by following this menu path: DISPLAY IMG (SPRO) • SAP GLOBAL TRADE SERVICES • SAP RISK MANAGEMENT • 'PREFERENCE PROCESSING' SERVICE • ASSIGN DETERMINATION PROCEDURE FOR ACTIVE PREFERENCE AGREEMENTS.

Under PREFERENCE PROCESSING: ACTIVATE LEGAL REGULATIONS, you can activate the preferential service for import and export. Figure 9.8 displays the configuration steps for preference determination procedure and country group activation.

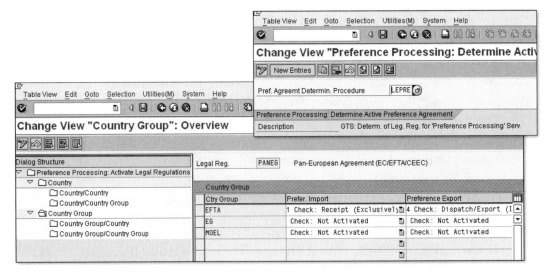

Figure 9.8 Preference Determination Procedure and Country Group Activation

When activating these preference agreements, specify which processes in the feeder system trigger preference processing in SAP BusinessObjects Global Trade Services. You can choose from the following processes:

▶ Dispatch (Exclusively)

▶ Export (Exclusively)

▶ Export (Excluding Domestic)

▶ Dispatch/Export (Including Domestic)

▶ Check: Not Activated

6. **Define and assign the rule set**

These rule sets are combinations of rules of all of the preference agreements that are valid for a jurisdiction. This allows you to control the attributes that are defined for preference rules and preference agreements for each jurisdiction. To get to the rule set, use Transaction SPRO, or follow this menu path: SAP GLOBAL TRADE SER-

VICES • SAP RISK MANAGEMENT • PREFERENCE PROCESSING SERVICE • DEFINE RULE SET. Enter a name, the rule set type, and a number scheme. In a later step, you assign the various preference agreements for a jurisdiction to the corresponding rule set. By defining the numbering scheme at rule set level, you ensure all of the preference agreements for a jurisdiction are based on the same numbering scheme. If you are uploading data from the data provider (e.g., customs information from NAFTA), the rule sets, preference agreements, country group, and legal regulation are automatically assigned. Figure 9.9 displays the configuration setup for the preference rule set.

Figure 9.9 Preference Rule Set

If you are uploading data from the data provider (e.g., customs information from NAFTA), the rule sets, preference agreements, country group, and legal regulation are automatically assigned. In the rule set, decide whether to use the rule set for NAFTA or EU preferential agreements. Enter the numbering schema for the rule set, and then assign the rule set to the preferential agreement. In a rule set, you can group all of the preference agreements that apply to a specific jurisdiction. You also need to specify a customs currency and an associated exchange rate type. Use the exchange rate type to define the type of currency translation that you are performing, such as translation between the currency of the threshold value and the document currency.

7. **Set control settings for the data scope in vendor declarations.**

For each administrative unit, define whether you can perform the following processes in relation to vendor declarations within preference processing:

- ► Requesting and dunning vendor-based vendor declarations
- ► Issuing and canceling vendor declarations for the customer's purposes
- ► Issuing detailed declarations for dutiable product components

Based on your indicator setting to activate the vendor-based declarations, the system prepares to send vendor declaration documents to your partners (e.g., vendors and customers). If you want to issue your customers with a detailed list of dutiable product components, you set the Detailed Declarations of Dutiable Products (Vendor Declaration for Customer Purpose) indicator. If you don't set up the indicator, the system issues a negative declaration. In the partner group, you need to define the specific partner functions for which you want to issue a vendor declaration in preference processing. Based on the partner function, the system determines the relevant data from the invoice document in the feeder system to create or cancel a request or dun a vendor declaration. If you define the consignor partner function (i.e., the receiver of goods who is the importer of record) in the partner group, the system issues vendor declarations for the customer's purpose for the partners who are flagged as consignors and who are shown on the invoice documents.

You can find the configuration steps by using Transaction SPRO and following this menu path: SAP RISK MANAGEMENT • PREFERENCE PROCESSING SERVICE • VENDOR DECLARATION:

- ► Control Settings for Long-Term Vendor Declarations and Administrative Unit
- ► Define Standard Texts and Logo for Printing Documents
- ► Control Settings for Vendor-Based Long-Term Vendor Declarations
- ► Control Settings for Long-Term Vendor Declarations for Customer's Purpose

Figure 9.10 displays, on the top left, Control Settings for Long Term Vendor Declarations and Administrative Units; on the top right, text definition for standard text with printing; on the bottom left, Control Settings for Vendor Based Long-Term Vendor Declarations; on the bottom right, Control Settings for Long-Term Vendor Declarations for Customer's Purposes. Control Settings for Long-Term Vendor Declarations and Administrative Unit configuration setup displays the setting for the administrative unit, which is responsible for the vendor declaration. Based on the administrative unit that you create, you can define whether it is meant as vendor-based or customer-based, as well as the applicable currency (USD or EUR) and exchange rate. Standard texts and logos for printing documents displays the details that you want printed in the declarations, including header, address, and any company-specific logo. Control settings for vendor-based long-term vendor declarations configuration setup displays the control settings you can apply to the administrative unit. These settings include the dunning levels (e.g., 1 – Request or 2 – Warning), residence time for retention, maximum dunning level, mode of communication (e.g., email or regulation mail), and layout of the print form (e.g., Smart Form, form text, or PDF). Control Settings for Long-Term Vendor Declarations for Customer's Purpose configuration step displays how the settings for the administrative unit apply to the vendor declarations that are managed for the customer's purpose.

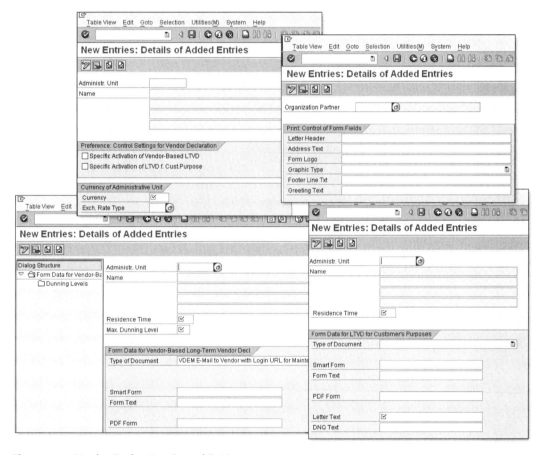

Figure 9.10 Vendor Declaration Control Settings

9.2   Preference Processing Business Processes

In the previous section, we went through the configuration steps required to set up communication between your SAP ERP ECC and SAP BusinessObjects Global Trade Services systems, as well as some Risk Management settings within SAP BusinessObjects Global Trade Services. Now we will go over the master data setup and the processing of the data within the transaction system. Preference processing involves processes within both the SAP ECC or SAP ERP system and the SAP BusinessObjects Global Trade Services system.

Following the configuration steps, there are master data to be set up that enable the preference processing. In this section, we will look at the transactions and functions to transfer data and review the information prior to submission to the customs authorities.

9.2.1   SAP Feeder System Process

SAP BusinessObjects Global Trade Services system depends on the feeder system for master data and the transaction data that are used for preferential processing. In other words, master data and transactions created in the feeder system are transferred to SAP BusinessObjects Global Trade Services system for preferential processing. In this section, we will go over these steps in detail. Follow these steps:

1. **Load initial and ongoing master data**

Load the master data that are required for processing Risk Management transactions from SAP ERP to SAP BusinessObjects Global Trade Services:

▶ Materials

▶ Bills of material (BOM)

▶ Vendors

▶ Customers

You can perform the initial load by using Transaction /SAPSLL/MENU_LEGALR3, clicking the Master Data tab, and then going to the section titled Initial Transfer of Master Data to SAP BusinessObjects Global Trade Services. Figure 9.11 displays the functions for initial and ongoing master data transfers from SAP ERP to SAP BusinessObjects Global Trade Services.

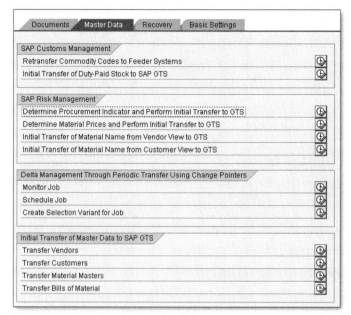

Figure 9.11 Functions for Initial and Ongoing Master Data Transfers from SAP ERP to SAP BusinessObjects Global Trade Services

2. **Set up the change pointers to recognize any new records and changes to the existing records.**

A *change pointer* is a function used by the SAP system that captures changes to the master data record or any new record addition into the master data. The change pointer uses the message type (i.e., master data template) to capture the information in which the target system is interested. With the help of Application Linking and Enabling (ALE), the system transfers the data. You can set up change pointers under the Basic Settings tab in the screen in Figure 9.11. First, check the box for global activation. Then you activate the change pointer for the following message types:

▸ Material Master Message Type: /SAPSLL/MATMAS_SLL

▸ Customer Master Message Type: /SAPSLL/DEBMAS_SLL

▸ Vendor Master Message Type: /SAPSLL/CREMAS_SLL

▸ Address Master Type: /SAPSLL/ADRMAS_SLL

▸ Change Pointers for Product BOM: /SAPSLL/BOMMAT_SLL

▸ Change Pointer for Product Price: /SAPSLL/PRCMAT_SLL

▸ Change Pointers for Procurement and Sales: /SAPSLL/PSDMAT_SLL

By activating the message types, the system captures the new records or changes to existing records and allows you to transfer them to SAP BusinessObjects Global Trade Services.

3. **Transfer master data from SAP ERP to SAP Risk Management**

You should consider five master transfers to SAP Risk Management, including three that are mandatory and two that are optional:

▸ **Determine procurement indicator (mandatory)**
The procurement indicator allows you to decide if you want to request the vendor declaration and use a preference calculation based on a part being made internally or procured externally.

▸ **Perform material price transfer (mandatory)**
The material price helps in performing the calculation for the threshold value for preference calculation. If the price of the part exceeds the threshold, then the higher-valued part might influence the preference determination.

▸ **Transfer BOM (mandatory)**
The structure of the BOM influences how the final product is determined. In other words, one of the component characteristics might change the final product's characteristics (e.g., country of origin, tariff), so this BOM structure is key in determining the preference.

▸ **Obtain the vendor's material number and description (company-specific scenario)**
The vendor material number allows you to map the number or name with your material number for identification.

▸ **Obtain the customer's material number and description (company-specific scenario)**
The customer material number allows you to map the number or name with your material number for identification.

The procurement indicators are in-house or sourced from a vendor, which helps in the preferential determination. The value or price of the part is used for the preferential determination and calculation of the threshold. The part number you have known within SAP ERP might have a different name or identification with your customer or vendor, and this transfer can provide you that information for the purposes of reporting. You can find this transaction under the SAP Risk Management section of the Master Data tab in Figure 9.11.

9.2.2 SAP BusinessObjects Global Trade Services Cockpit Process

You can validate the transfer for the procurement indicator, BOM, and material prices for any errors during the transfer process. Within the SAP BusinessObjects Global Trade Services area menu, click on Preference Processing - Master Data. This displays if there were any errors in the transfer of the material price, BOM, or procurement indicator. Similarly, you can review the log for the transfer of business partners under Systems Monitoring. Follow these steps:

1. **Assign the commodity code via the worklist**

The commodity code is necessary for material identity within preference processing. Use this material classification to identify the proper NAFTA rule of origin, and therefore determine the preference status of finished goods. To do so, follow this menu path, and then click the Execute icon: SAP GLOBAL TRADE SERVICES • SAP CUSTOMS MANAGEMENT – CLASSIFICATION • CLASSIFICATION WITH COMMODITY CODE • CLASSIFY PRODUCTS VIA WORKLIST. Figure 9.12 displays the numbering scheme assigned to the legal regulations (ACE, ATLAS). Now, assign the appropriate commodity code to the product. Select the product (e.g., US Schedule B Commodity Export/Dispatch), and click the Classify Multiple Products icon ( ) in Figure 9.12. A pop-up window appears (Figure 9.12). From the drop-down list in the Tariff Number field, select the commodity code.

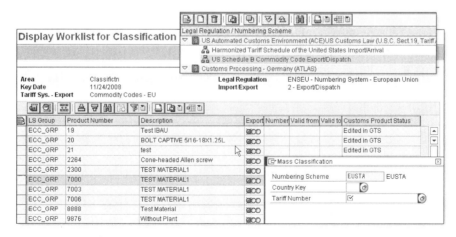

Figure 9.12 Numbering Scheme and Worklist for Product Classification

2. Display the worklist for vendor declaration

As soon as a purchase order or goods receipt document is created, the SAP BusinessObjects Global Trade Services system creates a worklist for vendor declarations. The worklist is the basis for the vendor declaration request. Within the SAP BusinessObjects Global Trade Services area menu, follow this menu path: Preference Processing • NAFTA Display • Worklist for Vendor Declaration. Enter the administrative unit in the Administr. Unit field, and the vendor number in the Business Partner Number field. Figure 9.13 displays the worklist for vendor declarations.

3. Request the vendor declaration

A vendor declaration must exist before a good can be eligible for preferential treatment. If there is no vendor declaration for a good, that good is always deemed to be a non-originating good. For this reason, you need to request vendor declarations from your vendors and send a reminder if a vendor does not send you a vendor declaration in time. Use Transaction /SAPSLL/PREVDI_03, or follow this menu path: SAP Global Trade Services • Preference Processing • Request Vendor Declaration. Figure 9.14 displays the transaction that allows you to run the report to request vendor declaration. Enter the Administrative Unit, the Business Partner Number, and the Validity Period. Select Print Preview and Simulation Run if you want to preview the results. Otherwise, leave Simulation Run unchecked, and check Create Log for updating. If you check the Request Initial LTVD check box, the system sends the request to the vendor. The worklist is based on existing purchase orders and goods receipts in the feeder system. Long-term vendor declarations that already exist are not taken into account.

You can request long-term vendor declarations from your vendors for each administrative unit and for a specified period of time. The system prints these requests for long-term vendor declarations based on the selection criteria you enter. You can limit the number of requests that are printed by entering the following parameters:

- Preference agreements
- Business partner number of the vendor
- Product number

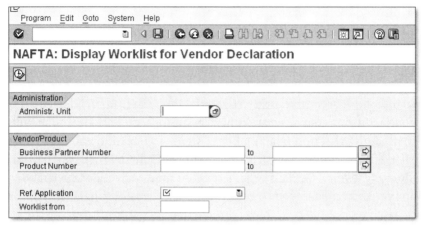

Figure 9.13 Worklist for Vendor Declarations

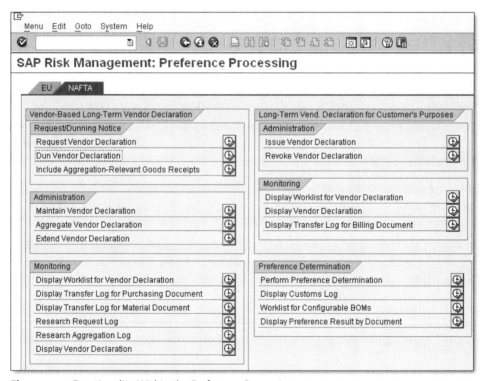

Figure 9.14 Functionality Within the Preference Processing

Figure 9.14 displays the different transactions, functions, and features within NAFTA preference processing. You can reach it by going to the SAP BusinessObjects Global Trade Services cockpit (Transaction /SAPSLL/MENU_LEGAL), clicking on Preference Processing, and selecting the NAFTA tab. In Figure 9.14, you can also see the Dun Vendor Declaration function in the Vendor-Based Long-Term Vendor Declaration section. If you do not receive the long-term vendor declaration you requested from your vendor within an appropriate period of time, you can dun the vendor declaration in a number of steps. You need to enter the same selection criteria as Request Vendor Declaration to generate the request. Depending on the dunning level (> 0), the system searches requested vendor declarations that have not yet been maintained. It prints these requests for long-term vendor declarations based on the selection criteria you enter.

4. **Maintain vendor declaration in SAP BusinessObjects Global Trade Services.**

You must manage and archive the vendor declarations that you receive from your vendors. If your organization is subject to an audit by the authorities, you have to show the vendor declarations to the relevant authorities. Long-term vendor declaration management maintenance involves determining the range of data and maintaining the indicators for each agreement. If a product is only partly qualified for preference, the vendor can provide a detailed negative vendor declaration. Therein the vendor quotes the number of the unqualified parts of the delivered product to the benefit of the preferential status. This could be the starting point for multiple vendor declaration maintenance.

You can also extend a long-term vendor declaration. If you have unprocessed goods from a vendor in stock, and the validity of the long-term vendor declaration has expired, the vendor-material relationship is considered inactive. You can reactivate this relationship by extending the existing long-term vendor declaration. Enter the vendor-based long-term vendor declarations that are received by your organization in SAP Risk Management. Figure 9.15 displays the maintenance for long-term vendor declarations.

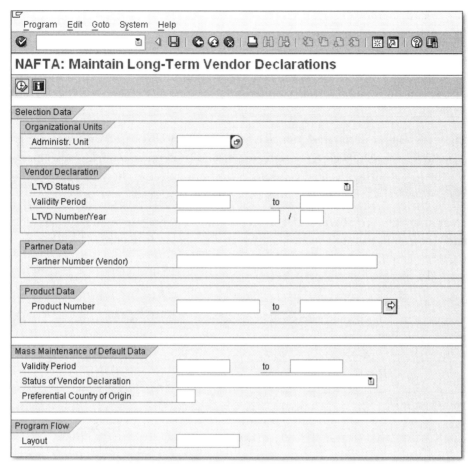

Figure 9.15 Long-Term Vendor Declaration: Maintenance

The following options are available with vendor declarations:

- Maintain a long-term vendor declaration
- Enter a vendor declaration for each administrative unit
- Maintain multiple long-term declarations
- Maintain for multiple administrative units at once, provided that the administrative units belong to a group of logical systems
- Extend a long-term vendor declaration

5. Aggregate vendor declarations

If there are several vendor declarations for the same material, use the aggregation process to specify which declaration should be used for determining preferential origin. The system uses the worst-case declaration (i.e., the least favorable vendor declaration for determining preferential origin) as default for reporting to customs.

Long-term vendor declaration management aggregation is based on the administrative unit, product, preference agreement, and preference model. It also maintains the log of the aggregated vendor declarations and uses the worst-case declaration, if several vendor declarations exist for one material.

Run Transaction /SAPSLL/PREVDI_15, and click on Aggregate Vendor Declaration under the Administration section shown in the screen in Figure 9.14. This produces the screen shown in Figure 9.16.

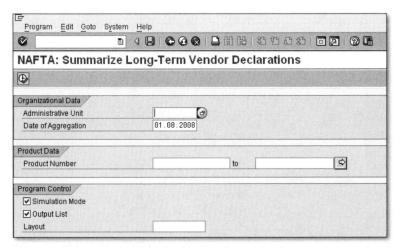

Figure 9.16 Long Term Vendor Declaration: Summarization

Figure 9.16 displays the transaction report to aggregate the vendor declarations. When you run the report shown in Figure 9.16, it pulls the material with multiple vendor declarations. The output generates a report of vendor declarations. Select the one you are interested in, and click the Save and Aggregate LTVDs button. Figure 9.17 displays the screen where the long-term vendor declaration is maintained for productions.

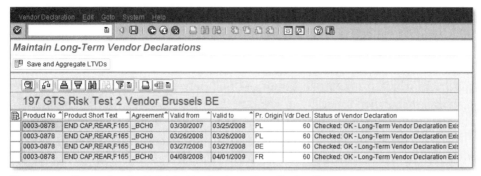

Figure 9.17 Transaction to Maintain Vendor Long-Term Declaration

6. **Determine preference**

Calculate the threshold value for determining preferential origin. This calculation is based on preference rules that you can define yourself or obtain from third-party data providers. You can store fundamental rules relating to a preferential agreement (e.g., a general tolerance rule, a minimum processing rule, or a set of goods rule). You can enter preference rules manually or upload them from a data provider. The system displays an overview of all of the preference rules for each preference agreement and lists the countries to which each agreement applies. The preference zones consist of the NAFTA countries and the country group belonging to the agreement. The preference rules consist of the commodity codes, standard rule, alternative rule, and the validity period.

You can perform preference determination by selecting the NAFTA tab from the screen shown earlier in Figure 9.14 and clicking Perform Preference Determination under the Preference Determination section. In the Header data, enter the relevant data. Select the preference model from plant-based preference determination or cross-plant preference determination. The model selection depends on how you source from the product (i.e., if it is sourced from multiple plants, then the cross-plant model applies). In the model view, enter the plants, depending on the model and the plant group. In the parameter view, other entries are optional, except the BOM view for determining the BOM explosion. For this, you need to either enter "T" for a top-down method or "B" for a bottom-up method. For top-down, only primary material is relevant, and assemblies are not taken into account. For bottom-up, the system determines each assembly and stores the results in the product master.

The system stores the results of the determination in the customs product master. The Cross-Plant Preference Model shown in the screen in Figure 9.18 enables preferential result optimization in the case of distribution production and mixed reference. The processing of the procurement information follows a two-stage approach, which results in an optimized preference statement compared to the individual determination for each plant. In the preference determination function, you determine whether products are sourced from multiple vendors or countries of origin. Those manufactured in-house are authorized for preferential custom duty. First, you execute the preference determination for each BOM alternative per plant defined in your company. Then the system aggregates the results on plant level. If you're determining preference on plant group level, the plant level results are then aggregated to get the result per product and plant group.

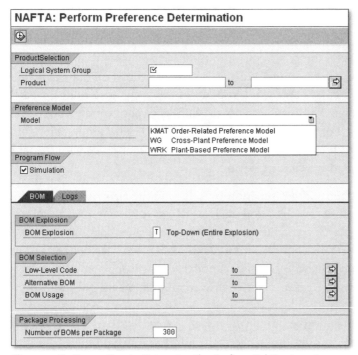

Figure 9.18 Transaction to Determine the Preferential Treatment

7. Evaluate preference results

Use the results of preference determination in the sales documents (e.g., orders and billing documents) to determine eligibility for preferential treatment. You can compare the threshold value (e.g., preference price) with the ex-works price (i.e., the price of the product to be delivered until it reaches the buyer's door) of the material. If the ex-works price is greater than or equal to the preference price, the product is eligible for preferential treatment. If the ex-works price is lower than the preference price, the product is not eligible for preferential treatment. The determination of preference eligibility in SAP BusinessObjects Global Trade Services happens by comparing the preference price of the material with its ex-works price.

Figure 9.19 displays the preference determination for documents. Depending on the result, SAP BusinessObjects Global Trade Services flags the product as eligible or ineligible. To reach the screen in Figure 9.19, from the NAFTA tab in Figure 9.14, click Display Preference Result by Document under the Preference Determination section.

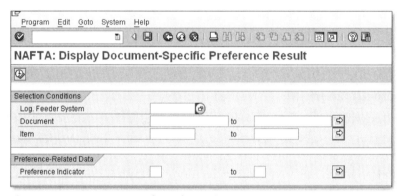

Figure 9.19   Document Specific Preferential Determination

8. **Print preference documents**

You use movement certificates as proof that a product is eligible for preferential treatment when it passes through customs. Within the European Union, for example, you need movement certificates for goods traded with countries with which the European Union has concluded free trade agreements, preferential agreements, or cooperation agreements. You also use movement certificates for states that are associated with the European Union (e.g., developing countries, South Africa, Mexico). You can perform this task by clicking Display Vendor Declaration in the Monitoring section of Figure 9.14. Figure 9.20 displays the transaction for monitoring the long-term vendor declarations for customer's purposes. SAP BusinessObjects Global Trade Services can take a billing document as a basis for printing out movement certificates that you can present to customs authorities.

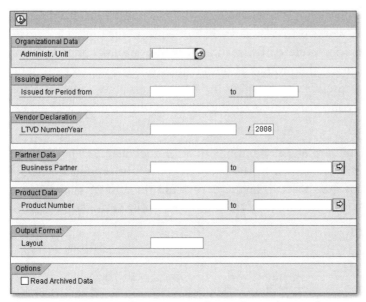

Figure 9.20 Transaction for Monitoring the Vendor Declaration for Customer Purposes

9. **Issue vendor declarations**

Vendor declarations for customer purposes are the final link in the vendor declaration loop. The company itself assumes the role of the vendor and makes a vendor declaration available to its customer. SAP BusinessObjects Global Trade Services offers the option of generating a vendor declaration per customer, product, and agreement. Under the Administrative section of Figure 9.14 shown earlier, click on Issue Vendor Declaration. This will bring up the report that allows you to issue the long-term vendor declarations for customers, as shown in Figure 9.21.

When issuing the vendor declarations for the customer's purposes, you must enter the validity period, partner number, product number, printer control, and additional options. You can issue long-term vendor declarations for customers provided that the aggregation results and preference determination results for the delivered goods indicate that the customer can obtain such a vendor declaration.

You can use this function to issue long-term vendor declarations for a specific administrative unit and a defined period of time as well as to enter additional details. The assignment of external product and partner numbers from the feeder system helps you communicate with other user departments because you can use these numbers when responding to inquiries from other departments about the partners or products for which vendor declarations have been issued.

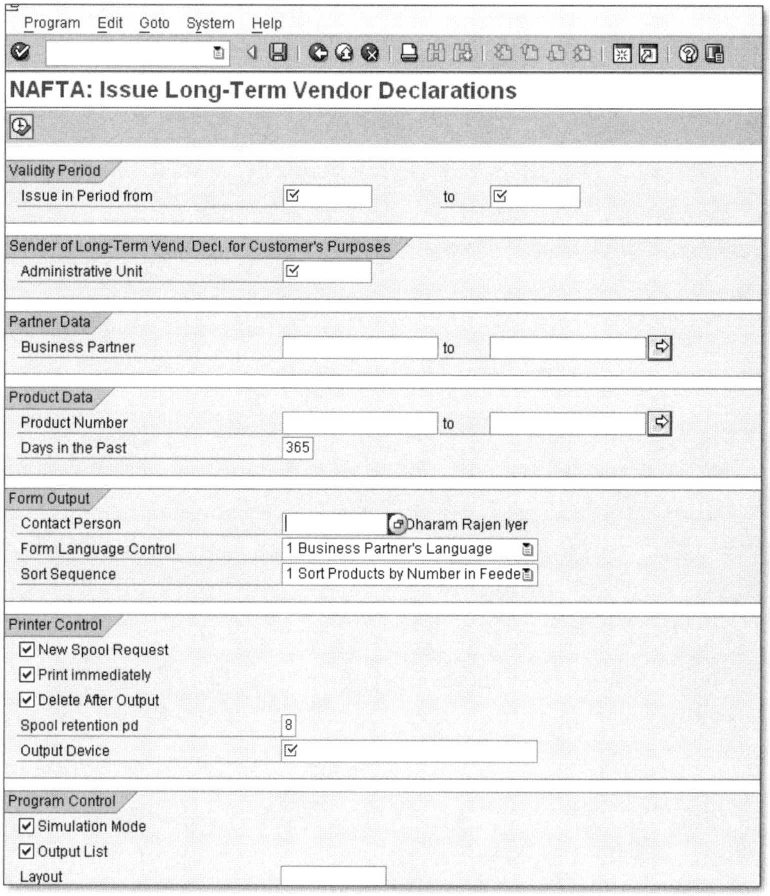

Figure 9.21 Issue of Long-Term Vendor Declaration

9.3   Summary

This chapter discussed the configuration steps required to set up legal regulations, procedures, and preference service activation in SAP BusinessObjects Global Trade Services and SAP ERP. We also discussed the business process and functionality that supports preferential treatment with export and import processing. In the next chapter, we review the steps for configuring electronic compliance reporting.

Intrastat and Extrastat reporting, which allows the European Union to keep track of monetary movements, was formerly part of the SAP Sales and Distribution (SD) Foreign Trade component. Starting with SAP BusinessObjects Global Trade Services 7.1, this functionality is enhanced in the SAP Electronics Compliance Reporting (SAP ECR) module.

10   Intrastat Reporting with SAP Electronics Compliance Reporting (SAP ECR)

Intra European Community Trade Statistics (*Intrastat*) is a system for collecting statistics on exchange of goods among member states of the European Union (EU). It became operational on January 1, 1993, with the creation of the EU single market. When the customs check on the EU internal borders disappeared, the opportunity to use the data from customs declarations for the compilation of the foreign exchange of goods statistics also disappeared. Consequently, the requirement for collecting data directly from the economic operator involved in the intra-community exchange of goods came into force. This system provides direct collection of information from economic operators and communities engaged in internal exchange of goods and registered in the Value Added Tax (VAT) system. Intrastat refers only to the exchange of goods with other EU member states. Statistics on the exchange of goods with non-EU countries are compiled by the Extrastat system, based on customs declarations.

You need a corresponding SAP ERP plug-in to identify the transaction, for example, billing document, goods receipt, and so on, and push it into SAP BusinessObjects Global Trade Services. In this chapter, we discuss SAP ECR functionality, including the master data requirement and setup, the processes in SAP ECR that help identify the transactions to transfer to SAP BusinessObjects Global Trade Services for declaration, and the functionality in SAP BusinessObjects Global Trade Services that processes them for declaration. In a later section of this chapter, we walk through the steps for configuring Intrastat and Extrastat reporting.

In this chapter, we will go over the data set to enable SAP ECR, transactions to push the reporting information to SAP BusinessObjects Global Trade Services and follow the transfer review and preparation of data prior to reporting. We will follow up with the detailed configuration steps to set up the functionality.

10.1 Data Setup for Intrastat Reporting

Arrivals for Intrastat declaration include goods dispatched from another EU member state, and dispatches for Intrastat declaration include goods exported from one EU country to another. Operations that are subject to reporting need not necessarily have a commercial character. Return of goods and dispatch of replacement goods are reported in the direction in which the returned or replacement goods are actually dispatched. In practice, this means that an Intrastat declaration has to be prepared for the flow of incoming goods (arrivals) or the flow of outgoing goods (dispatches) for the following transactions:

- Purchased or sold goods
- Goods intended for processing under contract (processing)
- Goods returned after processing under contract, that is, after processing operations are completed
- Goods received, shipped, and exceptionally returned as a part of financial leasing
- Goods dispatched and arrived as a part of claims of unsatisfactory performance of purchase contract, including return of defective goods, and goods dispatched and arrived as replacement defective goods under complaint
- Goods delivered for free, if they are not goods that are exempted from reporting (such as commercial free samples or advertising material)
- Goods supplied as a part of building and construction works
- Goods supplied as a part of a service, if VAT is applied to the goods as goods acquired from or supplied to another member state
- Goods shipped or received as part of deliveries to central and distribution warehouses
- Goods shipped or received into consignment stock
- Goods shipped out of or received into the storage location, where the storage time exceeded the two-year time period and the goods are returned

The main components of SAP ECR are Intrastat and Extrastat, commodity codes or classification, and master data. The Intrastat component allows you to edit documents, and display, import, or delete a worklist. Commodity codes or classification lets you maintain commodity codes and assign them to the products. Master data provides the functionality to edit the provider information, the default values, and business partners.

In the following sections, we discuss the data setup within the SAP BusinessObjects Global Trade Services system to receive the reporting data for review, edit, and declarations.

10.1.1 SAP BusinessObjects Global Trade Services Data Setup

Master data setup is a prerequisite for accepting transactional data from SAP ECC. Within the SAP BusinessObjects Global Trade Services cockpit, click on Master Data, or use Transaction /SAPSLL/MENU_LEGAL to see the screen in Figure 10.1.

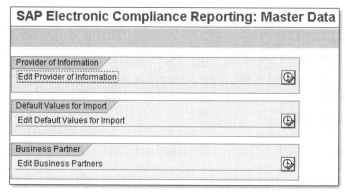

Figure 10.1 Transaction /SAPSLL/MENU_LEGAL

To set up data for Intrastat and Extrastat reporting, follow these steps:

1. **Maintain the provider's information master data using Transaction /ECRS/ POI_EDIT**

Figure 10.1 displays the transaction and reports that allow you to set up master data associated with electronics compliance reporting. First, identify providers as the entity responsible for reporting the transaction information to the authorities, for example, the dispatching company code or the receiving company code. Transaction /ECRS/POI_EDIT allows you to maintain the provider information.

Figure 10.2 shows the information that is available for maintaining or editing information. Click on the Create icon (the page image) to create a new provider, or on the Change for Editing icon (the pencil image) to change existing provider information.

Edit Providers of Information: Overview

In	N	Country	VAT Reg. Number	Addit. No.	Currency	Received Decl. Level	Dispatch Decl. Level	C	Created on	Created at	Changed by	Changed on	Chngd at
A	Ap	DE	DE811381130	001	EUR	Standard Declaration	Standard Declaration	X	11.10.2007	20:18:13		15.02.2008	18:51:12
AMI	Ap	FR	FR83389706771	00000	EUR	Standard Declaration	Standard Declaration	X	12.10.2007	12:11:01		30.01.2008	14:58:01
AMI	Ap	GB	GB593095414		GBP	Standard Declaration	Standard Declaration	X	12.10.2007	11:48:10		30.01.2008	14:58:11
AMI	Ap	IE	IE6517161J		EUR	Standard Declaration	Standard Declaration	X	17.10.2007	19:24:20		30.01.2008	14:58:23
AMI	Ap	IT	IT10746490159		EUR	Standard Declaration	Standard Declaration	X	17.10.2007	19:21:57		30.01.2008	14:58:32
AMI	Ap	NL	NL006790872B02		EUR	Standard Declaration	Standard Declaration	X	12.10.2007	12:17:19		30.01.2008	14:58:40
AMI	Ap	DE	DE129287217	000	EUR	Standard Declaration	Standard Declaration	X	24.10.2007	20:46:22		30.01.2008	14:58:47
AMI	Ap	FR	FR32385124862	00000	EUR	Simplified Declaration	Simplified Declaration	X	23.10.2007	18:05:46		30.01.2008	13:07:01
AMI	Ap	GB	GB911196736		GBP	Standard Declaration	Standard Declaration	X	24.10.2007	20:58:33		30.01.2008	14:58:58
AMI	Ap	IE	IE6595578L		EUR	Standard Declaration	Standard Declaration	X	24.10.2007	20:56:53		30.01.2008	14:59:06
AMI	Ap	IT	IT02621810965		EUR	Standard Declaration	Standard Declaration	X	24.10.2007	20:59:36		30.01.2008	14:59:12
AMI	Ap	FR	FR32385124862	00000	EUR	Simplified Declaration	Simplified Declaration	X	30.01.2008	15:03:08		30.01.2008	15:13:13

Figure 10.2 Transaction /ECRS/POI_EDIT

Maintain the provider information on the screen shown in Figure 10.3. You can change the tax office, VAT number, tax number, name of the company, address, declaration currency, exchange rate type, declaration type, format of the file that you send to the declaration authorities, and the contact information for the receiver of the declaration data.

2. **Maintain the provider's default values for the declaration purpose using Transaction /ECRS/DVI_EDIT**

This helps you set the data that you need for the transaction reporting; if you don't maintain this data, the transaction appears incomplete, and you cannot submit it to authorities. The system automatically provides the values when the transactions are transferred to SAP BusinessObjects Global Trade Services from SAP ECC. Use Transaction /ECRS/DVI_EDIT to maintain the default data (Figure 10.4). You can change the default information, for example, business transaction type, mode of transport, region, and country of origin.

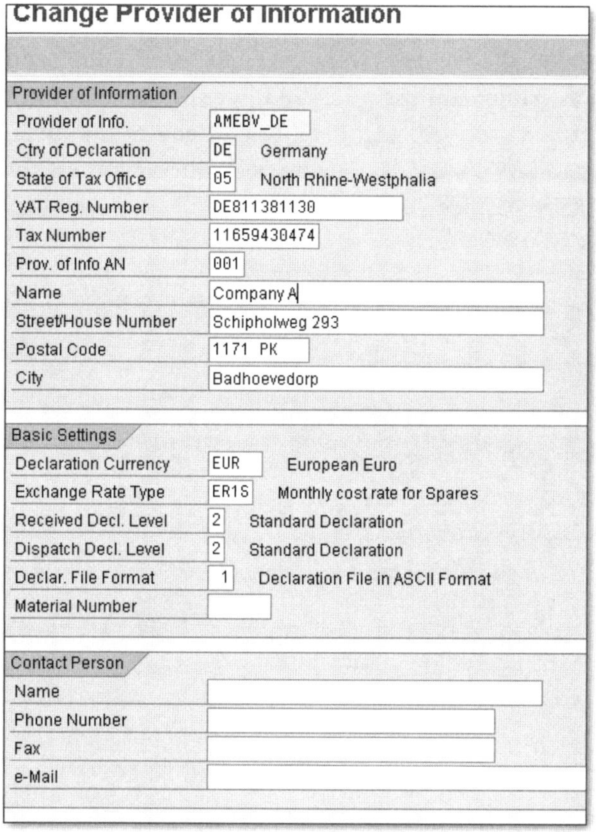

Change Provider of Information

Provider of Information	
Provider of Info.	AMEBV_DE
Ctry of Declaration	DE Germany
State of Tax Office	05 North Rhine-Westphalia
VAT Reg. Number	DE811381130
Tax Number	11659430474
Prov. of Info AN	001
Name	Company A
Street/House Number	Schipholweg 293
Postal Code	1171 PK
City	Badhoevedorp

Basic Settings	
Declaration Currency	EUR European Euro
Exchange Rate Type	ER1S Monthly cost rate for Spares
Received Decl. Level	2 Standard Declaration
Dispatch Decl. Level	2 Standard Declaration
Declar. File Format	1 Declaration File in ASCII Format
Material Number	

Contact Person	
Name	
Phone Number	
Fax	
e-Mail	

Figure 10.3 Maintain Provider Information

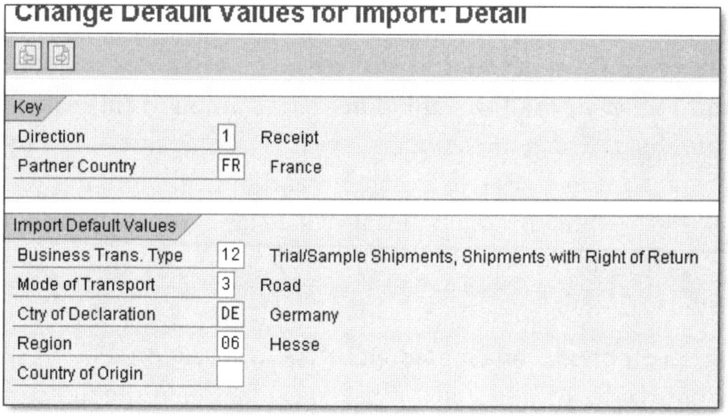

Change Default Values for Import: Detail

Key	
Direction	1 Receipt
Partner Country	FR France

Import Default Values	
Business Trans. Type	12 Trial/Sample Shipments, Shipments with Right of Return
Mode of Transport	3 Road
Ctry of Declaration	DE Germany
Region	06 Hesse
Country of Origin	

Figure 10.4 Transaction /ECRS/DVI_EDIT

3. Edit the business partner, which is transferred from SAP ECC

Business partners are maintained in the feeder system (SAP ECC or SAP R/3) and information about them (such as name, address, role, VAT, etc.) is transferred to SAP BusinessObjects Global Trade Services. If you need to edit any of the transferred information, use Transaction BP. Figure 10.5 displays business partners for which the VAT registration number has been updated.

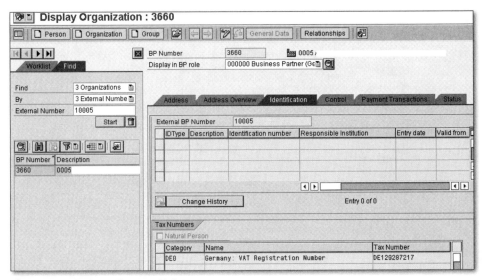

Figure 10.5 Business Partners Maintenance

4. Maintain the commodity codes/classification using Transaction /SAPSLL/ LLNS_102

Commodity codes are the classification codes published for international trade. In the case of Intrastat and Extrastat, the EU commodity codes are used (instead of material and product numbers, which are company-specific). Companies can buy these codes (which are standard by country) as content and upload them to their system. For a subscription fee, outside companies provide classification information, either as an XML or a text file. SAP BusinessObjects Global Trade Services can upload these files into the system.

The commodity code is comprised of eight digits. Use Transaction /SAPSLL/ LLNS_102 to maintain this code. In this step, you can also maintain the units of measure for commodity codes. Figure 10.6 displays Unit 1 through Unit 3 for maintaining the unit of measure.

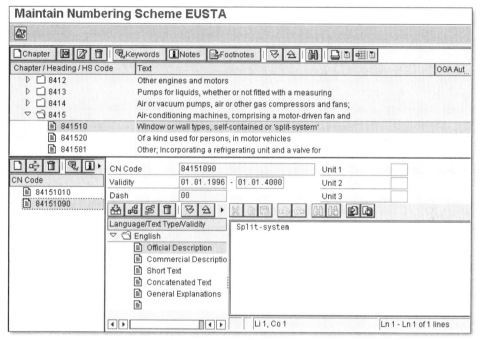

Figure 10.6 Maintain Commodity Code Transaction

5. Assign the commodity codes to each product

As mentioned earlier, material and product numbers are internal to the company; thus, for customs authorities, you must use the numbering scheme or code that is understood by the government. If you misclassify a product, your declaration is not complete, and you cannot submit it. Products are classified with the commodity codes that were maintained in step 4. To assign commodity codes, use Transaction /SAPSLL/PR_TRAPROC02. Figure 10.7 displays the product classification for EU commodity codes.

When you transfer a document to SAP BusinessObjects Global Trade Services, the system automatically copies the commodity code assignment of the product to the transaction (purchase order, shipping notification, etc.) and sales documents (delivery, billing document, etc.) at the item level. You can change the proposed entry manually by editing the declaration.

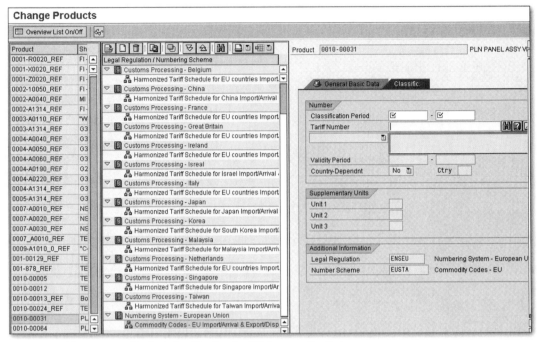

Figure 10.7 Product Classification for EU Commodity Codes

In the next section, we discuss the different reports that help identify transactions that need to be reported.

10.1.2 SAP ECR Data Preparation and Processes for Feeder Systems

To create Intrastat declarations for SAP ECR, you need information about the relevant goods movements. This declaration-relevant data are available in the logistics documents in the feeder system, which means you can reuse this data after you transfer the logistics documents from SAP ERP to SAP BusinessObjects Global Trade Services ECR.

Four specific transactions push transactional data from SAP ECC to SAP BusinessObjects Global Trade Services. Figure 10.8 displays the transaction that pushes receipts to SAP BusinessObjects Global Trade Services, which are delivered as part of the SAP BusinessObjects Global Trade Services plug-in. Running these transactions ensures that all necessary transactions are reported.

The business transactions that need to be reported are as follows:

- ▸ Receipts based on your purchase order
- ▸ Returns and credits
- ▸ Outbound and dispatch billing documents
- ▸ Inter-company billings

Some or all of these transactions are created in the SAP feeder system, and we will go over these functions to transfer the information from SAP ECC to SAP BusinessObjects Global Trade Services system. To perform the transfer, follow these steps:

1. **Report the vendor purchase order, indicating cross-border potential receipts in your warehouse**

Goods can be procured from a vendor or sourced from one location to another. In the case of the former, you might issue a PO to the vendor, and the vendor will then issue the product against the PO. When the goods arrive, you receive the goods against the PO. The system reports the purchase order after you use Transaction /SAPSLL/IS_MM, which transfers purchase orders from SAP ECC to SAP BusinessObjects Global Trade Services (Figure 10.8).

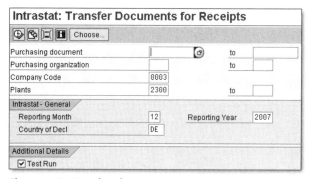

Figure 10.8 Transfer of Receipt Documents

When you execute the report shown in Figure 10.8 with the appropriate selections, including the mandatory Reporting Month and Country of Decl. (country of declaration), the system selects the document that meets the criteria. You can narrow down the selection by purchase order, purchasing organization, company code, and plants. Make sure the Test Run box is unchecked. When you execute this report, you receive a response with the document numbers that are selected for transfer, as shown in Figure 10.9.

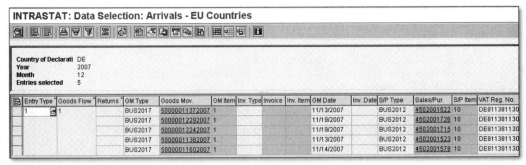

Figure 10.9 Document Numbers Selected for Transfer

Based on the goods receipt, the report lists the goods movements against the PO and associated data, such as goods movement date and PO. Double-click on an item to see the details.

2. **Transfer returns and credit memos**

Returns to vendor are goods moving out of your inventory to the vendor location, and *credit memos* are financial transactions issued for returns, both of which need to be reported to the European Union. The SAP BusinessObjects Global Trade Services plug-in provides Transaction /SAPSLL/IS_MM_RET: Materials Management (MM) returns and MM credit memos. These returns are associated with the purchase order. You use this transaction code if, after you have received goods from a vendor, you decide to send a part back and issue a credit memo against the returns. Figure 10.10 displays the transactions for vendor returns and associated credit.

Intrastat: Transfer Documents for MM Returns and MM Credit Memos

Choose...

Purchasing document		to		
Purchasing organization		to		
Company Code				
Plants		to		

Intrastat - General

Reporting Month 12   Reporting Year 2007

Country of Decl

Additional Details

☑ Test Run

Figure 10.10 Transfer of Return and Credit Memos

3. Identify outbound or inbound transactions in terms of the billing document using a transaction (documents for dispatch)

Outbound transactions can be shipped to your internal or external customer using sales orders, stock transfer orders, and deliveries. For declaration to the customs authorities, billing documents are used, for example, the proforma, credit, and debit memos. You can transfer invoices, proforma invoices, inter-company billing, cancellations, and credit and debit memos to SAP BusinessObjects Global Trade Services using this report. The reporting month and the country of declaration are required to identify the selection. Figure 10.11 shows the report for transferring billing documents and credit and debit memos associated with the outbound movement of goods. The lower section displays the documents that are identified for transfer to SAP BusinessObjects Global Trade Services.

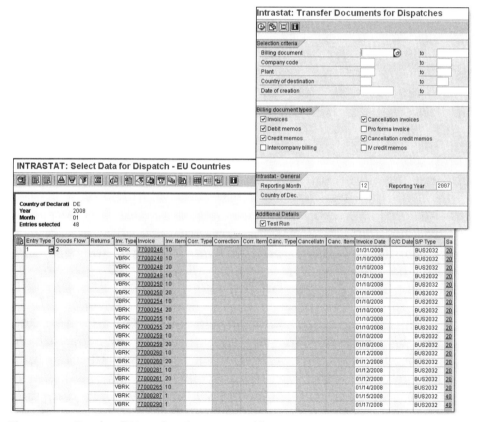

Figure 10.11 Transfer of Dispatch and Intrastat Worklist

4. **Identify inter-company transactions, and push them to SAP BusinessObjects Global Trade Services**

If you move inter-company goods around within the European Union (which needs to be reported), you might use inter-company billing to post the financials. Transaction /SAPSLL/IS_SD_IB is for outbound and inbound goods within the company. Figure 10.12 shows the report for transferring inter-company billings, proforma, and credit memos.

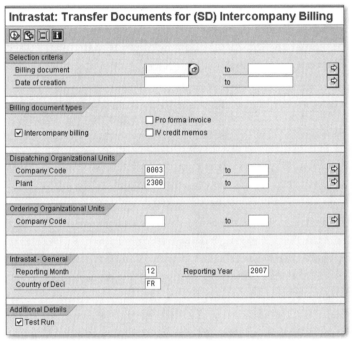

Figure 10.12 Transfer Billing Documents

10.1.3 SAP ECR Processing Within SAP BusinessObjects Global Trade Services

Following the transfer of the transactional data into the SAP BusinessObjects Global Trade Services system, these needs to be reviewed, updated with missing data, and subsequently reported to customs authorities. To configure SAP ECR processing within SAP BusinessObjects Global Trade Services, follow these steps:

1. **Import the worklist with Transaction /ECRS/WL_IMPORT**

The transactions that were transferred to SAP BusinessObjects Global Trade Services need to prepared for reporting; Transaction /ECRS/WL_IMPORT allows you to import the transactional data that was transferred in steps 6 to 9 (Figure 10.13). When you execute this transaction, you get a response like the one shown in the lower section of Figure 10.13. The worklist import reports the number of processed entries for a specific provider, which typically would be the company code of the company that issues the purchase order.

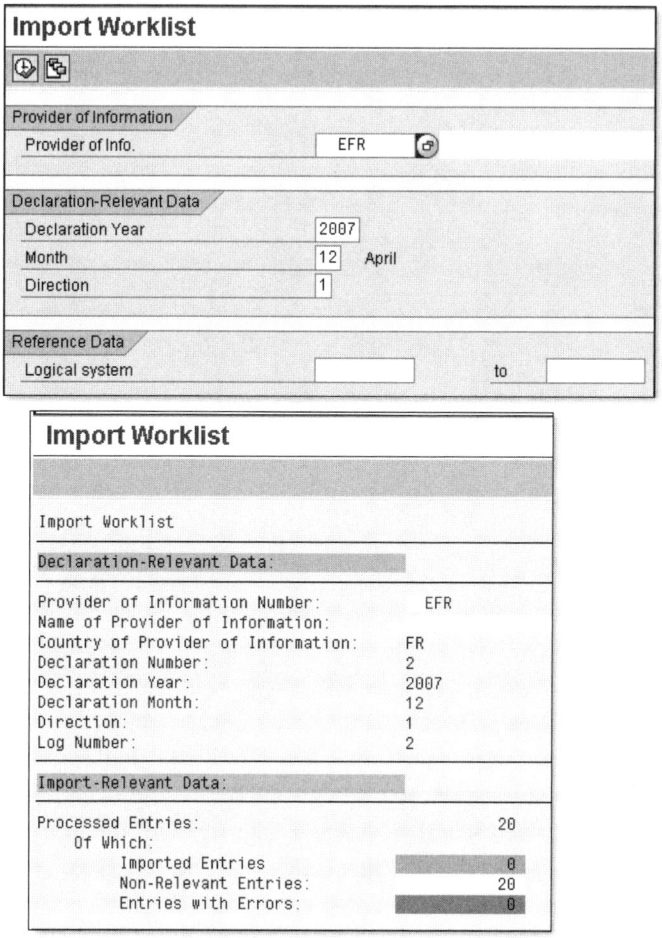

Figure 10.13 Import Worklist of the Transactions Transferred to SAP BusinessObjects Global Trade Services

After the system imports the worklist, you can click on Display Import List to view the data, or you can use Transaction /ECRS/WL_IMPORT (Figure 10.14). The imported transactional data is listed in the format shown in Figure 10.14 — by provider, VAT registration number, and country of declaration.

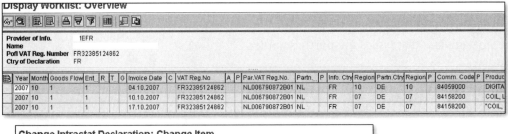

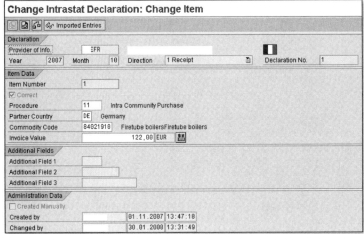

Figure 10.14   Edit of the Worklist to Update Information

2. Edit the Intrastat declaration

The data imported into SAP BusinessObjects Global Trade Services needs to be reviewed and updated with any missing data. Transaction /ECRS/RP_EDIT lists all of the imported transactions and allows you to edit the worklist. When you select the line item and click on the Change icon, the system brings up all of the items in the document. If you select the line item and click on the magnifying glass icon, the system displays item details, which allows you to review the information, and, where necessary, make changes. The lower section of Figure 10.14 shows the changes that can be made prior to Intrastat submission.

3. **Release the transaction**

After review and editing, save your report by clicking on the Save icon. When you save, the system prompts you for the release of the selected declaration. Click on Yes if you want to save the results to ensure that the system releases the document for declaration. You can now submit the information to the authorities.

10.2 Business Process Procedure for Intrastat Reporting

As with any SAP system implementation, you must configure the system. To this end, SAP provides the Reference Implementation Guide, which provides configurations that define business processes. SAP ECC configuration allows you to set up these processes and send data for reporting.

In the following sections, we discuss the configurations for both SAP BusinessObjects Global Trade Services and the feeder system.

10.2.1 SAP BusinessObjects Global Trade Services Configuration

SAP BusinessObjects Global Trade Services configuration can be divided into the following high-level areas:

▶ Basic setup

▶ SAP ECR-specific setup

In the following sections, we describe each of these areas in more detail.

Basic Setup

SAP offers pre-delivered configurations for SAP ECR (Figure 10.15). When using these pre-delivered configurations, list the country from where the regulation will be active. The following are the key steps for the basic setup of SAP ECR in SAP BusinessObjects Global Trade Services.

1. **Define legal regulations**

Select External Application for the Type of Legal Code and Import/Export for Import/Arrival and Export/Dispatch. Access this step via the following menu path: SPRO • SAP GLOBAL TRADE SERVICES • "LEGAL CONTROL" SERVICE • DEFINE LEGAL REGULATIONS.

2. Define the determination procedure

The determination procedure allows you to define the parameters for determining the legal regulations. These are pre-delivered, with the country default setting being the key piece of information. The menu path for this step is SPRO • SAP GLOBAL TRADE SERVICES • "LEGAL CONTROL" SERVICE • DEFINE THE DETERMINATION PROCEDURE FOR LEGAL REGULATION.

3. Activate the legal regulation

List the countries you want required. Use the following menu path: SPRO • SAP GLOBAL TRADE SERVICES • "LEGAL CONTROL" SERVICE • ACTIVATE LEGAL REGULATIONS.

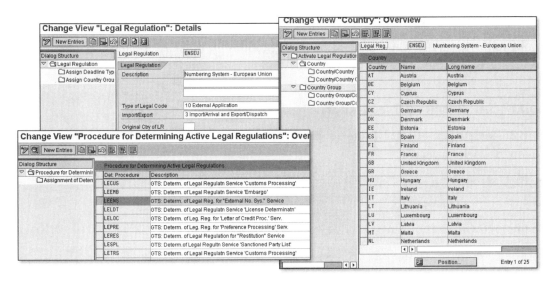

Figure 10.15 Pre-Delivered Configurations for SAP ECR

4. Define the numbering scheme for commodity codes

SAP ECR reporting is based on the commodity code. The numbering scheme for commodity codes is defined via: SPRO • GENERAL SETTINGS • NUMBERING SCHEMAS • DEFINE NUMBERING SCHEMA FOR COMMODITY CODES. Figure 10.16 displays the definition and assignment of the numbering scheme. This information can be manually maintained or loaded as an XML file from the content provider. In Figure 10.16, you can see the structure this content requires to be loaded; if you are using files from a content provider, you must have the structure defined per those files.

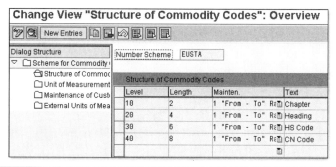

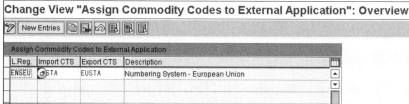

Figure 10.16 Numbering Scheme Structure

5. Link to external applications (activate legal regulation)

This configuration step allows you to activate SAP ECR for the countries defined in the activation step. You have the option to activate for both outbound and inbound goods movements. Use the following menu path: SPRO • GENERAL SETTINGS • NUMBERING SCHEMAS • LINK TO EXTERNAL APPLICATIONS • ACTIVATE LEGAL REGULATION FOR EXTERNAL APPLICATION.

6. For Intrastate codes, verify and use default settings where possible

This step is a collection of pre-delivered configuration verification, validation, and updates for relevant countries. These default settings are delivered as of SAP BusinessObjects Global Trade Services 7.1 and higher. You can find these configuration settings under SAP ELECTRONICS COMPLIANCE REPORTING • INTRASTAT CODES, SPECIAL SETTINGS AND IMPORT FROM WORKLISTS. To review the pre-delivered configurations, let's look at the IMG configuration node where the Intrastat codes for the procedures are populated. These procedures define the use direction, with 1 meant for receipt and 2 meant for dispatch. These are officially required codes in Intrastat declarations for receipts and dispatches. The codes are specified by the respective national authorities and can vary depending on the country of declaration. This configuration is listed under INTRASTAT CODES • DEFINE INTRASTAT CODE

273

FOR PROCEDURE. Figure 10.17 shows the pre-delivered Intrastat codes for the SAP BusinessObjects Global Trade Services system.

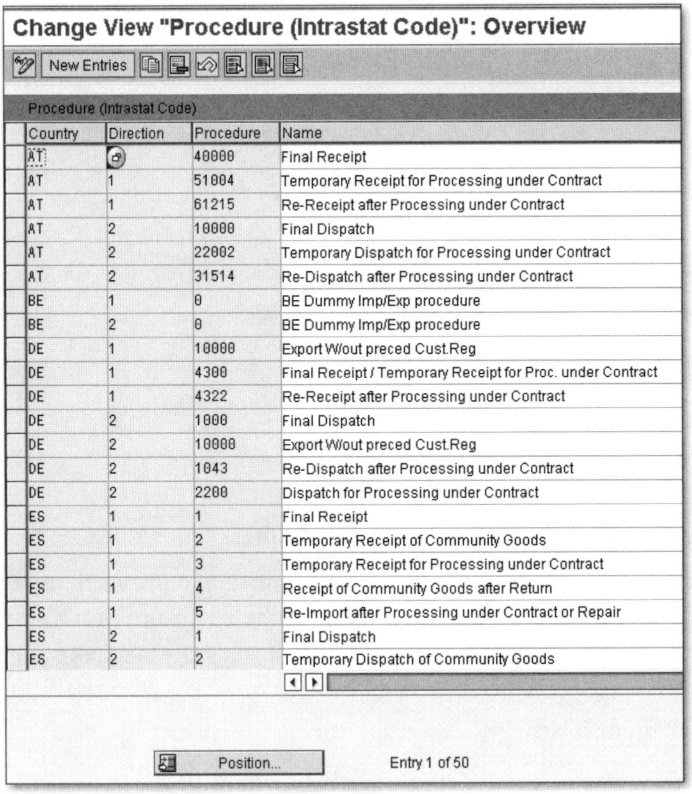

Change View "Procedure (Intrastat Code)": Overview

New Entries

Procedure (Intrastat Code)

Country	Direction	Procedure	Name
AT		40000	Final Receipt
AT	1	51004	Temporary Receipt for Processing under Contract
AT	1	61215	Re-Receipt after Processing under Contract
AT	2	10000	Final Dispatch
AT	2	22002	Temporary Dispatch for Processing under Contract
AT	2	31514	Re-Dispatch after Processing under Contract
BE	1	0	BE Dummy Imp/Exp procedure
BE	2	0	BE Dummy Imp/Exp procedure
DE	1	10000	Export W/out preced Cust.Reg
DE	1	4300	Final Receipt / Temporary Receipt for Proc. under Contract
DE	1	4322	Re-Receipt after Processing under Contract
DE	2	1000	Final Dispatch
DE	2	10000	Export W/out preced Cust.Reg
DE	2	1043	Re-Dispatch after Processing under Contract
DE	2	2200	Dispatch for Processing under Contract
ES	1	1	Final Receipt
ES	1	2	Temporary Receipt of Community Goods
ES	1	3	Temporary Receipt for Processing under Contract
ES	1	4	Receipt of Community Goods after Return
ES	1	5	Re-Import after Processing under Contract or Repair
ES	2	1	Final Dispatch
ES	2	2	Temporary Dispatch of Community Goods

Position...   Entry 1 of 50

Figure 10.17   Pre-Delivered Intrastat Codes

The export/import procedure is used in documents or transactions. The export procedure is only necessary when the authority expressively requires it. If this is not the case, only one entry (a dummy entry) is needed because the incompletion procedure in SAP requires that an export procedure is filled in. You should review the following list of pre-delivered configurations for Intrastat codes:

▸ Define Intrastat Code for Partner Country

▸ Assign Intrastat Code for Partner Country to Country of Declaration

▸ Define Intrastat Code for Country of Origin

- Assign Intrastat Code for Country of Origin to Country of Declaration
- Define Intrastat for Region
- Define Intrastat for Business Transaction Type
- Define Intrastat Code for Mode of Transport at the Border
- Define Intrastat code for INCO terms
- Define Intrastat Code for Ports and Airports
- Define Intrastat Code for Special Movement Code
- Define Intrastat Code for Collection Center

You must encode certain information in your Intrastat declarations of receipts and dispatches. The codes are specified by the respective national authorities and can vary depending on the country of declaration. Therefore, you have to define the Intrastat codes for your business transactions separately for each country. Dependent on the country of declaration, the system proposes the country-specific values for creating the Intrastat declaration in the application. SAP ECR in SAP Business-Objects Global Trade Services already contains the required Intrastat codes and their country-specific assignment for all countries in which you can create Intrastat declarations using SAP ECR. Check the provided codes, and supplement them as necessary.

SAP ECR-Specific Setup

Follow these steps for configuring SAP ECR in SAP BusinessObjects Global Trade Services:

1. **Define Foreign Currency in Partner Country**

Another pre-delivered setting where you need to verify or add new entries is in the foreign trade currency. Figure 10.18 shows the default settings for country currency by year and fiscal month. Go to SPECIAL SETTING • DEFINE FOREIGN CURRENCY IN PARTNER COUNTRY. These might be delivered by default for the respective country currency, but if you have a special need that is different – for example, if you have a company-wide currency you use for transaction – then you might want to make a change.

Change View "Foreign Currency in Partner Country": Overview

Country	Country VAT Reg. No.	From Year	From Month	Foreign Currency
IT		2006	01	CYP
IT	CZ	2006	01	CZK
IT	DK	2006	01	DKK
IT	EE	2006	01	EEK
IT	GB	2006	01	GBP
IT	HU	2006	01	HUF
IT	LT	2006	01	LTL
IT	LV	2006	01	LVL
IT	MT	2006	01	MTL
IT	PL	2006	01	PLN
IT	SE	2006	01	SEK
IT	SI	2006	01	SIT
IT	SI	2007	01	EUR
IT	SK	2006	01	SKK

Figure 10.18 Default Settings for Country Currency by Year and Fiscal Month

In addition to the data involving consignments of goods – such as recipient, quantity, and statistical value — the authorities in Italy also require information regarding the parties with whom you conducted financial transactions for a given consignment of goods. The information for this value flow contains the business partner's VAT registration number, along with the invoice value in the currency of the country where the business partner for the value flow is located. To specify the invoice value in the local currency of the business partner with whom you conducted financial transactions for a consignment of goods, you have to specify the currency codes dependent on the country key in your partner's VAT registration number.

This information determines the invoice value in the foreign currency and is independent of the figure for the invoice value in the local currency. Accordingly, you have to assign the country keys of your partners' VAT registration numbers to the currencies of the partner country. However, you only have to define this assignment for foreign currencies other than the Italian declaration currency, the Euro. If the system does not find an entry for a country in this activity, it uses the Euro as the declaration currency for the business partner's financial transactions.

2. **Import from the worklist**

Intrastat declarations are based on business transactions in your logistics systems. When SAP ECR is integrated with SAP ERP as a logistics system, you can transfer the logistics documents in SAP ERP that are relevant for Intrastat declarations directly to SAP ECR. To do so, the system creates an entry in the SAP ECR worklist for each document item. When you create an Intrastat declaration, you can import the entries from the worklist to the declaration, which copies the item data from the logistics documents to the Intrastat declaration. The country and region information in the logistics documents may differ from the information required in Intrastat declarations. This is the case, for example, for countries that are independent politically but which the authorities consider part of a neighboring country for statistical, intra-European trade purposes.

There are pre-delivered entries with the configuration for this. When the system imports data from the worklist to the Intrastat declaration, the country and region information from the logistics documents is adjusted to comply with the official requirements for Intrastat declarations. You can configure these adjustments in the following areas:

▸ **Define Regions for Exclusion from Intrastat Declaration**
In this area, you can define the regions that belong to a country from a political standpoint but which are not relevant for intra-European trade statistics and therefore must not be included in Intrastat declarations. The overseas departments of France, for example, are part of France politically, which is why France is listed as the country in the business partner data. You are not supposed to include these areas in Intrastat declarations, however, so you can exclude these regions. Entries involving excluded regions are not transferred to the Intrastat declaration.

▸ **Define Exception for Mapping Partner Country**
When goods deliveries from or to a business partner are relevant for Intrastat declarations based on its headquarters, but the business partner data for the partner country does not comply with the modeling required by the statistics authorities, you can map exceptions to the partner country here. To do so, you define which country key the system will use instead of the partner country in the business partner data in the Intrastat declaration. This is relevant, for example, for business partners from Northern Ireland. Although Northern Ireland belongs to the United Kingdom from a political standpoint, the intra-European statistics consider the regions of Northern Ireland to be different. Accordingly, you have to assign an artificial country key for Northern Ireland to the regions of the United Kingdom that represent Northern Ireland.

▶ **Define Exception for Mapping the Country of Origin**
You have to define the exceptions for modeling the country of origin, analogous to the partner country.

▶ **Assign Region in Worklist to Regions for Intrastat Declaration**
This setting is only relevant for countries of declaration in which the statistics authorities require information regarding a provider of the information's region. The entries in the worklist can contain information about the region information for a provider of information, from a logistics document, that does not meet the requirements of the statistics authorities. This is possible, for example, when the region information from the logistics document corresponds to the political borders of a country, but the authorities use a different region definition for their statistics. You have to define assignments between regions in documents and in Intrastat declarations regardless of whether your region information differs between the two documents.

Note

With currency translation, you are required to maintain the exchange rates, as these are used for converting document currency amounts into declaration currency, based on the customs rates prescribed by the customs officials (customs rate INTRASTAT). This involves three configuration steps with currencies setup that need to be matched with the feeder system:

1. Check exchange rates types.

2. Define translation ratios for currency translation.

3. Enter exchange rates.

The menu path for these three configuration steps can be found under: SPRO • SAP NETWEAVER • CURRENCIES.

10.2.2 Feeder System Configuration

You can configure Customizing settings to influence the total set of possible information in a logistics document, which means that you must check whether the logistics documents contains all of the information that is relevant for transfer to SAP ECR and creation of Intrastat declarations.

> **Note**
>
> The list also involves settings that are valid for areas other than the Intrastat declaration. Accordingly, settings may already be defined, and you must check whether they are relevant for Intrastat declarations with SAP ECR.

The following list contains the Customizing activities in the IMG that will ensure that the logistics documents in SAP ERP contain the necessary data:

▶ **Define the VAT registration number**

In this step, define the VAT registration number for your company, which your business partners and the authorities use as a unique identification. The VAT registration number is used in Intrastat declarations to identify the provider of information to a country's statistics authorities. If your company has a foreign plant for which you want to create Intrastat declarations, you need a separate VAT registration number for this legal foreign entity. You can define the number in this activity. This will help simplify your record-keeping, as you do not need an independent company code for this foreign plant. The menu path is FINANCIAL ACCOUNTING (NEW) • FINANCIAL ACCOUNTING GLOBAL SETTINGS (NEW) • GLOBAL PARAMETERS FOR COMPANY CODE • TAX • VAT REGISTRATION NUMBERS (VAT REG. NO.) • DEFINE DOMESTIC VAT REGISTRATION NUMBERS OR • DEFINE FOREIGN VAT REGISTRATION NUMBERS.

▶ **Define number ranges for import/export processing**

In this activity, define the number ranges that the system uses to identify foreign trade objects in logistics documents: SALES AND DISTRIBUTION • FOREIGN TRADE/CUSTOMS • DEFINE NUMBER RANGES • GENERAL IMPORT/EXPORT PROCESSING.

▶ **Incompleteness check**

This activity is optional. If you want the system to check document data for the completeness of foreign trade data, this configuration step or scheme will help you carry out this activity. Configure the control data for the checks, and assign the incompleteness schemas for foreign trade data. The menu path is SALES AND DISTRIBUTION • FOREIGN TRADE/CUSTOMS • CONTROL FOREIGN TRADE DATA IN MM AND SD DOCUMENTS • INCOMPLETENESS SCHEMAS FOR FOREIGN TRADE DATA AND FOREIGN TRADE DATA IN MM AND SD DOCUMENTS.

▶ **Import code by country**

This activity is optional. You need the settings in this step if you want to transfer commodity codes from your feeder system to SAP ECR. If you want to perform classification in SAP ECR, you can leave out this step. The menu path is SALES AND DISTRIBUTION • FOREIGN TRADE/CUSTOMS • BASIC DATA FOR FOREIGN TRADE • DEFINE COMMODITY CODES / IMPORT CODE NUMBERS BY COUNTRY.

▶ **Material groups for import/export**
This activity is optional. It helps you prepare the default setting for the automatic determination of the procedure. After it has determined the procedure, the system can set the document field to the appropriate value by default. The menu path is SALES & DISTRIBUTION • FOREIGN TRADE/CUSTOMS • BASIC DATA FOR FOREIGN TRADE • DEFINE MATERIAL GROUPS FOR IMPORT/EXPORT.

▶ **Define procedures and default values**
In this IMG activity, you define import/export procedures and determine defaults for SD and MM. The menu path is SPRO • SALES AND DISTRIBUTION • FOREIGN TRADE/CUSTOMS • BASIC DATA FOR FOREIGN TRADE • DEFINE PROCEDURES AND DEFAULT VALUES. The default code procedures are assigned to a country, as shown in Figure 10.19, with an indicator for Error (E) with exports and imports.

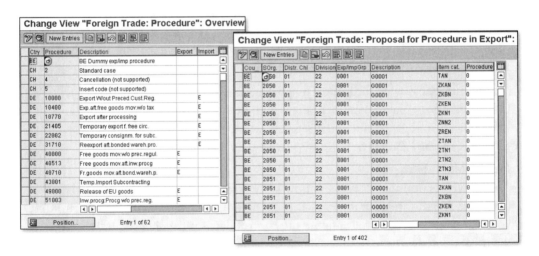

Figure 10.19 Default Code Procedures Assigned to Country

▶ **Define default procedures**
The proposal depends on the following criteria for SD Export/Dispatch: country, sales organization, distribution channel, division, export/import material group, and item category. Figure 10.19 displays the proposals for the export or import group for different item categories.

▶ **Define business transaction types and default values**

Business transactions are assigned by country, sales organization, distribution channel, and item category. They are the codes defined for different countries, and they represent the different transactions in reporting. In this activity, you configure the transfer of logistics documents to SAP ECR to include the business transaction type for the Intrastat declaration. You can also simplify document processing in the feeder system by defining default values for the business transaction type, which the system then uses automatically.

Here, you can maintain the default settings for business transactions used in SD documents. First you must define the business transaction types for a specific country. *Business transaction type* is a standard term and classifies the type of business transaction that is carried out. In this table, you can enter the default values per combination of sales area/item category. If you create a sales order for distribution channel 10, using sales order item category TAN (Normal Sales), this will be reported by Intrastat as a purchase/sale (business transaction type 11). If you use item category KLN (Free of Charge Item), this is reported by Intrastat as Article on Approval/Sample (business transaction type 12). The values in the table are default values and can be changed during the sales order processing. Figure 10.20 displays the business transactions for item categories used within the transactions.

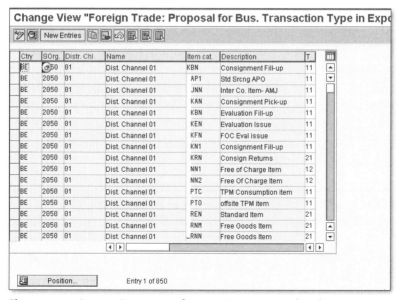

Figure 10.20 Business Transactions for Item Categories Used Within Transactions

There are also a number of conversion activities, listed here:

▶ **Convert business transaction type**
In this activity, configure the system to convert the business transaction type it determined automatically into the relevant business transaction type for the Intrastat declaration, for internal activity allocation in Sales and Distribution (SD). This conversion is required because you post issues as receipts for internal activity allocation. The menu path for this is SALES & DISTRIBUTION • FOREIGN TRADE/CUSTOMS • BASIC DATA FOR FOREIGN TRADE • CONTROL/CONVERSION • CONVERT EXPORT INTO IMPORT BUSINESS TRANSACTION TYPE.

Inter-company sales invoices don't have a purchase order on the incoming side. Therefore, some codes on the purchasing side have to be converted from the codes on the sales side. One of these is the business transaction type. The conversion is one-to-one, so every entry has been marked as the default conversion.

▶ **Convert export procedures into import procedures**
Similar to conversion of the business transaction type (previous item), in this activity, you configure the conversion of the automatically determined procedure to the relevant procedure for the Intrastat declaration. The menu path for this is SALES & DISTRIBUTION • FOREIGN TRADE/CUSTOMS • BASIC DATA FOR FOREIGN TRADE • CONTROL/CONVERSION • CONVERT EXPORT INTO IMPORT PROCEDURES.

▶ **Convert export customs office into import customs office**
Similar to conversion of the business transaction type and export/import procedures (preceding items), in this activity, you configure the conversion of the automatically determined customs office to the relevant customs office for the Intrastat declaration. The system uses the customs office information to determine the port or airport, which some declaration countries require you to specify in your Intrastat declarations. The menu path for this is SALES & DISTRIBUTION • FOREIGN TRADE/CUSTOMS • BASIC DATA FOR FOREIGN TRADE • CONTROL/CONVERSION • CONVERT EXPORT INTO IMPORT CUSTOMS OFFICE.

▶ **Convert export mode of transport into import mode of transport**
Similar to conversion of the preceding elements, in this activity, you configure the conversion of the automatically determined mode of transport to the relevant mode of transport for the Intrastat declaration. The menu path for this is SALES & DISTRIBUTION • FOREIGN TRADE/CUSTOMS • BASIC DATA FOR FOREIGN TRADE • CONTROL/CONVERSION • CONVERT EXPORT INTO IMPORT MODE OF TRANSPORT.

▶ **Define customs office and mode of transport**

Customs Office: In this activity, define the customs offices that can be selected later in document processing. The system uses these customs offices to determine port/airport information, which some declaration countries require you to specify in your Intrastat declarations. The menu path for this is SALES AND DISTRIBUTION • FOREIGN TRADE/CUSTOMS • TRANSPORTATION DATA • DEFINE CUSTOMS OFFICES.

Mode of Transport: In this activity, define the modes of transport that can be selected later in document processing. The menu path for this is SALES AND DISTRIBUTION • FOREIGN TRADE/CUSTOMS • TRANSPORTATION DATA • DEFINE MODES OF TRANSPORT.

▶ **Define valid combinations of mode of transport and customs office (optional)**

In this activity, you can define possible combinations of mode of transport and customs office to reduce the likelihood of errors in manual document entry. The system uses the defined combinations to check manual entries during document processing and prevents any combinations that you have not defined from being used in the document. The menu path for this is SALES AND DISTRIBUTION • FOREIGN TRADE/CUSTOMS • TRANSPORTATION DATA • DEFINE VALID COMBINATIONS: MODE OF TRANSPORT – CUSTOMS OFFICE.

▶ **Default values (optional)**

In this activity, you can simplify document processing in the feeder system by defining default values for the foreign trade header data for transportation data for sales document and stock transport orders, which the system then uses automatically. During the export or import document creation, the default procedure is used (sales order or purchase order). The menu path for this is SALES AND DISTRIBUTION • FOREIGN TRADE/CUSTOMS • TRANSPORTATION DATA • DEFAULT VALUES FOR FOREIGN TRADE HEADER DATA. MENU PATH SALES AND DISTRIBUTION • FOREIGN TRADE/CUSTOMS • TRANSPORTATION DATA • DEFINE DEFAULT VALUES FOR STOCK TRANSPORT ORDERS.

▶ **Define the exceptions for regions**

In this activity, you define the exceptions for region/country assignment. This involves defining exceptions for the regions that belong to one country politically but require a different assignment (or count as a separate country) for Intrastat declarations. The menu path for this is SALES AND DISTRIBUTION • FOREIGN TRADE/CUSTOMS • PERIODIC DECLARATIONS • CONTROL DATA • SPECIAL RULE COUNTRY / REGION.

▶ **Define data selection control**

In this activity, define the documents — for each direction — whose data the Intrastat declaration contains after the transfer of documents to SAP ECR. The menu path for this is SALES AND DISTRIBUTION • FOREIGN TRADE/CUSTOMS • PERIODIC DECLARATIONS • CONTROL DATA • DATA SELECTION CONTROL • DATA SELECTION CONTROL.

▶ **Define exclusion/inclusion indicators**

In this activity, you generally define whether documents from SD or MM should contain exclusion/inclusion indicators in the document UI. If this flag is set in document processing, you can exclude individual documents from transfer to SAP ECR. The menu path for this is SALES AND DISTRIBUTION • FOREIGN TRADE/CUSTOMS • PERIODIC DECLARATIONS • CONTROL DATA • INCLUSION AND EXCLUSION INDICATORS • DEFINE EXCLUSION/INCLUSION INDICATORS.

▶ **Assign item categories**

You can define whether or not the system automatically sets an inclusion/exclusion indicator for individual item categories in a sales order. If it does, you can reset the indicator for individual documents in document processing. The menu path for this is SALES AND DISTRIBUTION • FOREIGN TRADE/CUSTOMS • PERIODIC DECLARATIONS • CONTROL DATA • INCLUSION AND EXCLUSION INDICATORS • ASSIGN TO ITEM CATEGORIES FOR SD SALES ORDERS. The following is the menu path for deliveries: SALES AND DISTRIBUTION • FOREIGN TRADE/CUSTOMS • PERIODIC DECLARATIONS • CONTROL DATA • INCLUSION AND EXCLUSION INDICATORS • ASSIGN TO ITEM CATEGORIES FOR SD DELIVERIES.

▶ **Select transportation connection point**

This step is only relevant for dispatches and must only be carried out if you have defined routes. You can omit this step if you have maintained your own default objects using Transaction VI95. A mode of transport can be a general address, a trans-shipment center, a border with a customs office, or a reference to a location defined in the master data (shipping point, plant, customer, or vendor). You can select a transportation connection point as the border crossing point as part of the leg, which, in turn, is part of the route. The system automatically transfers the office of exit entered or the transportation point to the foreign trade header data only if the point is marked as the border crossing point, and the address for the point is maintained (especially the Country field). Transaction 0VTD is used for the transportation connection point.

> **Note**
>
> You must configure the pricing to make sure that the reporting transactions have statistical pricing conditions defined in the pricing procedure. Then, when the documents are transferred, the pricing conditions are transferred along with the document. For calculation in SD documents, the menu path is SALES AND DISTRIBUTION • BASIC FUNCTIONS • PRICING • PRICING CONTROL • DEFINE CONDITION TYPES AND DEFINE AND ASSIGN PRICING PROCEDURES. FOR CALCULATION IN MATERIALS MANAGEMENT (MM) DOCUMENTS UNDER MATERIALS MANAGEMENT • PURCHASING • BASIC FUNCTIONS • CONDITIONS • DEFINE PRICE DETERMINATION PROCESS; DEFINE CONDITION TYPES; DEFINE CALCULATION SCHEMA.
>
> In these activities, you define the criteria the system uses to calculate the statistical values that are reported in Intrastat declarations.

10.3 Summary

For statistical reporting within the European Union, you can configure your SAP ECC and SAP BusinessObjects Global Trade Services system to capture the transactions from your logistics system. Set up the reporting requirement within the SAP BusinessObjects Global Trade Services system, and ensure the transactions within the feeder system are moved to SAP BusinessObjects Global Trade Services. In this chapter, we discussed the process of preparing the data for reporting, as well as some different functionalities that facilitate submission. We also discussed the configuration steps within SAP BusinessObjects Global Trade Services and SAP ERP to enable SAP ECR reporting, and reviewed the pre-delivered configurations that enable Intrastat reporting.

In the next chapter, we explain how to prepare for an upgrade of the SAP BusinessObjects Global Trade Services and associated SAP ERP plug-in, and discuss some high-level functionality differences with the different releases. We also discuss data retention exercises and review the technical aspects of the SAP BusinessObjects Global Trade Services system.

SAP BusinessObjects Global Trade Services has come up with many releases since 1.0 and has considerably enhanced functionality with each one. We discuss these enhanced functionalities in this chapter and also cover the topics of data retention and archiving, table structures, BAdIs, user exits, and copy control.

11 Functionality Release, Upgrade, Archiving, and Technical Overview of SAP BusinessObjects Global Trade Services

The first version of SAP BusinessObjects Global Trade Services, release 1.0, introduced sanctioned party list screening, a function that was not available with SAP ERP Sales and Distribution Foreign Trade. SAP BusinessObjects Global Trade Services is now at release 8.0, and every new version has included significant increases in functionality. SAP BusinessObjects Global Trade Services 2.0 introduced Compliance and Customs Management. SAP BusinessObjects Global Trade Services 3.0 introduced Risk Management, table structure changes, and improvement in performance. The next release, SAP BusinessObjects Global Trade Services 7.0, introduced the Human Resources and Finance integration, as well as the Logistics integration for bonded warehouses and letters of credit. SAP BusinessObjects Global Trade Services 7.1 introduced electronics compliance reporting for Intrastat reporting. SAP BusinessObjects Global Trade Services 7.2 introduced the Environment, Health & Safety integration, and the new concept of a plug-in.

With a SAP BusinessObjects Global Trade Services upgrade, just like any SAP product upgrade, it's important to understand new functionality and make a technical and functional assessment of its use to your business. Depending on the year of implementation and the volume of your master and transactional data, your SAP BusinessObjects Global Trade Services could be very data intensive. As such, you must plan a strategy for data retention and archiving.

Performing upgrades involves technically understanding the system and eventually the functionality upgrade. Archiving involves reviewing the data stored in the

SAP BusinessObjects Global Trade Services tables. It is important to understand the technical aspect of SAP BusinessObjects Global Trade Services, including the tables, structure, functions, and BADIs. In this chapter, we will look at the key functionality and delta features with the different SAP BusinessObjects Global Trade Services releases. Because it is important to make an assessment of the system for data volume and planning archiving, we will review the archiving process. Last but not least, we will discuss the technical aspect of SAP BusinessObjects Global Trade Services.

11.1 Functionality Releases and Delta Features

In the following sections, we discuss some of the high-level functionality releases and delta functions of SAP BusinessObjects Global Trade Services.

11.1.1 SAP BusinessObjects Global Trade Services 1.0 Versus SAP BusinessObjects Global Trade Services 2.0

SAP BusinessObjects Global Trade Services 2.0 introduced archiving for key objects, customs documents, logs, and business partners, as well as email notification for blocked documents. Compliance Management – Legal Control was enhanced with license determination for exports and imports; export license requirement could now be managed with attributes for products, including ECCNs, business partners, destination countries, and more.

SAP BusinessObjects Global Trade Services 2.0 also enabled users to pull volume configuration mapping from the feeder system (SAP ERP) using the automatic transfer function, which helped to reduce manual configuration work. (SAP BusinessObjects Global Trade Services screenings are only performed with documents that have complete data; otherwise, the system captures the information within the technically incomplete documents.)

Finally, SAP BusinessObjects Global Trade Services 2.0 enabled data conversion for legacy transactional data. It introduced transactions to transfer documents from SAP ECC, including delivery notes, purchase orders, and sales orders. It also offered an XML upload interface for denied party list content, and storage for future reference and auditing purposes. Sanctioned party list screening logic was enhanced to allow periodic screening with detailed analysis.

11.1.2   SAP BusinessObjects Global Trade Services 2.0 Versus SAP BusinessObjects Global Trade Services 3.0

SAP BusinessObjects Global Trade Services 3.0 offered a recovery procedure that allows you to manage documents in the feeder system when SAP BusinessObjects Global Trade Services is down. Sanctioned party list screening was enhanced with expert mode, multiple addresses, two-way matches, and delta screening (which resulted in a performance improvement).

Integration with Logistics introduced the automatic transfer and cancellation of billing documents. Prior to the SAP BusinessObjects Global Trade Services 3.0 system, the customs declaration interface had to be implemented with technical changes, and there was not auto-cancellation of billing document triggered based on the cancellation in the feeder system. Customs Management was enhanced by the ability to submit declarations online. Customs declarations for inbound documents and goods receipts were also introduced, as were pre-delivered templates for trade documents, such as shipper export declarations, certificates of origin, export packing lists, shipper letters of instruction, and more. Default data determination and incompleteness check were introduced for trade document submission (both print and online).

Finally, SAP BusinessObjects Global Trade Services 3.0 introduced Risk Management, which included the preference processing functionality that allowed you to manage vendor declarations and preference determination for NAFTA and the European Union. Additionally, SAP NetWeaver BW content was updated with SAP BusinessObjects Global Trade Services Compliance and Customs Management export and import reports.

11.1.3   SAP BusinessObjects Global Trade Services 7.x

In the following sections, we discuss each of the SAP BusinessObjects Global Trade Services 7.x releases.

SAP BusinessObjects Global Trade Services 7.0

With SAP BusinessObjects Global Trade Services 7.0, Compliance Management was enhanced with country group activation for legal regulation activation and license determination. It also allowed you to flag documents for archiving. Transfer logs for master and transactional data were enhanced for applications, which allowed you to configure retention and capture error details. With sanctioned party lists, you could now maintain positive and negative lists. BAdIs were introduced to replace user exits. Human Resources and Finance integration for sanctioned party list screening became available for the screening of financial institutions and your internal workforce. Finally, Logistics integration was enhanced for bonded warehouses, and Risk Management provided letter of credit functionality.

SAP BusinessObjects Global Trade Services 7.1

SAP BusinessObjects Global Trade Services 7.1 introduced electronic compliance reporting for Intrastat reporting within EU countries. Case Management with sanctioned party list screening was released, and an online submission procedure for specific countries (such as the US, DE, FR, BE, CH, and AT) were now available as part of pre-delivered configurations. It also allowed the configuration of functionality involving International Traffic in Arms Regulations (ITAR), including agreements and nested licenses.

SAP BusinessObjects Global Trade Services 7.2

With SAP BusinessObjects Global Trade Services 7.2, SAP released a separate plug-in for SAP BusinessObjects Global Trade Services, which had the advantage of being independent from other application plug-ins. Sanctioned party list screening was enhanced with the TREX search engine. SAP ERP Environment, Health and Safety is now integrated with SAP BusinessObjects Global Trade Services Compliance Management for tracking and reporting. To support import declaration, this version of SAP BusinessObjects Global Trade Services has pre-delivered messages, IDocs, and Customs Management configurations.

11.1.4 SAP BusinessObjects Global Trade Services 8.0

SAP BusinessObjects Global Trade Services 8.0 is the latest release, and the following high-level functionalities have been added or upgraded:

- Master data transfer: When transferring master data from SAP ECC to SAP BusinessObjects Global Trade Services, you can now add product fields to the standard delivered product fields.

- Sanctioned party list screening of individual contacts, and tighter integration with HR.

- Import compliance checks on inbound deliveries.

- Enhancement to support ITAR: Project tracking with BOM explosion and sub-items are now transferred to SAP BusinessObjects Global Trade Services. License checks can now be performed at the component level.

- Re-export: To support re-export, the BOM explosion in Compliance Management service activation is checked in the SAP ECC plug-in for re-exports based on the originating country and dual-use status.

- SAP Transportation Management integration: SAP TM 7.0 is integrated with SAP BusinessObjects Global Trade Services 8.0 to support the export process. Transportation execution is initiated based on the export compliance check and released from SAP BusinessObjects Global Trade Services. Transport execution takes information from SAP BusinessObjects Global Trade Services; when the export declaration is generated based on the proforma creation in SAP ECC, the system triggers a block removal and transport leg execution in SAP TM. Interface with SAP TM uses the route information for screening embargo situations as the goods move from one country to another.

- Import process enhancement to support inward processing relief, where you can reclaim duties for components of imported goods.

11.2   Data Retention and Archiving

Data in SAP systems are stored in database tables, which you can view through transparent tables. Archiving objects form the data structure and context and are predefined in the system for each application component. The archiving procedure is divided into three main steps: (1) creation of archive files, (2) storage of archive files, and (3) deletion from the database after the data are archived. As with any system, data retention is a very important aspect of system implementation and is available in SAP BusinessObjects Global Trade Services using trade and customs reporting. Plan on archiving data that you no longer require because you may need to show it to customs authorities.

In the following sections, we discuss some examples of archiving objects and how to review the data and set up for archiving the data.

11.2.1 Archiving Objects

Prior to upgrading, we recommend that you archive non-essential data to free up the system database. Some of the key SAP BusinessObjects Global Trade Services objects to consider for archiving are as follows:

► **CHANGEDOCU**
Change documents, which consist of table data from tables, CDCLS (cluster structures for change documents), CDHDR (change document headers), CDPOS_STR (additional change documents – table for STRINGS), and CDPOS_UID (additional tables for inclusion).

► **CUHD**
Customs documents, which consist of a series of tables associated with the customs declaration documents, changes, addresses, and so on. This object keeps track of all manually created customs documents.

► **IDOC**
Intermediate documents, which get logged in the system during creation.

► **PREVD**
Preference configuration enabled with the data created for vendor declarations.

► **PRFCALC**
Logs created with preference determination.

► **PRPREF**
Preference statement for product. When you have preference processing enabled, the system captures records for product statements.

► **SPL_AT**
Sanctioned party list audit trail data. This object consists of the following tables: /SAPSLL/SPLAUD (SPL-audit), /SPLSLL/SPLAUDD (Details), and /SAPSLL/SPLAUDK (comments).

► **SPL_MD**
Sanctioned party list master data or the content itself.

11.2.2 Archiving General Steps and Procedures

The main archiving transaction, which takes you to the archiving administration, is SARA. Follow these steps to use the transaction:

1. **Check for the archiving session sequence**

Before you start archiving an object, you should check to see what the archiving session sequence is for that object. This helps you to understand the document flow within your SAP system and where this object falls in the sequence. Before you can archive and delete a material master record, you must archive other objects (such as purchasing documents) that refer to this material. Network graphics gives you the view of such dependencies between objects.

2. **Check for database tables that will be archived against this object**

Click on the Database Tables button. This shows the details of the tables behind the object SPL_AT. You can view all of the tables, or just the tables with deletions. Figure 11.1 displays the tables associated with the archive object SPL_MD.

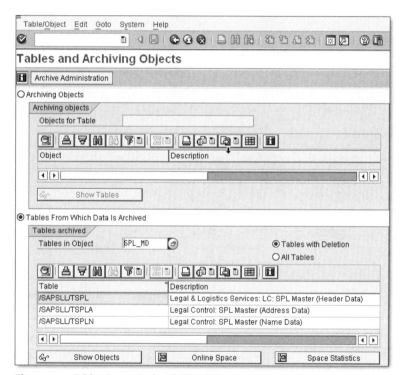

Figure 11.1 Tables Associated with SPL_MD

After completing these steps, you can begin the archiving process. Follow these steps:

1. **Set up archiving customizing**

Use Transaction SARA, and then click on the Customizing button shown in Figure 11.1. This displays a pop-up screen that allows you to customize data archiving. It has four main sections: Cross-Archiving Object Customizing, Archiving Object-Specific Customizing, Basis Customizing, and Application-specific Customizing. In the pop-up screen, complete all of the steps for customizing. When you click on Technical Settings under Cross-Archiving Object Customizing, it results in Change View "Cross-Object Customizing Data Archiving": Details, as shown in the pop-up in the top-right of Figure 11.2. Accept all of the defaults and appropriate selections in the area, or review the defaults and update them appropriately. For example, you may want the system to check for files in the file system or for stored files, have the system verify the archive file existence before deleting, indicate the maximum amount of data you can write to the archive file, and give the name of the server group name for a background job.

Select the Technical Settings under Cross-Archiving Object Customizing, if you want to archive an object in one client that in turn triggers archiving in another client. Use the green arrow button to return to the customizing pop-up shown in Figure 11.2. Click on Technical Settings under Cross-Archiving Object Customizing.

2. **Set up the production variant**

You can choose to set up a test variant along with the production variant. The test mode variant does a simulation (or, in other words, a test run) and shows the results. The production variant does the actual write job for the archive. On the Change View "Customizing View for Archiving": Details screen (Figure 11.2), click on the Variant button next to the Production Mode Variant button. This brings up the screen shown in Figure 11.2. Deselect Test Run if it is a real production run, and save.

3. **Define the logical file path definition in the Cross-Client File Names/Paths**

Archive files are stored in the file system under a physical path and filename that is derived from the user-defined logical path or filename. In this step, you define a platform-specific physical path and name where the archive files will be stored. You can find this under the Basic Customizing section shown in Figure 11.2. Click on Cross-Client File Names/Paths to get to the screen shown in Figure 11.2, where you configure the file names and paths.

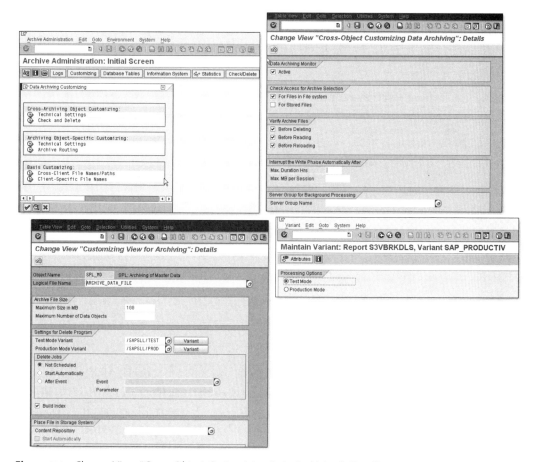

Figure 11.2 Change View "Cross-Object Customizing Data Archiving": Details

Click on Client-Specific File Names to configure the filenames and file paths. Basic customizing for File Names/Paths has two options. You can either set it up with client-specific settings so that the file names are only available for the client you want to archive, or you can make it client independent (cross-client), as shown in Figure 11.3. In this case, customizing for filename and path are available across all clients. First, click on Write to extract the data from the different tables in the object into a file.

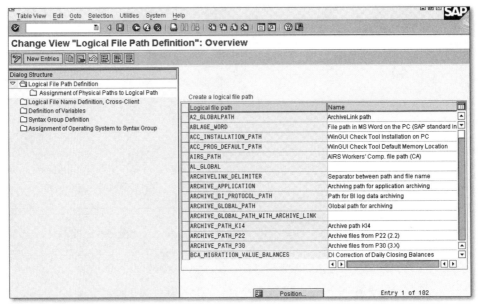

Figure 11.3 Client-Specific File Names

4. Set up archiving jobs

Now set up the archiving job for the Write step. Transaction SARA provides the view of the steps involved in archiving, as shown earlier in Figure 11.1. Before you can run the Write job, you need to set up a job variant, which involves data selection. Enter the archiving object "SPL_MD" in the screen shown earlier in Figure 11.1, and click on the Write icon. This brings up the screen where you enter the variant name (see Figure 11.4). Enter the name of the variant that you want to set up ("TEST123", in this example), and then click on the Maintain button. Next, select the variant criteria. The selection data shown in Figure 11.4 will be archived (i.e., written to a file). Use the Restrict Selections section to exclude other fields from the selection.

Now set the start date. In the Archive Administration: Create Archive Files screen (see Figure 11.5), click on the Start Date button. Click on the Immediate button, and then click on the Save button. This stipulates that your job will be executed as soon as you submit it. Set the spool parameters. Click on the Spool Params. button from the Archive Administration: Create Archive Files screen you saw in Figure 11.5. On the next screen, enter your output device, select Print Immediately, and select New Spool Request. If you want to, you can also name your spool file.

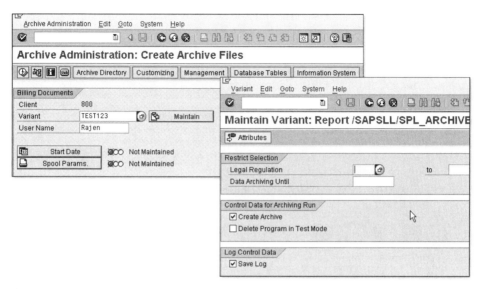

Figure 11.4 Enter the Variant Name

Figure 11.5 Archive Administration: Create Archive Files

Green lights next to the respective buttons indicate that your job start and spool parameters are set up.

5. **Execute your job**

Execute your job from the initial administration screen, shown in Figure 11.5, by clicking on the Execute icon.

6. **Review the output from your job as well as the spool list**

Click on the job icon on the Archive Administration: Create Archive Files screen, which displays the Job Overview screen (Figure 11.6) and allows you to display each job as well as the associated spool files.

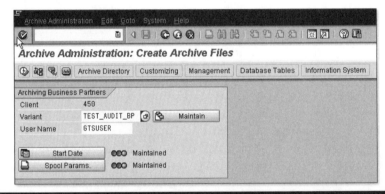

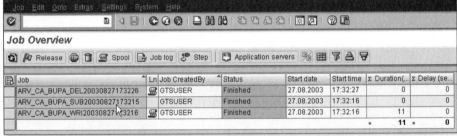

Figure 11.6 Archiving Run Job Overview

7. **Review the job log**

When you click on the job icon in the preceding step, it takes you to the list of jobs with the status of each (i.e., Finished for a successful run or Cancelled for a failed execution), as shown in Figure 11.6. Select the job from the overview screen, and then click on the Job Log button.

8. **Review the spool list**

A spool request is the document attached to a job run containing application data that you can send to a printer or other output. Spool file review gives you a summary of the write job execution. The resulting spool list screen shows your output report.

> **Note**
>
> After you run the Write job, this will create an archive file that you can store in a storage device and delete later. When you click on the Delete icon, it will provide the archive selection from the list of files you have archived, and you can select to delete it.

11.3   SAP BusinessObjects Global Trade Services Table Structure

SAP BusinessObjects Global Trade Services is one of the new dimension products, and, unlike traditional SAP systems, tables are accessed and data are stored with the GUID (Global Unique Identifier) primary key. Unlike SAP ERP, where there are header and item tables for most objects, SAP BusinessObjects Global Trade Services stores this information in multiple tables. As such, you can make use of pre-delivered function modules to retrieve information.

When transactions are transferred and saved in SAP BusinessObjects Global Trade Services, the master data associated with the transactions are captured through the GUID. Unlike the traditional SAP ERP system, if you keep your cursor on the field and press F1, the system provides the table structure rather than table details. While displaying the transaction information, the master data associated with it is retrieved based on the GUID, not the specific transaction.

In the following sections, we will demonstrate how the information is stored in the SAP BusinessObjects Global Trade Services tables and how they are linked for data retrieval.

11.3.1   Linking Product and Classification Information

To understand this concept, let's look at an example of a linking product and the classification information. Table /SAPSLL/PR records information for a product being transferred or created and saved in SAP BusinessObjects Global Trade Services. It generates a GUID PR, PRNUM (SAP BusinessObjects Global Trade Services internal number for the product), ERNAM (created by), CRTSP (created on), AENAM (changed by), ORGSYS (originating system), PRBUM (base unit), WEIGHT UNIT, and VOLUME UNIT. Table /SAPSLL/PNTPR stores information related to the feeder system product number and is linked to the previous table with the GUID PR.

If you have a country-specific classification, you must refer to Table /SAPSLL/PRCTSC. If you have used a classification that is not country-specific, you must refer to Table /SAPSLL/PRCTS. With PR GUID, you can retrieve the classification numbers GUID and CTSNUMC GUID, associated with Tables /SAPSLL/PRCTSC and /SAPSLL/PRCTS, respectively. Using CTSNUMC GUID, you can retrieve the classification information from Table /SAPSLL/CTSNUMC (field - STCTS). Similarly, using CTSNUM GUID, you can retrieve the classification information from Table /SAPSLL/CTSNUM (field – STCTS). Table 11.1 demonstrates the linkages between these tables and within SAP BusinessObjects Global Trade Services. All this information can be accessed through Transaction /SAPSLL/PRODUCT_03 (display).

Table	Purpose	Linkage
/SAPSLL/PR	SAP BusinessObjects Global Trade Services Internal Product Number	GUID PR
/SAPSLL/PNTPR	Feeder System External Product Number and SAP BusinessObjects Global Trade Services Internal Product Number	GUID PR
/SAPSLL/PRCTSC	Country-Specific Product Classification Number association	GUID PR, CTSNUMC GUID
/SAPSLL/PRCTS	Non-Country-Specific Product Classification Number association	GUID PR, CTSNUM GUID
/SAPSLL/CTSNUMC	Country-Specific Classification Number	CTSNUMC GUID
/SAPSLL/CTSNUM	Non-Country-Specific Classification Number	CTSNUM GUID

Table 11.1 BusinessObjects Global Trade Services Tables and Linkages for Data Retrieval

Figure 11.7 shows the information displayed using this transaction. The preceding example shows how many tables are being accessed using this GUID.

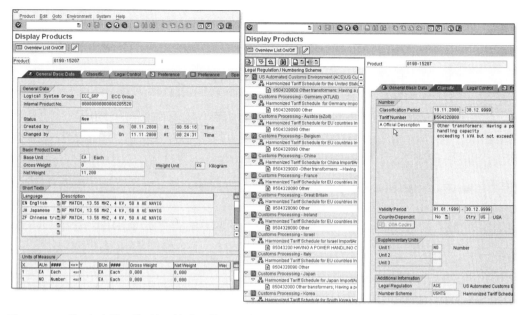

Figure 11.7 Product Classification Update Transaction

11.3.2 Transaction Information

Let's take an example of transaction information to understand how it is tied to master data and presented within the transaction data display. Using the feeder system document number, you can go to Table /SAPSLL/CORREF and get the GUID of Preded. (the preceding document) and MAIN Obj. GUID 16. This table keeps track of document flow, in other words, the preceding document reference and the subsequent document reference. With the GUID Preced., you can access Table /SAPSLL/CUHD and gather the field GUID_CUHD to get the Customs Doc No (CORDER). /SAPSLL/CUHD is the header table. With Main Obj. GUID. 16, you can access Table /SAPSLL/CUIT with GUID_CUHD for item details. From this table, you can also retrieve GUID PR. With GUID PR, you can access /SAPSLL/PRCTS and get CTSNUM GUID, and with CTSNUM GUID, you can access Table /SAPSLL/CTSNUM. Table /SAPSLL/CTSNUM has the GUID CTSNUM and the classification information. With CTSNUM GUID, you can go to /SAPSLL/LCLICC and get GUID LCLIC. With the GUID LCLIC field, you can access /SAPSLL/LCLIC and get the license information. Table 11.2 displays the tables, their purposes, and their linkages.

Table	Purpose	Linkages
SAPSLL/CORREF	Document Reference	GUID of Preded., MAIN Obj. GUID 16
/SAPSLL/CUHD	Document Header	GUID of Preded., GUID_CUHD
/SAPSLL/CUIT	Document Item	GUID_CUHD, GUID PR
/SAPSLL/PRCTS	Product Classification	GUID PR, GUID CTSNUM
/SAPSLL/CTSNUM	Classification	GUID CTSNUM, GUID LCLIC
/SAPSLL/LCLICC	License Details	GUID LCLIC

Table 11.2 SAP BusinessObjects Global Trade Services Transactional Table and Data Retrieval

Now that you understand the construction and concept of the SAP BusinessObjects Global Trade Services system, we will move on to another important technical aspect, BAdIs, user exits, and copy control. With every SAP BusinessObjects Global Trade Services implementation, some or all of these might be used. In the next section, we will discuss these technical objects and review some cases in which they are applied to the implementation.

11.4   BAdIs, User Exits, and Copy Control

With the new dimension products, SAP is moving from user exits to BAdIs. User exits are ABAP code placeholders, which allow customers to write their own code to meet custom requirements. BAdIs can be used in the similar fashion as user exits, but they use a different methodology in building the custom enhancement. Copy control is available within the SAP ERP system and is used very effectively for checking the SAP BusinessObjects Global Trade Services services and blocking the processing of supply chain transactions, if the previous document is blocked in the SAP BusinessObjects Global Trade Services system.

11.4.1   BAdIs

SAP BusinessObjects Global Trade Services provides BAdIs that allow customers to create their own enhancements. With release 7.0 and higher, you can use BAdIs to access enhancement builders. Prior to 7.0, you were able to use the BAdIs as a substitute for user exits. SAP BusinessObjects Global Trade Services has pre-delivered BAdI implementations, which may consist of multiple enhancement spots that you must activate.

Example

Let's discuss one example of an enhancement spot for transferring additional pricing conditions from SAP ECC proforma documents to SAP BusinessObjects Global Trade Services for customs declarations. The menu path for BAdI activation in SAP ECC is REFERENCE IMG • SALES & DISTRIBUTION • FOREIGN TRADE/CUSTOMS • SAP GLOBAL TRADE SERVICES – PLUG-IN • CONTROL DATA FOR TRANSFER TO SAP GLOBAL TRADE SERVICES • BUSINESS ADD-INS FOR GLOBAL TRADE SERVICES • EDIT CONTROL OF DOCUMENT TRANSFER • BADI TO CONTROL INTERFACE CALLS FROM BILLING DOCUMENTS (SD0C) • BADI NAME /SAPSLL/IF_EX_CTRL_SD0C_R3.

▶ ECC Structure: KOMV, Document number, Condition type = ZCOND.

▶ Condition base currency: WAERS, Condition base value = KAWRT.

▶ SAP BusinessObjects Global Trade Services destination for both pricing conditions: Table (View) /SAPSLL/V_TLCRVS, data element: PRCND.

In SAP BusinessObjects Global Trade Services, maintain a duty type (ZCOND) to bring in the condition value from the SAP ECC proforma document. This is populated into the condition - W001 (Value for Foreign Trade Statistics (Statistical Value).

11.4.2   User Exits

User exits are getting replaced with BAdIs, but, in some cases, you might have to use the traditional user exits, as there may not be equivalent BAdIs available. *User exits* are placeholders where custom codes can be written; while performing the relevant function, this code is called.

Let's look at a user exit example, where the business application is to ignore the transfer and screening of text items because text items are not physical products and are not shipped as goods. Use Transaction SE38, and access the user exit EXIT_SAPLSLL_LEG_CDPIR3_002. Go to Include - ZXSLLLEGCDPIR3U02. The following is the sample code:

```
* if IS_MM0A_HEADER-ebeln = '4500001335'.
*    BREAK-POINT.
DATA:wa_gen_work TYPE /sapsll/api6800_itm_r3_s,  " Work Area  of type
table CS_API6800-ITEM-GEN.
        lmtart LIKE mara-mtart .
                    " FILED FOR STORING THE MATERIAL TYPE.
   IF it_mm0a_item[] IS NOT INITIAL. "CHECKING WHETHER THE P.O LINE
ITEMS ARE PRESENT ARE NOT .
```

```
      LOOP AT it_mm0a_item.
        IF it_mm0a_item-matnr IS INITIAL. " CHECKING WHETHER THE
MATERIAL MASTER IS PRESENT OR NOT .
*          read table CS_API6800-ITEM-GEN into WA_GEN_WORK  WITH KEY
ITEM_NUMBER = IT_MM0A_ITEM-EBELP.
          wa_gen_work-legal_active = ' '.
          MODIFY cs_api6800-item-gen FROM wa_gen_work TRANSPORTING
legal_active WHERE item_number = it_mm0a_item-ebelp.
          IF sy-subrc <> 0.
        MESSAGE 'UNABLE TO FILTER THE REQUIRED LINE ITEM ' TYPE 'I'.
          ENDIF."AT SY-SUBRC.
*     ELSEIF IT_MM0A_ITEM-MATKL BETWEEN 7 AND 17   .
**           SELECT SINGLE MTART FROM MARA
**                    INTO LMTART
**                      WHERE MATNR = IT_MM0A_ITEM-MATNR .
**        IF LMTART = 'NLAG'. " CHECKING THE MATERIAL TYPE
***        IN THIS CASE THE LINE ITEMS SHOULD BE TRANSFERED
**         ELSE.
**          read table CS_API6800-ITEM-GEN into WA_GEN_WORK   with key
ITEM_NUMBER = IT_MM0A_ITEM-EBELP.
*          WA_GEN_WORK-LEGAL_ACTIVE = ' '.
*          MODIFY CS_API6800-ITEM-GEN FROM WA_GEN_WORK TRANSPORTING
LEGAL_ACTIVE WHERE ITEM_NUMBER = IT_MM0A_ITEM-EBELP.
*          IF SY-SUBRC <> 0.
*          MESSAGE 'UNABLE TO FILTER THE REQUIRED LINE ITEM ' TYPE
'I'.
*          ENDIF."AT SY-SUBRC
**         ENDIF. " IF FOR LMTART = 'NLAG'.
      ELSE .
*         IN THIS CASE THE LINE ITEMS SHOULD BE TRANSFERED
      ENDIF. " AT IT_MM0A_ITEM-MATNR IS INITIAL
    ENDLOOP. "LOOP AT IT_MM0A_ITEM.
   ENDIF."AT IT_MM0A_ITEM [].
* ENDIF. "AT BREAK POINT
```

11.4.3   Copy Control

Copy control is a function used in SAP ERP for performing requirement checks, data transfers, and validation when moving from one document to another (e.g., sales order to delivery note). If you want a process that stops delivery note creation when a sales order is blocked, you can use the copy control item order requirement to do so. The application of this change is described in SAP Note 444204.

The configuration is maintained within SAP ECC: SAP Reference IMG • Logistics
Execution • Shipping • Copy Control • Specify Copy Control for Deliveries.
Figure 11.8 displays this configuration step.

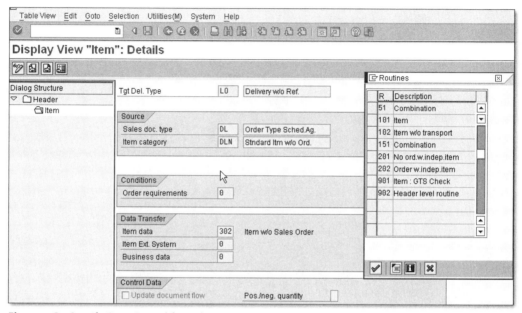

Figure 11.8 Specify Copy Control for Deliveries

One important point to make here is that copy control does not apply to *stock
transport orders*, which is when companies move goods from one plant to another.
As they cross borders, trade checks are applied to these transactions. You can make
use of the shipping function for delivery note creation and further processing of
the delivery note, but the copy control function to stop the delivery note does not
apply.

> **Case Study: Stop Delivery Note Creation with Reference to Stock Transport Orders**
>
> Make use of the function module GN_DELIVERY_CREATE. Create an enhancement im-
> plementation using Z-GN_DELIVERY_CREATE_GTS and the description. The following
> are the high-level steps of ABAP programming:
>
> ▸ Check for the Purchase Order document type or Stock Transport Order (NB or UB),
>   and check on the table field, VBTYP equals to V or UB).
>
> ▸ Get the RFC destination of the SAP BusinessObjects Global Trade Services system by
>   calling function module /SAPSLL/CD_ALE_RECEIVER_GET_R3.

▶ Get the purchase order SAP BusinessObjects Global Trade Services statuses by doing an RFC to function module /SAPSLL/API_6800_STATUS_GET. Use the destination retrieved in the preceding step.

▶ Export the following parameters:

hdr_reference_data-dual_r	= 'EXTID'.
hdr_reference_data-refno	= temp table$-vgbel.
hdr_reference_data-org_logsys	= concatenation of sy-sysid + 'CLNT' + sy-mandt
hdr_reference_data-objtp	= 'BUS2012'.
hdr_reference_data-refapp	= 'MMOA'.
langu_iso = sy-langu.	

▶ LOOP at search result, where the document is blocked, and then stop the delivery note creation. If there are qualifying entries, issue a Legal Control in Global Trade error message with the following service response: DN creation prevented by SAP BusinessObjects Global Trade Services blocked.

11.5   Summary

In this chapter, we reviewed some of the high-level functionality changes in various SAP BusinessObjects Global Trade Services versions with the purpose of preparing you for an upgrade. We also discussed data retention, which is a very important requirement in trade business. Finally, we covered BADIs, user exits, and copy control.

In the next chapter, we conclude the book by discussing data transfers and the interface of functions and processes. This will help you understand the key interfaces with content providers, SAP systems, and non-SAP systems. We will also go over some of best known methods in preparing and managing an SAP BusinessObjects Global Trade Services project.

In this chapter, we review the key functions and processes that enable the interface between feeder systems and SAP BusinessObjects Global Trade Services. We end the book with the best known methods to prepare you for SAP BusinessObjects Global Trade Services project implementation.

12 Data Transfer Between Standard, and Non-SAP Interfaces, and Best Known Methods

The communication between SAP ERP (or any feeder system) and SAP Business-Objects Global Trade Services is primarily carried out by two methods, through Application Linking and Enabling (ALE) for master data, and remote function calls (RFCs) for transactional data. For the initial transfer of master data, the system uses a real-time RFC connection. Additions and changes to master data are identified and transferred to SAP BusinessObjects Global Trade Services by making use of change pointers. The standard interface between SAP ERP and SAP BusinessObjects Global Trade Services is pre-delivered as part of a plug-in; SAP ERP utilizes different function modules to make a call to SAP BusinessObjects Global Trade Services, transfer data, and extract information and updates. In addition to the standard interfaces, there are other ways to interface with SAP BusinessObjects Global Trade Services; for example, by utilizing XML interfaces for trade data loads and BAPI (Business Application Programming Interface).

There are pre-delivered SAP standard interfaces, as well as pre-delivered BAPI, which allow you to build non-SAP system interfaces. In this chapter, we review some of the non-standard interface methods to understand how the interfaces are invoked and how their processes work. We then conclude the book by discussing the most effective methods for executing an SAP BusinessObjects Global Trade Services project implementation. We will also consider some cases of best-known methods on supply chain processes and how to manage your projects.

12.1   Master and Transactional Data Interface

As mentioned earlier, master data transfers use *change pointers*, which identify changes in fields of interest — whether they are brand new or edited — and then schedule these changes for transfer. Fields of interest are identified and associated with *message types*. Message types are like structures or templates made up of segments, elements, and control information for capturing data elements from the tables or objects of interest. Like a template, the information is retrieved and transferred to the table for storage.

Transaction transfers to SAP BusinessObjects Global Trade Services use RFC connections and are completed during the transaction save, following the creation or change of a document. The transaction saves invokes a function module, which transfers the data to SAP BusinessObjects Global Trade Services. In the following sections, we will discuss change pointers in more detail and then discuss a few different types of interfaces.

12.1.1   Change Pointers

Change pointers save information identified using message types, keeping track of objects, keys, change categories, timestamps, last changes, associate changes, statuses, and details of changes. The change pointer restricts the change that is transferred to the target system. In the following sections, we discuss both the configuration steps and the process steps involved in change pointers.

Configuration Steps

Configuration is done within the SAP ERP system via the following menu path: Global Trade Services Area Menu (Transaction /SAPSLL/MENU_LEGALR3) • Basic Settings • ALE Change Pointer. Follow these steps:

1. **Activate the change pointer function within the SAP ERP system**

This step enables the change pointer for all functional areas. While you are in Basic Setting, click on Activate Change Pointer Globally, or use Transaction BD61. Check the Change Pointers Activated – Generally box.

2. **Click on Activate Change Pointers for Reduced Messages, or use Transaction BD53**

Select the message types that are pre-delivered within SAP ECC, and click on Activate Change Pointers. Table 12.1 identifies some of the pre-delivered reduced message types for SAP BusinessObjects Global Trade Services.

Message Type	Reference/Reduced From	Purpose
/SAPSLL/MATMAS_SLL	MATMAS	Material Master
/SAPSLL/CREMAS_SLL	CREMAS	Vendor Master
/SAPSLL/DEBMAS_SLL	DEBMAS	Customer Master

Table 12.1 Message Types for Key Data Transfer

Reduced message types are copied with reference to the basic message type and modified to select only the fields that are of interest to SAP BusinessObjects Global Trade Services. Figure 12.1 shows the fields that are identified for the material master message type /SAPSLL/MATMAS_SLL for transfer to SAP BusinessObjects Global Trade Services.

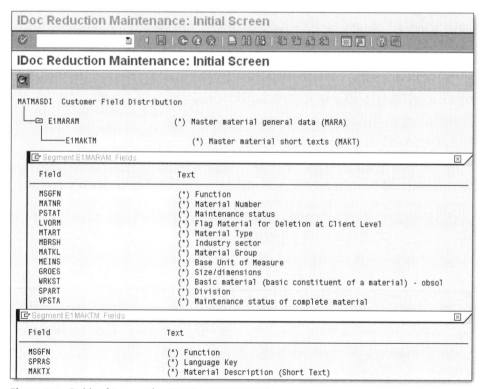

Figure 12.1 Fields of Interest for /SAPSLL/MATMAS_SLL

After following these steps, you can review the message types that are activated within Activate Change Pointers for Message Type (or Transaction BD50). The message type will have Active checked. Use Transaction BD52 to ensure that the key relevant fields are listed with their respective message types. Then verify the function module; use Transaction BD60, select the message type, and validate the table entries for message types found in Table 12.2.

Message Type	Reference	Function Module	Object	ALE Object
/SAPSLL/ CREMAS_SLL	CREMAS	/SAPSLL/ CREMAS_ DISTRIBUTE_ R3	LFA1	LIFNR
/SAPSLL/ DEBMAS_SLL	DEBMAS	/SAPSLL/ DEBMAS_ DISTRIBUTE_ R3	KNA1	KUNNR
/SAPSLL/ MATMAS_SLL	MATMAS	/SAPSLL/ MATMAS_ DISTRIBUTE_ R3	MARA	MATNR

Table 12.2 Function Modules Associated with Key Message Types

Process Steps

After you set up the configuration, the SAP ERP system logs the changes into the change pointer Tables BDCP and BDCPS. Table BDCP provides the details of the change with regards to the table name, key object number (vendor number, customer number), time of change, changes made by (user ID), field, and so on, and associates each change with a change pointer ID. Table BDCPS keeps track of the status (processed or yet-to-be processed) of the logged change pointer. After configuration, you must set up the batch job with the program (RBDMIDOC) that will look at the table entry in Table BDCPS for specific message types and schedule these transfers. You can use Transaction SE38 or SA38, and enter the program (RBDMIDOC). Create a variant with the relevant message type for material, customer, or vendor. With Transaction SM36, you can create a job and schedule it to transfer change pointer entries for different message types. Figure 12.2 displays the process flow for the data transfer from SAP ECC or R/3 to SAP BusinessObjects Global Trade Services.

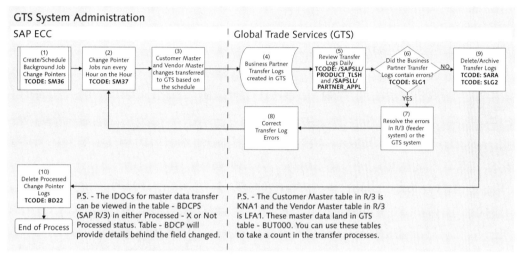

Figure 12.2 Process Flow for Data Transfers

12.1.2 Non-SAP Interface

Like other SAP applications, you have pre-delivered SAP BusinessObjects Global Trade Services BAPIs (Business Application Programming Interface) that allow you to build a standard interface with a non-SAP System. Let's look at some standard BAPI examples where you can build your key interfaces, the most important of which are the products, business partners, and transactions. The following code explains some of the important functions or BAPI and key interface fields.

```
Function Module: /SAPSLL/API_6800_SYNCH (Documents)
```

▶ HDR_DATA (Header Data) Fields input

  ▶ APPL (APPLICATION_LEVEL) > SDOA / SDOB (Sales, Delivery, etc)

  ▶ DOCUM (DOCUMENT_TYPE) > OR (Document Type from feeder system)

- ► COMP (COMPANY_CODE) > Company Code from the feeder System
► HDR_REFERENCE_DATA (Header reference data) input fields
  - ► QUAL_R (QUAL_REFNO) > EXTID (for external id)
  - ► REFNO (Reference Number) > Customs Document Number created in SAP BusinessObjects Global Trade Services
  - ► ORG_LOGSYS (ORG_LOGSYSTEM) > Feeder system
  - ► OBJTP (OBJECT TYPE) > Sales Order, Delivery (BUS2032, LIKP, etc)
► ITM_DATA (Item Data) input fields
  - ► ITEM_NUMBE (ITEM_NUMBER) > Item number from the feeder system document (# 10, 20, etc)
  - ► L (LEGAL_ACTIVE) > X to check for active regulation
  - ► R (RECHECK_INDICATOR) > X for rechecking
  - ► ITEM_(ITEM_CATEGORY) > Item category from the feeder system (ex. TAN)
  - ► ARR (ARRIVAL_COUNTRY) > Country key (US, CN, etc)
  - ► AR (ARRIVAL_COUNTRY_ISO) > ISO code of the country
  - ► PRODUCT_ID > Product #
  - ► PLAN (PLANT) > Plant from the feeder system

Function Module: /SAPSLL/API_6850_SYNCH_MASS (Product Interface), key interface fields are listed below:

► IV_LOGID_EXT > Created by
► API6850_KEY
  - ► Product_ID > Product #
  - ► ORG_LOGSYS > Feeder System Group
► API6850_HDR interface fields
  - ► Product_ID > Product #
  - ► DATAB > 05/03/2005
  - ► DATBI > 12/31/2006
  - ► PRBUM_ISO > EA (UOM)

▶   API6850_TXT (text) fields

   ▶ Product_ID > Product #

   ▶ LANGU_ISO > EN (English)

   ▶ PRODUCT_TEXT > Text Description

   ▶ PRODUCT_TXTG > Text Description

Function Module: /SAPSLL/API_1006_SYNCH_MASS > Business Partner transfer and screening

Interface fields for inputs:

▶ IV_APPLOG_POSITIVE (Screening results – negative or positive)

▶ API1006_KEY

   ▶ PARTNER_ID

   ▶ PARTNER_TYP > 02 (Customer)

   ▶ ORG_LOGSYSTEM

▶ API1006_HEAD Header fields

   ▶ PARTNER_ID

   ▶ PARTN_CAT > 2

   ▶ EXTERN_NO > External Business Partner Number

▶ API1006_CENTRAL Add-on header fields

   ▶ PARTNER_ID

   ▶ SEARCHTERM1 >

   ▶ SEARCHTERM1 > External Term

▶ API1006_CENTRAL_ORG

   ▶ PARTNER_ID

   ▶ NAME1

▶ API1006_ADDRESS Address fields

   ▶ PARTNER_ID

   ▶ STANDARDADDRESS > S

   ▶ CITY

   ▶ STREET

   ▶ COUNTRY

- ▶ EXTADDRESSNUMBER > External Address Number
- ▶ API4001_AD1VL: Add-on Fields
  - ▶ ADDR_NO > External Address number
  - ▶ FROM_DATE >
  - ▶ TO_DATE
  - ▶ NAME
  - ▶ CITY
  - ▶ STREET
  - ▶ COUNTRY
  - ▶ COUNTRYISO

12.1.3 Content Load and Screening Interface

SAP BusinessObjects Global Trade Services has an XML interface for loading content such as key components of trade data; for example, the denied party list, which is used for screening business partners against different lists published by governments. Once loaded into the system, you can use the indexing functions to index this data and screen your business partner database.

You may want to have a process in place to load this content on a regular basis with delta information. Table 12.3 lists different screenings that happen based on database changes from the feeder system or SAP BusinessObjects Global Trade Services.

Process	Screening	Purpose
New business partners or changes to business partners	A1	Screening of new business partners and changes to business partners against existing denied party list content
New documents or changes to documents	A2	Screening of new documents and changes to documents against existing denied party list content
Existing business partners in SAP BusinessObjects Global Trade Services and sanctioned party list data	B1	Screening of existing business partners against existing denied party list content

Table 12.3 Sanctioned Party List Screening Scenarios

Process	Screening	Purpose
Existing document in SAP BusinessObjects Global Trade Services and SPL data	B2	Screening of existing documents against existing denied party list content
Delta denied party list screening of business partners	C1	Screening of existing business partners against delta denied party list content loaded
Delta denied party list screening of documents	C2	Screening of existing documents against delta denied party list content loaded
Simulation screening	S1	Screening simulation of business partners

Table 12.3 Sanctioned Party List Screening Scenarios (Cont.)

Figure 12.3 displays the process involved in loading content, building indexes, and screening business partners, as well as the different tables that are updated within SAP BusinessObjects Global Trade Services.

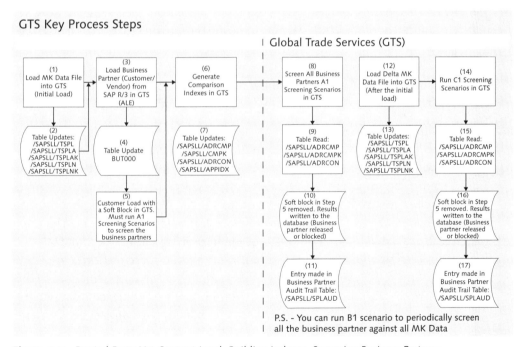

Figure 12.3 Denied Party List Content Load, Building Indexes, Screening Business Partners

12.2 Best Known Methods for Managing Your Trade System Project Implementation

With globalization and low-cost sourcing, your supply chain processes are becoming more complex and unpredictable. SAP BusinessObjects Global Trade Services can help companies execute their global sourcing strategy when, for example, choosing providers based on low duty rates, looking for preferential treatment, or making considerations based on special importing or exporting requirements. It can also help mitigate the risk of doing business internationally based on each country's import and export regulations requirements. This, in turn, helps businesses maintain their brand equity and comply with each country's import and export regulations.

With SAP BusinessObjects Global Trade Services, you have a centralized repository for all trade processes, and this information is available consistently across your supply chain. This helps reduce the fulfillment cycle times and increase customer service levels. SAP BusinessObjects Global Trade Services facilitates the import/export entry with necessary and accurate documentation.

Many companies that do business globally have automated their supply chains, yet they continue to rely on costly manual import/export trade processes. Manual processes are not only error prone but also require high maintenance on day-to-day operations and business processes. They are difficult to deploy across the company and to integrate with the supply chain. Manual processes create bottlenecks within supply chain processes and add unpredictable lead times to the cycle.

When implementing SAP BusinessObjects Global Trade Services, it is important to understand company-wide global requirements and to assess the scope of the project to achieve maximum benefit for your investment. Make use of standard delivered configurations and recommended practices. Pay attention to trade requirements, which are well established and documented. Spend resources and time to ensure that you have a good process in place for system deployment. The trade system is embedded within your supply chain process and has dependencies on other processes and function, so you must ensure that these processes are ready to support the SAP BusinessObjects Global Trade Services implementation. In this section, we discuss some of the best known methods in understanding requirements, assessing the scope of your project, and planning for project deployment.

12.2.1 Supply Chain Processes: Preparation Work

There are processes and functions managed within your supply chain areas that feed into the SAP BusinessObjects Global Trade Services system and are necessary for successful implementation. Let's look at a typical process flow within a logistics or SAP ERP system. Start the customer relationship by establishing an opportunity, which hopefully leads to an inquiry or request for a quote. Now perform a compliance check for sanctioned party list screening of business partners and expected transactions, embargo services, and license requirements. When you are ready to sign the contract with the customer, you can initiate the required compliance checks and take appropriate action based on the compliance check results; for example, the compliance check might show that you need a license to ship a part.

When you deal with your vendor, you might have to enable your import functions. For example, you might start with a purchase requisition and confirm procurement with the purchase order. This purchase order document can be used for a compliance check and also as information for expected goods. You can get advanced shipment notification to prepare for your import clearance, and, when you make a goods receipt, you can confirm the goods imported and use a customs declaration to report this back to the customs authorities.

In the following sections, we give some examples of supply chain key processes or dependencies that are important and critical for the success of your trade system implementation. It is not a comprehensive list, but it gives you an idea of how a trade system implementation depends on other processes and functions.

Country of Origin

The simple definition of *country of origin* is the country where the product, goods, or commodity was originally grown, mined, or manufactured. Certification of Origin is one document that is required by certain countries during the entry process for tariff purposes, certifying the country of origin of specific goods. Customs offices use this document to determine whether or not a preferential duty rate applies on the products being imported. Certificates are also important for trade agreements and regulations that might apply to goods being imported.

Customs expects all imported goods to be marked permanently or prominently with the country of origin. There are some products that are exempt from these marking requirements; these are included in the *different list* (e.g., needles, cigarettes, and wire) for duty exemptions. The country of origin can also determine whether there are any restrictions that might apply, regardless of where the item was acquired. For example, an Iranian rug acquired in the United States might be prohibited. This can also happen when the commerce of the goods happens in a sanctioned country; for example, a UK-made piece of jewelry acquired in Iran may be considered to be of Iranian origin if returned to the United Kingdom.

Rules of origin help determine the duty calculations, necessary permits, quotas, and any other restrictions. The country of origin is also the country where the majority of the value was added to the product, regardless of where it is bought or sold. Companies risk losing import and export privileges and incurring significant fines, if they don't mark their goods with country of origin or represent the information incorrectly. If challenged by authorities, this can also cause delays, fines, penalties, and further scrutiny to clear customs.

It is the responsibility of the exporter, manufacturer, or vendor to provide country of origin of the product being imported information. It is important that this is captured during the product receipt and then associated with the goods through the processing and inventory. When it is exported out, this information can be printed in the export trade document. As a customer, you expect this information from your vendor, and you are expected to provide this information to your customers.

> **Note**
>
> For exporting, the country of origin information is captured within the delivery note line item. With batch split, the country of origin information is captured within the batch split item.

Figure 12.4 displays the view and the country of origin field where the information is maintained. This can be accessed through Transactions VL01N (delivery note create), VL02N (change), or VL03N (display). Double-click on the item number of interest, select the Foreign Trade/Customs tab, and select the Origin/Destination/Business sub-folder. The bottom section shows the country of origin maintenance with the batch split items. With batch split items, you must select the item and click on the Batch Split icon. Then you can double-click on the batch item, which brings up the Origin/Destination/Business view. The country of origin from the delivery note is carried over to the proforma billing document, and the proforma billing document is transferred to SAP BusinessObjects Global Trade Services for generation of the customs declaration document.

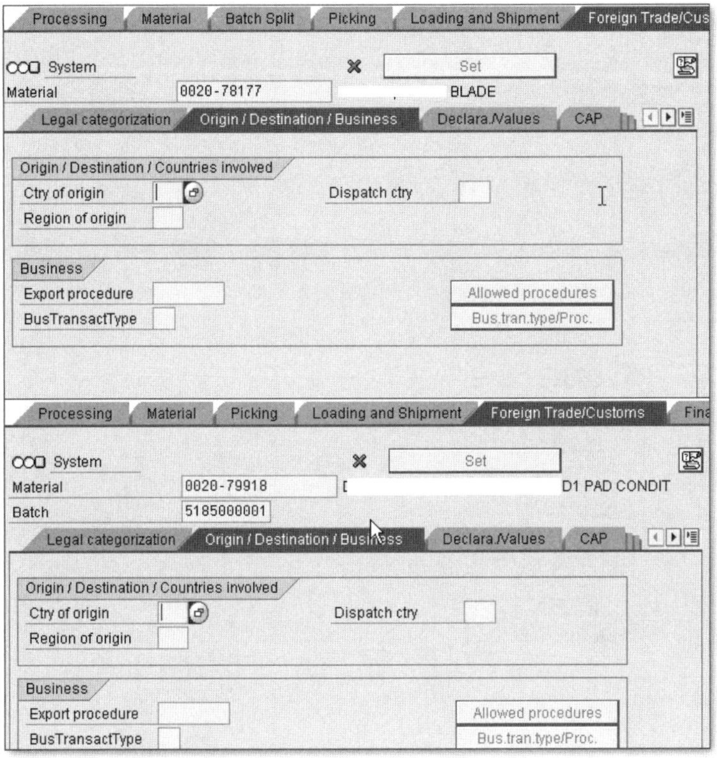

Figure 12.4 Country of Origin Field

Shipment Consolidation

With SAP BusinessObjects Global Trade Services implementation, trade documents are generated from the SAP BusinessObjects Global Trade Services system. We recommend that you let them reside there and print from the SAP BusinessObjects Global Trade Services system. Trade documents represent shipments leaving the country, either in single shipments or consolidated shipments. These shipments are generated within your logistics system and can result in a single delivery note or consolidated delivery notes. Figure 12.5 displays the process flow from delivery notes through billing and shows how the SAP BusinessObjects Global Trade Services system is interfaced with other logistics processes.

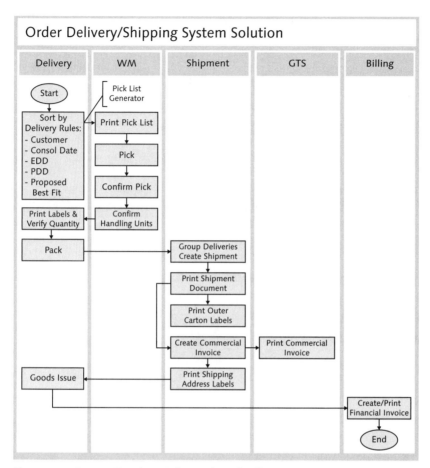

Figure 12.5 Process Flow from Delivery Through Billing

> **Note**
>
> The proforma billing document is the recommended document for interfacing with the SAP BusinessObjects Global Trade Services system, as these document don't generate any accounting entries and can be used for generating the customs declaration document in SAP BusinessObjects Global Trade Services. A shipment document represents consolidation in SAP ERP and is used by your operations group; the proforma document should represent or mirror the shipment document.

Consolidating proforma documents is based on multiple delivery notes, and is carried out within the SAP ERP system. With SAP BusinessObjects Global Trade Services 7.2 and higher, Transaction /SAPSLL/CUS_INV_CREATE_R3 facilitates the consolidation of delivery notes into one proforma document within the SAP ECC plug-in. With earlier versions, you can use Transaction VF01 (billing document create) or Transaction VF04 (billing due list) to consolidate proforma documents, but you need to ensure that the consolidated delivery notes reflect the shipment.

The following list describes some of the critical elements with the shipping process that might prevent you from consolidating. After that, we take those issues and show how you can address them:

▶ **Foreign trade number**
SAP ERP or your logistics system generates a unique number for every export delivery note, which may prevent you from consolidating them. This can be overcome by making use of a configuration selection or option. Using copy control from delivery notes to proforma billing documents, select option B (Redetermine the Export Data). Figure 12.6 displays the configuration selection. The menu path for this is SAP REFERENCE IMG • SALES AND DISTRIBUTION • BILLING • BILLING DOCUMENTS • MAINTAIN COPYING CONTROL FOR BILLING DOCUMENTS • COPYING CONTROL: DELIVERY DOCUMENT TO BILLING DOCUMENT. Select the source delivery document (e.g., LF) and target billing document (e.g., F8), and click on Details. This brings up the screen shown in Figure 12.6.

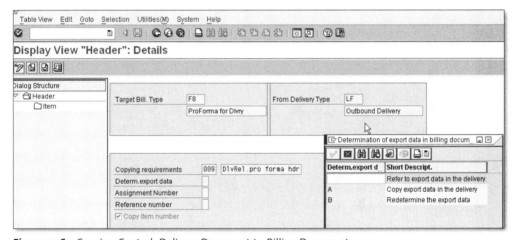

Figure 12.6 Copying Control: Delivery Document to Billing Document

▶ **INCO term**
International commercial term (INCO term) defines the terms of sales or procurement and passing the risk of export and import of the goods. This is a code used in international trade for the goods being shipped as the interpretation of the ownership of the goods. Some of the examples are EXW (Ex-Works), DAF

(Delivery at Frontier), DDU (Delivered Duty Unpaid), DDP (Delivered Duty Paid), CIP (Carriage and Insurance Paid to), CFR (Cost and Freight), and FOB (Free on Board). You should ensure that the INCO terms in all of the delivery notes are being consolidated.

▶ **Billing data**
One of the business and technical challenges you might face is when the billing date on the different delivery notes causes the proforma to split. You can write custom code to ignore the billing date or to ensure that billing dates are updated accordingly.

Shipment consolidation is key in increasing visibility and reducing transportation costs, cycle time, and manual work.

Controlled and Hazardous or Dangerous Materials

Hazardous materials calls for separate handling and also ensuring that they are packed and shipped separated, as required. The identification of the hazardous part is captured within the logistics system, so you need to ensure the process is in place to capture this information with the transactional or logistics system. Following the information capture, the handling of the material is managed within the SAP ERP system, and packing information is important in identified these part as hazardous. This also impacts the shipment of these parts, as they might need to be separately shipped and not mixed with the regular parts. So you might have to ensure that the shipment consolidation process can identify and separate out these dangerous goods for proper handling and reporting.

12.2.2 Requirement Analysis

Requirement analysis is important because it helps in mapping out a project plan. Requirement analysis allows you to discover the company's as-is process and how the trade system to be processed will map into their business. There are different approaches to the requirement analysis, and the following list provides some of the critical aspects and tools that can facilitate the process and guide you through. When assessing your requirements, pay attention to the following areas:

▶ **As-is process**
It is important to understand the current process from an end-to-end import and export process point of view, that is, how the company has been handling their trade and supply chain touch points.

▶ **To-be process**
This lays out the new planned process and lists the details behind achieving the deployment.

▶ **New implementation versus upgrade**
If you are upgrading, you should gather details of the current existing system, in terms of the feeder system and the currently implemented SAP BusinessObjects Global Trade Services components.

▶ **Business scenarios**
Understanding critical business processes is important to the success of the project. From sourcing to the customer shipment, understand the different functions impacted by the trade system and use change management. For example, from the import process point of view, you want to know if the screening of your vendor is important and if there is a requirement for import licenses.

▶ **Trade-related questions**
You should establish important trade business processes and function questions, such as

  ▶ Number of countries you export out of and import from

  ▶ Screening of types of business partners

  ▶ Import license requirement

  ▶ Export and import classification

  ▶ License and export control requirements

  ▶ Export and import documentations by country

  ▶ Preference agreement countries

▶ **Technical requirements**
It is important to understand the technical architecture of SAP BusinessObjects Global Trade Services; for example, you may use reporting from the SAP NetWeaver BW and require access through the portal. Based on volume and performance requirements, it is important to do the right sizing.

12.2.3 Scoping

Scoping is a very important exercise; as a project team, you must put together a realistic plan based on resources and timelines. Table 12.4 is a template that can help you gather the key aspects of the project and determine their complexity.

Components/Business Process	Compliance			Customs		Risk		Complexity (Small/Medium/High)
	Sanctioned Party List	EMB	Licensing	Document Print	Electronic Submission	Preferential	Others	
Export/Import								
Number of SAP Systems								
Other SAP Systems (CRM, SRM, etc.)								
Number of Non-SAP Systems								
Exporting/Importing Countries								
Content								
Classification Tool								
Types of Business Partners								
Different Types of Transactions/Business Processes (Sales Orders, Deliveries, STO)								
Other Requirements (Archiving)								
Upgrade/Migration from R/3								
SAP NetWeaver Components (BW, EP, etc.)								

Table 12.4 Matrix for Capturing High-Level Scope and Complexity

12.2.4 Managing the SAP BusinessObjects Global Trade Services Project

In all instances of SAP BusinessObjects Global Trade Services implementation (new, upgrade, etc.), we recommend that you have a separate plan for SAP BusinessObjects Global Trade Services and track the key dependencies (Table 12.5). Be aware of the standard interfaces and the data elements that are transferred from the feeder system to SAP BusinessObjects Global Trade Services, as you need to plan for the enhancement development work to bring in additional data or processes. You will likely require development work on the trade forms, as the pre-delivered forms may not meet all the data requirements.

High-Level Task	Resource Type	Remarks
Scope	Project Team, Business, and Functional	Use the high-level scope and prepare a detailed plan.
Business Requirement/ Analysis	Business and Functional	Use the questionnaire to drive the requirement analysis. Start with the functional specifications on the development work identified.
System Install – SAP BusinessObjects Global Trade Services	Technical and Functional	Start this activity ahead of time, so you can begin it while assessing scope and requirements.
Plug-In Install – Feeder System	Technical and Functional	Start this activity ahead of time, so you can begin it while assessing scope and requirements.
Build Activity/ Configuration in the Feeder System	Functional	Feeder system setup to support SAP BusinessObjects Global Trade Services.
System Communication Between SAP Feeder and SAP BusinessObjects Global Trade Services	Technical and Functional	Establish the system communication between SAP ECC and SAP BusinessObjects Global Trade Services.

Table 12.5 Key Elements, Tasks, and Milestones in the SAP BusinessObjects Global Trade Services Project Plan

High-Level Task	Resource Type	Remarks
Build Compliance	Business and Functional	Build the foundation to allow the configuration of other modules in parallel.
Build Customs	Business and Functional	Build the foundation to allow the configuration of other modules in parallel.
Build Risk, LOC, etc.	Business and Functional	Build the foundation to allow the configuration of other modules in parallel.
Unit Test (Compliance)	Business and Functional	With separate resources, you can perform the unit tests for different components in parallel.
Unit Test (Customs)	Business and Functional	With separate resources, you can perform the unit tests for different components in parallel.
Unit Test (Risk, Others)	Business and Functional	With separate resources, you can perform the unit tests for different components in parallel.
RICEWF	Functional and Technical	Development work can start with minimal build activity.
Security	Functional and Technical	Start on the security work, based on the requirement analysis performed.
QA Box Install and Build	Functional and Technical	Start the QA build when 80% of build is complete and unit tested.
Cut Over/Conversion	Business, Functional, and Technical	Use QA as a trial opportunity for cut over and conversion prior to production go-live, and measure the time for activities.

Table 12.5 Key Elements, Tasks, and Milestones in the SAP BusinessObjects Global Trade Services Project Plan (Cont.)

High-Level Task	Resource Type	Remarks
Integration Test	Business, Functional, and Technical	Plan on end-to-end testing with the feeder systems and other functions.
Performance Test	Business, Functional, and Technical	Some of the processes within SAP BusinessObjects Global Trade Services are performance-intensive; it is recommended that the SAP BusinessObjects Global Trade Services system is tested for stress.
User Acceptance Test	Business and Functional	Involve the users ahead of time, during the build and prototype. User acceptance makes validation and training easier. This also helps manage the change well ahead of time.
System Install Production	Functional and Technical	Start the install, following a successful integration test.
Build and Data Preparation	Business, Functional, and Technical	Plan on SAP BusinessObjects Global Trade Services preparation for configuration and trade data maintenance.
Go-Live	Business, Functional, and Technical	Plan on first-level support of trade super users, expect data-related issues, and manage the change.

Table 12.5 Key Elements, Tasks, and Milestones in the SAP BusinessObjects Global Trade Services Project Plan (Cont.)

12.2.5   Build and Testing Approach

While coming up with the build plan, review your plans for parallel tasks based on the resources available. For example, plan on the test plan and test case build while working on the build. Involve your business users ahead of time, with more informal sessions; do not wait until the user acceptance test.

> **Note**
>
> SAP pre-delivers configurations with Client 000, so when you install the SAP BusinessObjects Global Trade Services box, ensure that the system is built as a copy with reference to Client 000.

Make use of pre-delivered configurations, which will help you rapidly build a prototype. Involve the users in demonstrating the functions and identifying the gaps; address these as part of the requirement analysis and delivery. Make use of the build to rapidly deploy, unit test, and get acceptance from the business users.

You might want to plan on capturing the resource and time taken to build the quality system build, which can be a benchmark for your production system build. In other words, it can be a mock run system for a production system build, and this can be input into your pre-go live and cut over plan. Clients plan on having a different system build for stress tests and performance measures, but if you have resource constraints, you can make use of the same QA box for performance testing. Plan on multiple iterations for test cycles; jump start with pre-delivered configurations, and then fine-tune them.

12.3 Summary

Understanding the different interfaces with SAP BusinessObjects Global Trade Services is key to your trade system implementation success; it involves preparation of business processes and technical readiness. In this chapter, we discussed some of the key standard interfaces and functions that can enable non-SAP interfaces. We also discussed the best-known methods and practices to manage your SAP BusinessObjects Global Trade Services project effectively.

The Author

 **Rajen Iyer** is a business- and technology-focused professional with demonstrated success in systems implementation, support, product development and team leadership. He has significant experience with many SAP project implementations across different leading industries. Rajen has a Bachelor's degree in engineering and an MBA in Technology Management. He has authored the SAP PRESS bestseller, Effective SAP SD, several white papers, and best-known-methods articles. With extensive experience in supply-chain management applications and implementations, Rajen is focused on building a practice within many SAP niche areas via value-driven products and solutions with companies like, Kyrpt, Inc and Kryaa, Inc. Rajen Iyer can be reached at *Rajen@ kryptinc.com* or *Rajen.Iyer@kryaa.com*.

KRYPT is a GTS and Logistics value chain-focused consulting company that helps make effective and efficient utilization SAP and GTS investments, with a 100% reference-able client base. Krypt specializes in end-to-end projects with large and complex global roll outs as well as rapid and robust implementations.

KRYAA is focussed on identifying new niche areas with the SAP and associated solution space and providing clients with new innovative products, solutions and tools. KRYAA has to its credit products for Trade System Solutions and Interfaces (patents pending), GTS tools, and content for project accelerations and automated shipping solutions.

Index

A

action definition, 175
action profile, 175
Activate case management, 200
Activate Legal Regulation, 90
Activate the document type and item category, 236
Activate the preference agreement, 237
Activating the Business Partner, 89
Activation
   Customs Document, 170
Activations Specific to Embargo Service Checks, 81
activity function, 198
Add-On Functionality, 191
Address Comparison, 91
   License, 141
aggregate vendor declarations, 252
Agreements, 153
Application Integrations, 207
Application Linking and Enabling (ALE), 29, 307
   model, 44
   setup, 210
archiving customizing, 294
archiving jobs, 296
Archiving objects, 291
archiving steps, 291–292
Assigned Documents, 152
Assignment of Feeder Document Types, 77
Assignments
   Item Categories and Document Types, 164
Assign the logical system, 208
asynchronous, 104
Authorization, 168
Automated Export Submission, 173

B

BAdI, 302

C

BAPI (Business Application Programming Interface), 307
Baseline Settings, 59
Billing data, 322
billing documents, 40
Bill of Material (BOM) transfer, 229
Bills of product, 233
Block Dialog, 40
Blocked Document Report, 146
Blocked Report, 151
Build, 325
   Compliance, 326
   Customs, 326
   Risk, 326
Bureau of Industry Security (BIS), 24
Business Add-In (BAdI), 216, 302
Business partner, 261
   Definition, 189
   roles, 55
   SPL screening, 107
business process for intrastat, 271
Business Process preference, 242
Business scenarios, 323
business transaction types, 281

Cascade Activation, 137
Case Management, 197, 199
Case Type, 198
Change History and Transfer Logs, 62
change pointer, 45, 243, 308
   Processing, 48
Check Multiple Country Groups, 137
Checks, 221
Classification, 20, 187
Cockpit Setup, 184
combined nomenclature, 226
Commerce Control List (CCL), 24
Commercial Control List (CCL), 148
commodity code, 116, 245, 262
   product assignment, 263

communication from SAP ERP to SAP
Communication Setup, 173
Comparison Terms, 98
Compliance Management Fundamentals, 72
Condition, 177
Configuring Customs Management, 169
Content, 121
    Load and Screening Interface, 314
    Loading, 122
Control Data, 162
Control for Screening Business Partner, 91
Control Grouping, 136
Control Settings, 170
Control Settings for Embargo Service Checks,
82
Control Settings for Legal Control, 136
control settings for vendor declarations, 239
copy control, 41, 302, 321
Countries, 51
Country Chart, 134
Country Group, 130, 234
Country of Destination or Departure, 85
Country of Origin, 317
Cross-Application Components, 55
Cross-plant preference model, 237
Currencies, 54
Customs Codes, 120, 166
Customs Declaration, 19
Customs Document, 76
    type, 163
Customs Duty Setup, 171
Customs Management, 159
customs office, 283
customs processing, 160
Customs Product, 195
Cut Over/Conversion, 326

D

Dangerous Material, 322
Data Setup, 156
    for Intrastat, 257
Date Fields, 203
Default Data, 203
    by Business Partner, 203
default procedure, 200

Default values, 280, 283
Define legal regulations, 271
Define the Control Procedure, 91
Define the logical system, 208
Define the RFC destination, 210
Delta Features, 288
Depreciation Group, 131
Determination Procedure, 79, 90
    Legal Control, 140
determination setup, 180
Determine preference, 251
Distribute the distribution model, 215
distribution model, 213
document Specific preference determination,
253
Document Structures, 161
document transfer, 228
Document Type Activation, 79
Duty Corrections, 165
Duty Structure, 172

E

ECCN, 18, 113
ECR data set up, 275
edit ntrastat, 270
Electronics Compliance Report, 273
Electronics Compliance Reporting, 22
Email Notification, 197, 202
Embargo activation for import, 142
Embargo Applications, 84
Embargo Business Partners and Documents,
106
Embargo Country — Global, 84
Embargo Service Checks, 78
Enabling Embargo, 83
End Uses, 119
ERP system, 14
evaluate preference, 252
Exclusion Indicator, 284
Export, 14
Export control, 24
    classification number (ECCN), 72
export customs office, 282
Export/Import Data Setup, 148
Export Legal Control Setup

Baseline, 129
Export list, 114
Export Lists Assignments, 115
export mode of transport, 282
export procedures, 282
Export Process, 24
Extend Field List for Data Proposal, 204
External License Number, 138
Extrastat system, 257

F

Feeder System, 33, 325
  Foundation, 34
  Interfaces, 36
  Process, 242
  setup, 227
Field Labels, 166
filter, 213
Filter Group, 215
foreign currency, 275
Foreign Trade (SAP SD FT), 37
Foundations of Custom Management, 160
Functionality Release, 288

G

General settings, 59
Generate the partner profiles, 215
Geographical Codes, 52
Global trade, 13
Go-Live, 327
GTS table linkages, 299

H

Harmonized Tariff Number, 116
Harmonized Tariff System (HTS), 72, 113
Hazardous material, 322

I

Import, 14

code, 279
Process, 25
Process Flow, 26
worklist, 259
Import Customs Declarations, 165
import customs office, 282
Import Licenses, 143
Import Lists Assignments, 116
import mode of transport, 282
import procedures, 282
Inclusion Indicator, 284
Incompletion Checks, 206, 279
INCO terms, 322
Indexing, 101
Installation Components, 50
Integration Test, 327
Interface Points, 34
Intermediate Document (IDoc), 182
International Traffic in Arms Regulations (ITAR), 113
Intrastat, 22
  codes, 273
  Reporting, 258
ISO Codes, 53
Issue vendor declarations, 254
ITAR, 153
ITAR Business Scenarios, 153
Item Categories, 164
Item Category Activation, 131
Item Category Definition, Activation, and Mapping, 77

L

Landscape, 28
Legal Control
  Data, 147
  Export, 129
  Import, 129
  Embargo, 147
Legal Import Control, 142
Legal Regulation, 82
legal regulation activate, 235
Legal Regulations, 68
  Customs Management, 160
Legal Regulations ï Define, 234

Letter of Credit, 21
License Determinations, 18, 149
License Determination Table, 150
Licenses, 150
license statuses, 139
License Text, 193
License Type Determination Procedure, 137, 140
License Types, 133
Link to external applications, 273
List Type, 95
Log Control, 162
logistics process, 16
Long Term Vendor Declaration, 250

M

Maintain remote function call (RFC), 209
Maintain Vendor Long-Term Declaration, 251
Map document types, 236
Master and Transactional Data Interface, 308
Master Data, 45, 188, 242
master data load, 242
material documents, 39
material group, 280
material price transfer, 244
Message, 178
Message Parameters, 180
Messages, 187
message type, 45, 308
method calls, 210
Middleware Communication Setup, 181
mode of transport, 283
Monitoring, 100
    Legal Control, 146

N

Negative Lists, 107
Non-SAP Interface, 311
North America Free Trade Agreement (NAFTA), 28
Numbering Scheme, 71
Numbering Schemes, 114, 131, 160

Number Range
    documents, 162
Number Ranges, 63

O

One View Product Classification, 125
Operational Effectiveness, 105, 145
organizational parameters, 233
Organizational Structure, 65, 236
other government agencies (OGA), 119
outbound activity, 185
Output, 177

P

Partner Group, 136
Partner Groupings, 139
Partner Profile, 183, 211
partner profile inbound parameter, 216
Partner Structure, 66
Peculiarity Code, 136
Performance Test, 327
Plant-based preference model, 237
Plug-In Install, 325
port for partner profiles, 211
Positive Lists, 107
Post-Processing Framework (PPF), 174
preference documents, 252
Preference Management, 27
Preference model, 233
Preference Settings, 170
Preferential Determination, 253
Preferential model, 237
Preferential processing, 27, 237
preferential treatment, 237
printer determination, 181
Procedure for default data, 205
Process Template, 178
procurement indicator, 244
Product Classification, 113, 122
Product Content, 120
Product Master Maintenance, 136
Product Text, 195

provider information, 259
purchasing document, 38

R

Receipts, 166
Recheck, 146–147
Re-Check Import/Export Documents, 111
Reclassification, 124
Record Management, 197
Reference Type, 95
regions, 283
Regulatory, 221
release blocked documents, 110
releases, 288
Remote Function Call Port, 182
remote function calls (RFC), 44
request for vendor declaration, 246
RFC destinations for method calls, 210
rule set, 238

S

SAP Business Information Warehouse, 162
SAP ECC Configurations, 41
SAP EH&S Integration, 219
SAP ERP HCM Integration, 208
SAP FI Integration, 218
SAP NetWeaver Configurations, 51
Scoping, 323
Sending of Mail Activation, 137
Service Activation, 76
service activation for content, 61
Shipment Consolidation, 319
SPL, 315
SPL Activation for Import, 142
SPL audit trail, 103
SPL configurations, 88
SPL Content Loading, 99
SPL control settings, 89
SPL Control Settings, 94
SPL data set up, 99
SPL screening, 101
SPL Screening of Documents, 110
SPL Screening Reports, 107

substance volume tracking, 219
Supply chain, 13
    Extension, 23
    processes, 316
synchronous, 104
Syncing tables, 53
System Architecture, 28
System Communication, 44, 56, 200

T

Table Structure, 299
Tactical Reporting, 106
Technically Incomplete Documents, 111
technical medium, 175
Text Determination, 192
text ID, 192
Time Zones, 139
trade business processes, 17
Trade Checks, 16
trade compliance, 18
Trade Identification Numbers, 190
Trade process, 31
Trade Reporting and Monitoring, 151
transaction data, 242
transaction monitoring, 253
transactions to transfer for intrastat reporting, 260
transaction tables, 300
transfer billing document, 257
Transfer Leg. Contr. Data, 137
Transit Procedure, 19, 160
transportation connection point, 284

U

Units of Measure, 53
Unit Test, 326
    Compliance, 326
    Customs, 326
Upgrade, 287, 323
User Acceptance Test, 327
user exits, 302
U.S. Munitions List (USML), 113

V

Value Added Tax (VAT), 257
vendor-based long-term vendor declarations, 230
Vendor declaration, 27

W

Workflow, 97, 200
Worklist, 123
worklist for vendor declarations, 230

X

XML interface, 30

Provides an easy-to-read overview of all Business Objects client tools in an SAP environment

Explains which tools to use for which types of reporting

Offers simple and practical hands-on examples that leve-rage robust sample scenarios and case studies

Ingo Hilgefort

Reporting and Analytics with SAP BusinessObjects

This book provides comprehensive coverage of the major business intelligence tools in the SAP/BO toolset with a practical focus on the user experience and integration with SAP. Coverage includes detailed application features and functionality, as well as practical, how-to content geared toward end users hoping to maximize the benefits their BI investment by creating actionable, easy to read and disseminate reports, analytics and other business process metrics. The author will present the content in an easy to read, step-by-step fashion.

approx. 500700 pp., 79,95 Euro / US$ 79.95
ISBN 978-1-59229-310-0, Jan 2010

>> www.sap-press.com

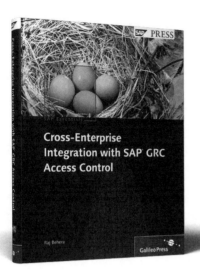

Configuration steps for
cross-enterprise integration of SAP
GRC AC RAR for SAP and non-SAP
systems

Use of Rule Architect, Data Extractor,
and Real Time Agent

Optimizing reporting, dashboard
creation, and advanced rule sets

Raj Behera

Cross-Enterprise Integration with SAP GRC Access Control

The book will provide the target group with the implementation
strategies, configuration steps, and best practices necessary to implement
a global SoD rule set across a multiple system landscape, including SAP
and non-SAP applications. Specific sections of the book focus on
configuring AC RAR for use with the most common non-SAP systems
(Oracle, PeopleSoft, and JDEdwards), configuring the Data Extractor for
failsafe movement of data from non-SAP systems, building a rule matrix
for a multi-system enterprise using the Real Time Agent, and managing
the entire integrated rule set with SAP ERP.

138 pp., 2009, 68,– Euro / US$ 85
ISBN 978-1-59229-250-9

>> www.sap-press.com

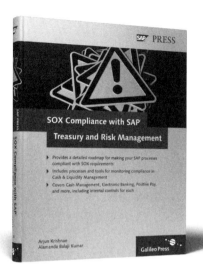

Roadmap for SAP Treasury processes compliant with SOX requirements

Processes, tools, techniques involved in Treasury & Risk Management and Cash & Liquidity Management

Application areas including Cash Management, Electronic Banking, Positive Pay

Balaji Kumar Alamanda , Arjun Krishnan

SOX Compliance with SAP Treasury and Risk Management

SOX Compliance with SAP Treasury Management provides Treasurers, CFOs, and Finance professionals with a roadmap for making their SAP TR processes compliant with SOX requirements. Combining comprehensive coverage of the major TR applications (Electronic Banking, Positive Pay, Cash Management & Liquidity, In-House Cash) with discussion of relevant control structures, processes, and compliance matrices for each, this book will lend guidance to those tasked with integrating SOX compliance into established or proposed SAP TR implementations.

437 pp., 2009, 79,95 Euro / US$ 79.95
ISBN 978-1-59229-200-4

>> www.sap-press.com

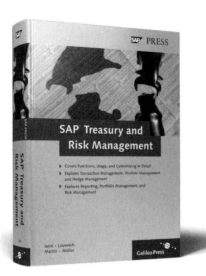

Uncover functionality, processes and complete customization details

Master transaction and position management with hedge management

Secrets of reporting, portfolio controlling and risk management

Fully up-to-date for SAP ERP 6.0

Sönke Jarré, Reinhold Lövenich, Andreas Martin, Klaus G. Müller

SAP Treasury and Risk Management

This guide introduces you to the functionality and helps you quickly master the usage of SAP Treasury and Risk Management. Learn about the most important customization settings as well as typical use cases and get straightforward solutions to many of the most common problems. With volumes of detailed screenshots, in-depth overviews and practical examples, all components of the tool are covered in detail – from transaction and position management, to risk and performance analyses, to reporting and beyond. The book is up-to-date for SAP ERP 6.0.

722 pp., 2008, 99,95 Euro / US$ 99.95
ISBN 978-1-59229-149-6

>> www.sap-press.com

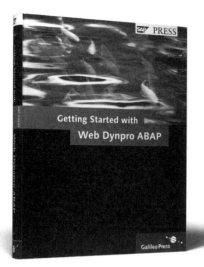

Covers all Finance-related processes, from purchasing and production to distribution

Teaches how to integrate Financial Accounting and Controlling with MM, PP, and SD

Details financial statement preparation and reporting

Andrea Hölzlwimmer, Andreas Vogelsang

Optimizing Value Flows with SAP ERP

This book is written to teach financial consultants, IT managers, and integration consultants how value flows can be enhanced across an organization's entire finance and logistics chain. It takes a process-oriented approach to the problems presented by non-integrated value flows in an organization and explains the solutions available in the SAP system. You'll explore the central processes of purchasing, production, distribution accounting, and reporting.

approx. 350 pp., 79,95 Euro / US$ 79.95
ISBN 978-1-59229-298-1, Jan 2010

>> www.sap-press.com

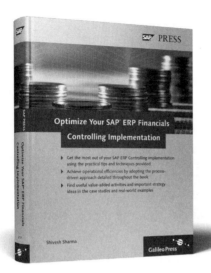

Practical tips and techniques for using your SAP Controlling implementation

Better management decisions by using the Controlling specific information

Investment Management, Funds Management, and more

Shivesh Sharma

Optimize Your SAP ERP Financials Controlling Implementation

This book will answer the question, What do I do with my SAP Controlling-related requirements once the implementation is complete? Therefore, it begins where implementation guides leave off. Using tested business processes it prepares readers to make the most of their Controlling implementation.

465 pp., 2008, 79,95 Euro / US$ 79.95
ISBN 978-1-59229-219-6

>> www.sap-press.com

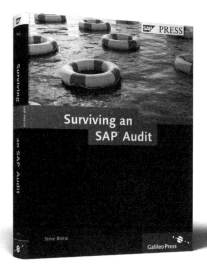

Helps understand typical requirements for an SAP system audit

Proven insight on how auditors approach a system audit, and how to prepare an SAP system for successful audit

Roadmap of audit objectives for FI, CO, SD, BI/BW, MM, PP, and HR

Steve Biskie

Surviving an SAP Audit

This book is written to help SAP project managers, implementation teams, administrators, and users understand the typical audit requirements related to SAP. The book will give you practical, proven advice for preparing your specific domains for an internal or external SAP system audit by helping you learn to "think like an auditor" while preparing for an SAP audit.

It provides an overview of how auditors approach an SAP audit, discusses typical audit techniques. It covers specific SAP applications and components and their related business processes in detail.

approx. 510 pp., 89,95 Euro / US$ 89.95
ISBN 978-1-59229-253-0, Dec 2009

>> www.sap-press.com

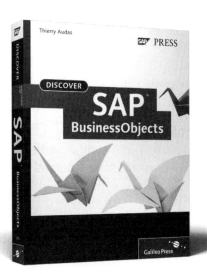

Learn the SAP BusinessObjects Strategy

Explore the SAP BusinessObjects portfolio of solutions

Understand the value for SAP customers and prepare to get started or transition to the new solutions

Thierry Audas

Discover SAP BusinessObjects

Discover SAP BusinessObjects will answer the many questions that decision makers and current SAP and BusinessObjects customers have about the new BI strategy from SAP. It will explain the business value of the new SAP BusinessObjects solutions and explain how to get started or transition to these solutions. The book will focus on describing and positioning all of the key solutions in the new SAP BusinessObjects portfolio, and explain how they fit together and into existing SAP customer landscapes.

approx. 500 pp., 39,95 Euro / US$ 39.95
ISBN 978-1-59229-315-5, Feb 2010

>> **www.sap-press.com**

Interested in reading more?

Please visit our Web site for all
new book releases from SAP PRESS.

www.sap-press.com